Construction Scheduling: Preparation, Liability, and Claims
Second Edition

by Jon M. Wickwire, Thomas J. Driscoll, Stephen B. Hurlbut, and Scott B. Hillman

Construction Scheduling: Preparation, Liability, and Claims, Second Edition, is a valuable resource for those who require a working knowledge of scheduling principles, their implementation under everyday circumstances, and the legal application of those principles. The authors place special emphasis not only on planning and implementing the construction schedule as a management tool, but also on the application of scheduling principles and procedures by the courts and boards of contract appeals. Some of the more salient issues that arise throughout the life of a construction project, which are addressed in this book, include: drafting scheduling specifications, identification of accepted and suggested techniques for CPM claims analysis; an in-depth look at software abuses; and alternatives for dispute resolution of claims.

2004 Supplement by Jon M. Wickwire

The following developments and issues are included in the 2004 Supplement:

- Analysis of the combined scheduling specification (Unified Facilities Guide Specification, "UFGS"), which directly addresses the issues of defective schedules and seeks to eliminate abuses;

- The landmark *Stone and Webster* decision recognizing the right of an owner on a major project to terminate a contractor for default due to the failure of the contractor to produce an acceptable schedule, thereby committing a material breach of contract;

- Decisions reflecting the application of *Daubert* rules to scheduling expert witness testimony, including disallowing certain unqualified scheduling experts and their testimony;

- Cases concerning the use of contemporaneous schedule updates to determine and calculate critical path delays;

- A poorly reasoned VA Board of Contract Appeals decision, *Fire Security Systems, Inc.*, on float and postcontract completion date delays, holding that the burden of proof is on the contractor to show that base contract work [performed after the current completion date] could or would have been performed sooner had owner delays not occurred; and

- Case studies on a Boston "Big Dig" procurement, addressing the need of an owner to be proactive and vigilant in all phases of the scheduling process; and on a National Oceanic and Atmospheric Administration facility in Boulder, Colorado.

The Table of Cases and Index have also been updated for this supplement.

11/03

For questions concerning this shipment, billing, or other customer service matters, call our Customer Service Department at 1-800-234-1660.

For toll-free ordering, please call 1-800-638-8437.

© 2004 Aspen Publishers

A WoltersKluwer Company

CONSTRUCTION SCHEDULING:
PREPARATION, LIABILITY, AND CLAIMS

2004 Supplement

CONSTRUCTION SCHEDULING:
PREPARATION, LIABILITY, AND CLAIMS
Second Edition

2004 Supplement

Jon M. Wickwire
Thomas J. Driscoll
Stephen B. Hurlbut
Scott B. Hillman

1185 Avenue of the Americas, New York, NY 10036
www.aspenpublishers.com

This publication is designed to provide accurate and authoritative information in regard to the subject matter covered. It is sold with the understanding that the publisher is not engaged in rendering legal, accounting, or other professional services. If legal advice or other professional assistance is required, the services of a competent professional person should be sought.

—From a *Declaration of Principles* jointly adopted by a Committee of the American Bar Association and a Committee of Publishers and Associations

© 2004 Aspen Publishers, Inc.
A Wolters Kluwer Company
www.aspenpublishers.com

All rights reserved. No part of this publication may be reproduced or transmitted in any form or by any means, electronic or mechanical, including photocopy, recording, or any information storage and retrieval system, without permission in writing from the publisher. Requests for permission to reproduce content should be directed to the Aspen Publishers website at *www.aspenpublishers.com,* or a letter of intent should be faxed to the permissions department at 646-728-3048.

Printed in the United States of America

1 2 3 4 5 6 7 8 9 0

Library of Congress Cataloging-in-Publication Data

Construction scheduling: preparation, liability, and claims/Jon M. Wickwire ... [et al.].—2nd ed.
    p. cm.
Rev. ed. of: Construction scheduling/Jon M. Wickwire, Thomas J. Driscoll, Stephen B. Hurlbut. c1991.
Includes bibliographical references and index.
    ISBN   0-7355-2994-9 (hbk.)
    ISBN   0-7355-4233-3 (supplement)
    1. Construction contracts—United States. 2. Construction industry—Law and legislation—United States. 3. Production scheduling. I. Wickwire, Jon M. II. Wickwire, Jon M. Construction scheduling.

KF902.W55 2002
343.73'078624—dc21

2002151680

About Aspen Publishers

Aspen Publishers, headquartered in New York City, is a leading information provider for attorneys, business professionals, and law students. Written by preeminent authorities, our products consist of analytical and practical information covering both U.S. and international topics. We publish in the full range of formats, including updated manuals, books, periodicals, CDs, and online products.

Our proprietary content is complemented by 2,500 legal databases, containing over 11 million documents, available through our Loislaw division. Aspen Publishers also offers a wide range of topical legal and business databases linked to Loislaw's primary material. Our mission is to provide accurate, timely, and authoritative content in easily accessible formats, supported by unmatched customer care.

To order any Aspen Publishers title, go to *www.aspenpublishers.com* or call 1-800-638-8437.

To reinstate your manual update service, call 1-800-638-8437.

For more information on Loislaw products, go to *www.loislaw.com* or call 1-800-364-2512.

For Customer Care issues, e-mail CustomerCare@aspenpublishers.com; call 1-800-234-1660; or fax 1-800-901-9075.

Aspen Publishers
A Wolters Kluwer Company

SUBSCRIPTION NOTICE

This Aspen Publishers product is updated on a periodic basis with supplements to reflect important changes in the subject matter. If you purchased this product directly from Aspen Publishers, we have already recorded your subscription for the update service.

If, however, you purchased this product from a bookstore and wish to receive future updates and revised or related volumes billed separately with a 30-day examination review, please contact our Customer Service Department at 1-800-234-1660, or send your name, company name (if applicable), address, and the title of the product to:

ASPEN PUBLISHERS
7201 McKinney Circle
Frederick, MD 21704

CONTENTS

Sections listed below appear only in the supplement and not in the main volume.

Preface		ix

PART I SCHEDULE PREPARATION AND IMPLEMENTATION

Chapter 4	**Legal Aspects of Schedule Specifications**	3
§ 4.14A	Federal Unified Facilities Guide Specification	3
Chapter 5	**Rights and Obligations in Scheduling**	19

PART II CLAIM RECOGNITION, PREPARATION, AND PROOF

Chapter 8	**Time Impact Analysis Procedures**	23
Chapter 9	**Applying CPM Techniques to Contract Claims**	35
§ 9.11	Failure to Provide Acceptable Network Analysis Schedule as Material Breach of Contract Justifying Termination/Relevance of Defective Schedules to Default Terminations	68
Chapter 10	**Standards of Proof for Contractor Time Delay Claims**	77
§ 10.08	Negative Inferences Drawn from Claimant's Failure to Call Witnesses with Actual Knowledge of Project	77
Chapter 11	**Scheduling Industry Crisis—"Rotten Bananas in Software Paradise" or "The Return to the Uncertainty of the Bar Chart"**	79
Chapter 12	**Calculating Contractor's Damages for Delay, Disruption, and Loss of Efficiency**	81
Chapter 13	**Calculating Owner's Damages for Delay**	87
Chapter 15	**Legal Decisions Affecting Experts—Expert's Role in Preparing and Defending Schedule Claims**	93
Chapter 16	**Case Histories**	107

§ 16.08	Big Dig	107
§ 16.09	NOAA Facility	109

Appendix L   **PMI's College of Scheduling**   **115**

Appendix M   **Unified Facilities Guide Specifications for Network Analysis Systems (Feb. 2003)**   **119**

Appendix N   **Unified Facilities Guide Specifications for Network Analysis Systems (Apr. 2002)**   **145**

Table of Cases   *171*

Index   *173*

PREFACE

The last year since the publication of the second edition of *Construction Scheduling* has seen a variety of significant developments. These developments concern actual scheduling practices and procedures as well as the legal principles that apply to the scheduling field.

Developments in the field of scheduling practices and procedures include:

- The continued growth of the PMI College of Scheduling (as well as the growth of the PMI COS Board of Directors to include software and industry leaders), *www.pmicos.org*, to address needs of the field of scheduling in education, training, guidelines, and best practices (see new **Appendix L** for information on the College).

- The commitment by AACE to develop a certification test for schedulers.

- The development by key federal agencies (the Navy, Air Force, Corps of Engineers) of a combined scheduling specification, the Unified Facilities Guide Specification or UFGS, which directly addresses the issues of defective schedules and seeks to stamp out abuses (whether arising from software features, negligence, or deliberate manipulation). We analyze this specification in new **§ 4.14A** (see also **Appendix M** for the 2003 version). The most up-to-date version of the specification may be found at *http://www.ccb.org/ufgs/ufgs.htm*.

- The development by the English Society of Construction Law of a proposed scheduling standard, including a protocol for the calculation of delays; see *www.scl.org* and *www.eotprotocol.com*.

Developments in the legal arena of scheduling are extremely important. They include:

- The landmark *Stone and Webster* decision recognizing the right of an owner on a major project to terminate a contractor for default due to the contractor's failure to produce an acceptable schedule (open ends, unacceptable logic, omitted work), thereby committing a material breach of contract (see new **§ 9.11**).

- A number of decisions addressing the issue of apportionment/nonapportionment of liquidated damages in the context of concurrent delay. These decisions include a number of state and federal decisions. Significantly, these include the landmark *PCL* decision by Judge Horn of the Federal Claims Court, which directly addresses the apparent anomaly between cases stating that courts will not allocate damages between the parties when concurrent delays are present (during a given time frame) and cases in which courts actually apportion damages when alleged concurrent delays are present. This was followed by the *Manuel* decision by the same judge, giving us further guidance as to circumstances in which so-called apportionment will be allowed (see § **9.08[G][2]**).

- Decisions confirming that CPM proof is the preferred method of establishing delay (see § **9.08[A]**).

- Decisions confirming the refusal of courts and boards to accept as proof defective schedules that contain erroneous logic, omitted resource loading, omitted phasing, and unallowed constraints (see § **9.11**).

- Decisions reflecting the application of *Daubert* rules to expert witness testimony, including a ruling disallowing certain unqualified scheduling experts and their testimony (see § **15.02**).

- Decisions addressing the application of CPM principles to liquidated damages as well as penalties and concurrent delays (see § **13.03[A]** and **[B]**).

- Decisions reflecting the necessity for an owner to be proactive in dealing with preparation and accuracy of contemporaneous schedules (see §§ **9.06[E]**, **9.06[F]**, and **9.08[D]**).

- Decisions confirming the owner's duty to schedule and coordinate the work in a multi-prime setting (see § **5.04[C]**).

- Decisions allowing negative inferences to be drawn from the failure to call witnesses with actual knowledge (see new § **10.08**).

- Cases reflecting the use of contemporaneous schedule updates to determine and calculate critical path delays (see §§ **9.06[E]**, **9.06[F]**, and **9.08[D]**).

- Decisions involving lost efficiency calculation on CPM projects (see §§ **8.11** and **12.16**).

PREFACE

- Rulings confirming presumptions relative to compensable time derived from the execution of contract modifications (see § **9.08[M]**).

- Decisions reflecting the increasing sophistication of state courts in applying CPM principles to delay claims (see § **9.08[A]**).

- A poorly reasoned VA Board of Contract Appeals decision, *Fire Security Systems, Inc.*, on float and postcontract completion date delays, holding that the burden of proof is on the contractor to show that base contract work (performed after the current completion date) could or would have been performed sooner had owner delays not occurred (see §§ **9.08[G][3]** and **9.08[K]**); and

- *Eichleay* decisions reflecting the willingness of state courts to utilize the *Eichleay* standards, as well as federal decisions reflecting the continuing evolution of this important legal rule for calculating extended overhead expense (see § **12.14**).

Also included in the 2004 Supplement are two new case studies. The first concerns Boston's "Big Dig" procurement, and addresses the need for the owner to be proactive and vigilant in all phases of the scheduling process. The second case study is on a National Oceanic and Atmospheric Administration facility in Boulder, Colorado (see § **16.09**).

October 2003   JON M. WICKWIRE
                                                        Vienna, Virginia

CONSTRUCTION SCHEDULING:
PREPARATION, LIABILITY, AND CLAIMS

2004 Supplement

PART I
SCHEDULE PREPARATION AND IMPLEMENTATION

Chapter 4
LEGAL ASPECTS OF SCHEDULE SPECIFICATIONS

Page 107, add new section between §§ 4.14 and 4.15:

§ 4.14A FEDERAL UNIFIED FACILITIES GUIDE SPECIFICATION

The 2002 Unified Facilities Guide Specification for Network Analysis Systems, a copy of which is contained in **Appendix N**, has been adopted by the Corps of Engineers, Air Force, and Navy. It confronts the issues identified in this chapter with respect to: necessary elements of scheduling specifications, including the types of reports required during performance for transparency and visibility for the owner; the pitfalls and abuses of scheduling software and network analysis logic identified in **Chapters 2, 3,** and **11**; and the nature of float, major project revisions, and the calculation of project delays.

In this analysis we are working from the April 2002 version of the Guide Specification (**Appendix N**), because it sets out separately the requirements for a design/bid/build-type procurement. The later versions of the Guide Specification combine design-build provisions with design/bid/build provisions. This requires a greater effort to separate. The combined specification (dated February 2003) is, however, available in **Appendix M**.

For the latest version of the Guide Specification, visit the Web site *http://www.ccb.org/ufgs/ufgs.htm*.

In breaking down our analysis, we first examine the manner by which the April 2002 Unified Facilities Guide Specification (UFGS) addresses necessary elements of scheduling specifications. Second, we examine the means by which the specification deals with diagramming/software abuses, as well as with the potential conflict of precedence (activity on node) versus arrow (activity on arrow) diagramming methods in assuring good quality schedules. Third, we address the manner by which the specification deals with float, major project revisions, and calculation of project delays.

First, we turn to the manner by which the UFGS addresses necessary elements of scheduling specification. In the earlier examination (see **§ 4.01**), the following are identified as necessary elements for consideration: feasibility of the schedule; type of diagram used; number of activities; resource loading; approval; control of the record schedule; updating procedures; cost loading; float use and reporting; subcontractor involvement; major revisions and time extensions.

In § **4.13,** the following typical areas of conflict arising from scheduling specification are identified: unreasonable schedules; the approval/nonapproval issue; approval standoff; failure to require initial and continuing involvement of major trade contractors; vague and defective updating procedures; failure to require joint updating meetings to force proactive and timely engagement; defective procedures for approval and updating of logic revisions; failure to provide definite methodology for incorporation of logic revisions; failure to provide a definite baseline and methodology for approval and incorporation of time extensions; and submission of early completion schedules.

In this section we review the UFGS within the context of these issues and concerns. At the end of the discussion, there is an overall evaluation of the specifications; a full copy of the April 2002 Specification is provided in **Appendix N.**

A number of key facts appear in Section 1.1 of the specification. First, a schedule must be prepared on the basis of a network analysis system. This system is to include a network analysis schedule (diagram),[35.1] a mathematical analysis, and associated reports. Scheduling is the responsibility of the contractor, not the owner; submission of progress data will be used to assess progress and evaluate payment and time extension requests. The critical path method of network calculation will be used to generate the schedule and will use the precedence diagram technique to satisfy time and cost applications.[35.2] The schedule will be cost-loaded for payment purposes:

> 1.1 DESCRIPTION
> Prepare a progress chart pursuant to the clause entitled "FAR 52.236-15, Schedules for Construction Contracts" of the Contract Clauses that shall consist of a network analysis system. The network analysis system shall consist of the network analysis schedule (diagram), mathematical analysis, and associated reports. The scheduling of construction shall be the responsibility of the Contractor. Submission of progress and revision data will be used to measure work progress, aid to evaluate time extensions, and provide basis of all progress payments. The Critical Path Method (CPM) of network calculation shall be used to generate the project schedule and will utilize the Precedence Diagram technique to satisfy both time and cost applications. All progress payment amounts will be derived from and tied to the cost-loaded schedule activities.

[35.1] When the UFGS mentions a diagram, it should immediately be understood that the diagram is not a mere bar without logic ties.

[35.2] The reference to critical path calculation means that the forward and backward passes for finding the critical path are clearly required. Further, although this section of the specification refers to the use of precedence diagram technique, the UFGS specification in fact greatly limits use of precedence-type relationships (such as start-to-start or finish-to-finish or leads-and-lags with the consequent need for careful vigilance; see **Ch. 11**) where traditional predecessor successor relationships can be used.

LEGAL ASPECTS OF SPECIFICATIONS § 4.14A

Section 1.3 of the specifications confirms both that the schedule submission requires acceptance and that the contractor remains responsible for scheduling and prosecuting the work. Government acceptance extends only to activities for which the government is responsible:

> 1.3 SCHEDULE ACCEPTANCE
> Review comments made by the Government on the Contractor's construction schedule will not relieve the Contractor from compliance with requirements of the Contract Documents. The Contractor is responsible for scheduling, sequencing, and prosecuting the Work to comply with the requirements of the Contract Documents. Government acceptance extends only to the activities of the contractor's schedule that the Government has been assigned responsibility for and agrees it is responsible. <u>The Government will also review for contract imposed schedule constraints and conformance, and cost loading of the CPM activities</u>. Comments offered on other parts of the schedule which the Contractor is assigned responsibility are offered as a courtesy and are not conditions of government acceptance; but are for the general conformance with established industry schedule concepts. [Emphasis added.]

Section 1.3.1 confirms that the accepted network analysis system is *required before the contractor will be allowed to start work*:

> 1.3.1 Schedule Acceptance Prior to Start of Work
> The Accepted Network described in the paragraph entitled "Accepted Network Analysis Schedule" must be submitted and accepted by the government before the contractor will be allowed to start work.

Section 1.3.2 details the fact that once the network analysis schedule has been accepted, it becomes the *baseline schedule* for planning, executing, and reporting the work. The submission of monthly updates constitutes *a representation that the schedule meets all contract requirements and **accurately reflects the work accomplished**, and that the work will be **executed in the sequence indicated** on the submitted schedule:*

> 1.3.2 Acceptance
> a. When the Accepted Network Schedule is submitted and accepted by the Contracting Officer, it will be considered the "<u>Baseline CPM Schedule</u>". The Baseline CPM Schedule will then be used by the Contractor for planning, organizing, and directing the work; reporting progress; and requesting payment for work accomplished. The schedule will be updated monthly by the Contractor and submitted monthly with the progress pay request to reflect the current status of the work. [For payment requests made after the period covered by the Preliminary Schedule,] The submittal and acceptance of the Accepted Network Analysis Schedule and accurate updated schedules accompanying the

pay requests are both conditions precedent to processing pay requests. Only bonds will be paid prior to acceptance of the Accepted Network Analysis Schedule.

b. <u>Submittal of the Network, and subsequent updates</u>, will be understood to be the <u>Contractor's representation that the submitted schedule meets all of the requirements of the Contract Documents, accurately reflects the work accomplished, and that Work will be executed in the sequence indicated on the submitted schedule</u>. [Emphasis added.]

Section 1.4 calls for the use of Primavera software or software convertible to Primavera-readable format. However, a later section on activity properties severely restricts some of the user features.

Section 1.5 requires an experienced scheduler to be provided at a level commensurate with the nature of the project. If an acceptable scheduler is not provided, progress payments will not be processed.

Section 1.6, entitled "Network System Format," and its subsections are some of the most important provisions of the specification. These provisions make it clear that the Corps, Navy, and Air Force want real-time scaled logic diagrams with well-defined activity logic, not bar-chart reports. Further, the specifications make it clear that shortcut logic will not be allowed. Although the specifications earlier noted that precedence diagramming would be used, here the government requires that activities have predecessor and successor ties wherever possible—it is therefore looking for finish-to-start relationships and avoidance of open ends. Moreover, as shown from an examination of later activity properties, the government prohibits the kinds of manipulation discussed in **Chapters 10** and **11** (such as constraints, improper updating, incorrect calendars, etc.).

We start with Section 1.6, which requires a time scaled logic diagram and mathematical analyses:

> 1.6 NETWORK SYSTEM FORMAT
> The system shall consist of time scaled logic diagrams accompanying mathematical analyses and specified reports.

Section 1.6.1 specifies the diagram and makes it clear that finish-to-start relationships are desired,[35.3] as well as necessary reports and limitations on the duration of activities. This specification, by requiring that logic ties move from right to left only effectively prohibits the use of logic such as negative lags:

> 1.6.1 Diagrams
> Show the order and interdependence of activities and the sequence in which the work is to be accomplished as planned. <u>The basic concept

---

[35.3] This is shown by the language: "The basic concept of a network analysis diagram will be followed to show how the start of a given activity is dependent on the completion of preceding activities and how its completion restricts or restrains the start of following activities."

LEGAL ASPECTS OF SPECIFICATIONS § 4.14A

<u>of a network analysis diagram will be followed to show how the start of a given activity is dependent on the completion of preceding activities and how its completion restricts or restrains the start of following activities</u>. Diagrams shall be [organized by [Work Phase] [Area Code] and] sorted by Early Start Date and <u>will show a continuous flow from left to right with no logic (relationship lines) from right to left</u>. <u>With the exception of the Project Start and Project Completion</u> milestone activities, <u>no activities will be open-ended; each activity will have predecessor and successor ties</u>. The <u>diagram shall clearly show the activities of the critical path</u>. No onsite construction activity shall have duration in excess of 20 working days. Once an activity exists on the schedule it may not be deleted and must remain in the logic. No more than [20] [___] percent of the activities may be critical or near critical. Critical will be defined as having zero days of Total Float. "Near critical" will be defined as having Total Float in the range of [1 to 14] [[___] to [___]] days. Show the following information on the diagram for each activity:

    a. Activity/Event Number
    b. Activity Description
    c. Original Duration in work days
    d. Actual Duration in Work Days
    e. Early Start Date
    f. Early Finish Date
    g. Total Float (or Slack)
    h. Responsibility Code

Provide network diagrams on ANSI E sheets. Updated diagrams shall show the date of the latest revision. [Emphasis added.]

Section 1.6.2 covers the quantity and numbering of activities. Here the specification calls for the use, in general, of higher numbers for successor activities than predecessors.

Section 1.6.2.2 requires that procurement activities be included as separate activities.

Section 1.6.2.3 requires that the network identify government activities that could impact progress.

Section 1.6.2.4 requires that contractor activities be based on a calendar where Saturday, Sundays, and federal holidays are shown as non-work days.

Section 1.6.2.5 covers the requirement for taking into account normal weather delays. This specification requires that the number of allocated weather delays be reflected in the activity's calendar.

Section 1.6.2.6, entitled "Activity Properties," contains provisions extremely important to assuring the validity and integrity of the network schedule. These include subsections a through x, which cover such key requirements as: a standard activity coding dictionary; activity description; work phase; work category; area code; responsibility code; CSI code; drawing code; modification code (identifying activities that are modified or added by modification); REA (request for equitable adjustment) or claim code; project milestone dates; scheduled project duration; project start date milestones; constraint of last activity milestone; early completion milestone (if applicable with an unconstrained date with a zero duration milestone); substantial completion milestone (when the contractor elects to include one—again with an unconstrained date with a zero duration milestone); and phase start and end milestones.

Most significantly, Section 1.6.2.6 sets forth specific provisions in subsections v, w, and x, calling for the use of activities rather than shortcut diagramming techniques. These provisions also prohibit poor scheduling or potential abuses of the type noted in **Chapters 10** and **11** with leads and lags or incorrect logic or incorrect updating. (For example, the UFGS prohibits the use of automatic updating procedures; it requires that activities be updated by actual work progress rather than being cash-flow-driven).

> v. Activity/Event Constraints: <u>Date/time constraint(s)</u>, other than those required by the contract, <u>will not be allowed unless accepted by the Contracting Officer</u>.
> w. Leads and Lags. <u>Leads or lags will not be used when the creation of an activity will perform the same function</u> (e.g., concrete cure time). <u>Lag durations</u> contained in the project schedule <u>shall not have a negative value</u>. The use of any lead or lag will be explained in the Narrative Report.
> x. Default Progress Data Disallowed: Actual Start and Finish dates shall not be automatically updated by default mechanisms that may be included in the CPM scheduling software system. <u>Actual Start and Actual Finish dates on the CPM schedule shall match the dates provided from Contractor Quality Control and Production Reports. These reports will be the sole basis for updating the schedule.</u> Work activities will be updated by actual work progression rather than being cash flow driven. The updating of the percent complete and the remaining duration of any activity shall be independent functions; program features that calculate one of these parameters from the other shall be disabled. Out-of-Sequence progress (if applicable) shall be handled through Retained Logic, not the Default Option of Progress Override. Actual labor and equipment hours used on activities will be derived from the daily reports. [Emphasis added.]

Section 1.6.3 covers the requirement for mathematical analysis for each activity in the network, including total float, manpower required, early start/finish, late start/finish, actual starts/finishes, and so on.

> 1.6.3 Mathematical Analysis
> The network diagram mathematical analysis shall include a tabulation of each activity shown on the detailed network diagrams. Provide the following information as a minimum for each activity:

a. Activity/Event number
b. Activity/Event description
c. Estimated duration of activities (by work days)
d. Earliest start date (by calendar date)
e. Earliest finish date (by calendar date)
f. Actual start date (by calendar date)
g. Actual finish date (by calendar date)
h. Latest start date (by calendar date)
i. Latest finish date (by calendar date)
j. Total float or slack
k. Material/Equipment costs will be assigned to their respective Procurement Activities (i.e., the delivery activity). Costs for installation of the material/equipment (labor, construction equipment, and temporary materials) will be assigned to their respective Construction Activities. The value of inspection/testing activities will not be less than [10] [__] percent of the total costs for Procurement and Construction Activities. Evenly disperse overhead and profit to each activity over the duration of the project.
l. Responsibility code (including prime contractor, subcontractors, suppliers, Government, or other party responsible for accomplishment of an activity.)
m. Area Code
n. Manpower required (crew size)
o. Percentage of activity duration completed
p. Contractor's earnings based on accepted work-in-place.

The program or means used in making the mathematical computation shall be capable of compiling the total value of completed and partially completed activities. The program shall also be capable of accepting revised completion dates as modified by approved time extensions and recompilation of tabulation dates/codes and float accordingly. The total of all cost loaded activities; including costs for material and equipment delivered for installation on the project, and manpower and construction equipment loaded construction activities, shall total to 100 percent of the value of the contract.

Section 1.6.4 provides for additional information to track on-site manpower loading and equipment loading.

Section 1.6.5, entitled "Required Reports," contains provisions that are again important to make sure that the owner has real visibility as to what is happening on the project, including logic relationships and changes in schedule logic from month to month. This provision includes requirements for a monthly disk and reports, detailing activities: by preceding event number, by the amount of total float, by latest allowable start dates, by earned value report for all activities, by early start dates and by 30-day look ahead.

In addition, Subsections 1.6.5 g, h, i, and j specifically require a schedule comparison listing all changes made between the previous and current updated schedules (including changes for added and deleted activities, original durations, remaining durations, activity percent complete, total float, free float, calendars, constraints added or deleted, actual starts/finishes, resource information, changed relation lags, changed critical status); a predecessor/successor report; and manpower and equipment staffing reports and histograms.

g. With each updated schedule submission, provide a computer generated Log Report using a recognized schedule comparision [sic] software listing all changes made between the previous schedule and current updated schedule. Identify the name of the previous schedule and name of the current schedule being compared. This report will as a minimum show changes for: Added & Deleted Activities, Original Durations, Remaining Durations, Activity Percent Complete, Total Float (or Slack), Free Float, Calendars, Descriptions, Constraints (added, deleted or changed), Actual Starts/Finishes, Added/Deleted Resources, Resource Quantities, Costs, Resource Percents, Added/Deleted Relations, Changed Relation Lags, Changed Driving Relations, and Changed Critical Status.

h. By the activity number from lowest to highest, showing preceding and succeeding activity numbers for each activity (Predecessor/Successor Report), and showing the current status of each activity.

i. Manpower staffing report and histogram: With each update schedule, a planned early and planned late versus actual labor resource histogram will be provided. This histogram shall be based upon and shall be in agreement with, the number of shifts and crew sizes by craft, in the Accepted Network Analysis Schedule (planned) and the Monthly Network Update (actual). Included in the report will be a tabular report that will list each trade to the activities that were worked on during the construction period.

j. Equipment usage report and histogram: With each update schedule, a planned early and planned late versus actual equipment resource histogram will be provided. This histogram shall be based upon and shall be in agreement with the equipment allocation accepted on the Accepted Network Analysis Schedule (planned) and the Monthly Network Update (actual). Included in the report will be a tabular report that will list equipment (by make and model) to the activities that were worked on during the construction period.

Section 1.7 covers submission and acceptance of the schedule. Of significance here is the requirement for a schedule development session attended not only by the owner but also by major subcontractors. Further time cycles are called out for the submission and review process.

The next important provision is Section 1.7.7, "Monthly Network Analysis Updates." This provision covers the preparation of the monthly updates and

LEGAL ASPECTS OF SPECIFICATIONS § 4.14A

requires joint updating meetings to develop an accurate picture of construction progress and predictions of completion dates based on current status. Further submission of an error-free acceptable update is a condition precedent to processing the contractor's pay request.

1.7.7 Monthly Network Analysis Updates
At monthly intervals the Contractor, Government representatives and major subcontractors will meet to jointly update the project schedule and agree on percentage of payment for each activity progressed during the update period. The purpose of the meeting is to determine progress payment amounts for each activity, allow all parties to evaluate project status at the data date, provide a complete and accurate update of procurement and construction progress, create an historical record of the project and establish prediction of completion date(s) based upon current status. The Contractor is responsible to gather all supporting documentation[,] propose the update data for the schedule and record the meeting minutes. All progress payment amounts will be derived from and tied to the cost-loaded schedule activities. Submit at monthly intervals a report of the actual construction progress by updating the required reports, the time scaled logic diagram, and mathematical analysis. Meeting to update the schedule and the submission of an error free, acceptable updated schedule to the Government is a condition precedent to the processing of the Contractor's pay request. As a minimum, the following actions will be accomplished during the meeting:

a. Identify activities started and completed during the previous period and enter the Actual Start and Actual Finish dates.
b. Show estimated duration (in workdays) to complete each activity started but not completed (remaining duration).
c. Indicate percentage of cost payable for each activity.
d. Reflect changes in the network diagram. All changes (i.e., duration changes, logic changes, new logic, conformed change orders, new activities, changes due to Conformed Modifications, changes in work sequence, etc.) shall be recorded and a note added to the activity log field. The log shall include as a minimum, the date and reason for the change, and description of the change.
e. Submit [two] [___] copies of a Narrative Report describing: 1) Progress made in each area of the project; 2) Changes in the following: activities, original durations, logic interdependencies, milestones, planned sequence of operations, critical path, and resource and loading; 3) Pending items and status thereof, including permits, change orders, and time extensions; 4) Status of Contract Completion Date and interim milestones; 5) Current and anticipated delays (describe cause of the delay and corrective action(s)); and 6) Description of current and future schedule problem areas. Each entry in the narrative report will cite the respective Activity ID and Activity Description.

f. Submit [two] [___] copies of the required reports listed in paragraph entitled "Required Reports".
g. Submit [two] [___] copies of the Update Meeting minutes.

Section 1.7.8 covers the requirement for a summary network.

Section 1.7.9 requires the preparation of an accurate as-built schedule prior to the release of retention. It must include accurate logic ties as well as starts and finishes of activities.

1.7.9 As-Built Schedule
As a condition precedent to the release of retention, the last update of the schedule submitted shall be identified by the Contractor as the "As-Built Schedule". The As-Built shall reflect the exact manner in which the project was actually constructed (including actual start and finish dates, activities, sequences, and logic) and shall be certified by the Contractor's Project Manager and Construction Scheduler as being a true reflection of the way the project was actually constructed. If more than one person filled the position(s) during the course of the project, each person will provide certification for the period of time they were responsible.

Section 1.8 details the requirements for contract modification. This includes the submission of the proposed revisions to the schedule with a fragnet and cost proposal—as will be seen later, no reservation of rights is allowed. All modifications require separately identifiable activities and are inserted into the network in the first update following notice to proceed. This provision further requires *submission of the total float report and proposed time impact analysis on a disk to establish the change*. Unless allowed by the owner, only conformed modification fragnets will be added to later monthly updates.

1.8 CONTRACT MODIFICATION
When a contract modification to the work is required, submit proposed revisions to the network with a fragnet and a cost proposal for each proposed change. All modifications shall be incorporated into the network analysis system as separately identifiable activities broken down and inserted appropriately on the first update following issuance of a directive to proceed with the change. Submit [one copy] [___ copies] of the Total Float Report, Log Report and a copy of the proposed Time Impact Analysis on disk, with the cost proposal. Unless the Contracting Officer requests otherwise, only conformed contract modification fragnets will be added into the subsequent monthly updates. All revisions to the current baseline schedule activities that are necessary to further refine the schedule so that the changed work activities can be logically tied to the schedule shall be made. Financial data shall not be incorporated into the schedule until the contract modification is signed by the Contracting Officer.

LEGAL ASPECTS OF SPECIFICATIONS § 4.14A

Section 1.8.1 requires a time impact analysis to justify extensions of time and to illustrate the effect of the change or delay on the completion dates. This specification calls for use of the current monthly schedule accepted by the owner to display the impact of the change.[35.4]

> 1.8.1 Time Impact Analysis:
> Time Impact Analysis shall be used by the Contracting Officer in determining if a time extension or reduction to the contract milestone date(s) is justified. The Contractor shall provide a Time Impact Analysis to the Contracting Officer for any proposed contract change or as support for a Value Engineering Proposal, Clam or Request for Equitable Adjustment by the Contractor.
>
> a. The Contractor shall submit a Time Impact Analysis (TIA) illustrating the influence of each change or delay on the Contract Completion Date or milestones. <u>Unless the Contracting Officer requests an interim update to the schedule, the current monthly updated schedule accepted by the government shall be used to display the impacts of the change</u>. Unless requested by the Contracting Officer, no other non-conformed changes will be incorporated into the schedule being used to justify the change impact.
> b. <u>Each TIA shall include</u> a Fragmentary Network (<u>fragnet</u>) demonstrating how the Contractor proposes to incorporate the impact into the Project Schedule. A fragnet is defined as the sequence of new activities and/or activity revisions, logic relationships and resource changes that are proposed to be added to the existing schedule to demonstrate the influence of impacts to the schedule. The fragnet shall identify the predecessors to the new activities and demonstrate the impacts to successor activities. Include a narrative report describing the effects of new activities and relationship to interim and contract completion dates, with each TIA.
> c. Following the Contractor's receipt of a contract modification on a Standard Form 30 signed by the Government, all changes in the fragnet used to determine impacts, shall be incorporated into the schedule. Changes will occur during the next monthly schedule update meeting. [Emphasis added.]

Section 1.8.2 prohibits reservation of rights.

[35.4] This raises a question, in considering a delay purported to have occurred in May of 2002, which is not evaluated (for whatever reason) until November 2002, as to which update will be used to incorporate the time impact analysis. As we will see, this question becomes more interesting when we get to UFGS Section 1.11, "Time Extensions," which calls for granting time only in circumstances in which a given matter *actually* delays the project. Section 1.11, "Time Extensions," also requires that the purported delay affect the contract completion dates ***on the CPM network at the time of the delay.***

1.8.2 No Reservation-Of-Rights
All direct costs, indirect costs, and time extensions will be negotiated and made full, equitable and final at the time of modification issuance.

Section 1.9 covers changes to the network analysis schedule, requiring submissions to the owner when the contractor wants to make major changes in logic and particularly when the contractor is trying to shorten the schedule.

1.9 CHANGES TO THE NETWORK ANALYSIS SCHEDULE
If changes in the method of operating and scheduling are desired, the Contracting Officer shall be notified in writing stating the reasons for the change. If the Contracting Officer considers these changes to be of a major nature, the Contractor may be required to revise and submit for acceptance, without additional cost to the Government, the network diagrams and required sorts. A change may be considered of a major nature if the estimated time required or actually used for an activity or the network logic is varied from the original plan to a degree that there is a reasonable doubt as to the effect on the contract completion date(s) [or phase completion dates]. Change that affect activities with adequate float time shall be considered a major change when their cumulative effect could extend the contract completion date.

Section 1.10 and its subsections are some of the most important provisions in the entire specification. This section covers the topic of float. First, in Section 1.10 the specification *prohibits the use of potential gaming techniques, including the use of float suppression techniques, preferential sequencing, special lead/lag logic relationships, constraints to force dates and interrupt the math of the network, unreasonable resource leveling to manipulate float, and extended activity times to remove float.*

1.10 FLOAT
Use of float suppression techniques, such as: preferential sequencing (arranging critical path through activities more susceptible to government caused delay), special lead/lag logic restraints, zero total or free float constraints, extended activity times, or imposing constraint dates other than as required by the contract, shall be cause for rejection of the project schedule or its updates. The use of Resource Leveling (or similar software features) used for the purpose of artificially adjusting activity durations to consume float and influence the critical path is expressly prohibited.

Section 1.10.1 defines float.

1.10.1 Definitions of Float or Slack
Free Float is the length of time the start of an activity can be delayed without delaying the start of a successor activity. Total Float is the length of time along a given network path that the actual start and finish of

LEGAL ASPECTS OF SPECIFICATIONS § 4.14A

activity(s) can be delayed without delaying the project completion date. Project Float is the length of time between the Contractor's Early Completion (or Substantial Completion) and the Contract Completion Date.

Section 1.10.2 covers ownership of float, making it clear that this is a shared resource available to both parties. In addition, this specification deals with the issue of early completion schedules, identifying the time between an early completion and the contract completion date as float, and specifying that no time or delay damages will be granted unless a delay extends the project beyond the contract completion date.

> 1.10.2 Ownership of Float
> Float available in the schedule, at any time shall not be considered for the exclusive use of either the Government or the Contractor. During the course of contract execution, any float, generated due to the efficiencies of either party is not for the sole use of the party generating the float; rather it is a <u>shared commodity</u> to be reasonably used by either party. <u>Efficiencies gained as a result of favorable weather</u> within a calendar month, where the number of days of normally anticipated weather is less than expected, <u>will also contribute to the reserve of float</u>. <u>A schedule showing work completing in less time than the Contract time, and accepted by the Government, will be considered to have Project Float</u>. Project Float will be a resource available to both the Government and the Contractor. No time extensions will be granted nor delay damages paid unless a delay occurs which impacts the Project's critical path, consumes all available float or contingency time, and extends the work beyond the Contract Completion Date. [Emphasis added.]

Section 1.10.3 addresses the issue of negative float and notes that negative float by itself will not be a ground for requesting time extensions. This is entirely logical. When a project goes negative, the critical path does not end; rather, one needs to look for the path with the greatest amount of negative float to find the critical path.

> 1.10.3 Negative Float
> Negative float will not be a basis for requesting time extensions. Any extension of time will be addressed in accordance with the Paragraph "time extensions". Scheduled completion date(s) that extend beyond the contract [or phase] completion date(s) (evidenced by negative float) may be used in computations for assessment of payment withholdings. The use of this computation is not to be construed as a means of acceleration.

Section 1.11 covers time extensions. This section details the need for a time impact analysis, total float report, and the like to demonstrate that the critical path is actually affected, utilizing the dates shown on the CPM network at the time of the delay. This provision thus appears to require chronological and cumulative analyses of the updates to determine the effect of the delay and also to make certain (probably by looking both at the updates at the beginning of a period and at what happened during the update) that purported delays actually delayed the critical path.

> 1.11 TIME EXTENSIONS
> Extension of time for performance required under the clauses entitled "Changes," "Differing Site Conditions," "Default (Fixed-Price Construction)" or "Suspension of Work" <u>will be granted only to the extent that equitable time adjustments for the activity or activities affected exceed the total float or slack</u> along the network paths <u>involved at the time Notice to Proceed was issued for the change</u>. The <u>Contractor</u> acknowledges and <u>agrees that delays</u> in activities <u>which, according to the network analysis schedule, does [sic] not in fact actually affect any milestone completion dates</u> or the contract completion date shown on the CPM network at the time of delay, <u>will not be a basis for a contract extension</u>. Submit time extension requests with a Time Impact Analysis and three copies of the Total Float (or Slack) Report, Narrative Report and Log Report. [Emphasis added.]

Sections 11.12, 11.13, 11.14, and 11.15 cover requirements for meetings, reports, and correspondence.

When assessing the UFGS, we find that the necessary elements of scheduling specifications are addressed: feasibility of schedule; type of diagram; number of activities; resource loading; approval; control of the record schedule; updating; cost loading; subcontractor involvement; float use and reporting; and major revisions and time extensions. The UFGS does a very good job of covering these items. One area that could benefit from more attention is control of the record schedule: the contractor should not be running unapproved schedules or unapproved updates. However, this appears to be addressed by the requirement for the joint updating meeting; the requirement that actual starts and finishes be based only on the contractor quality control and production reports; and by the ability to withhold payments.

As noted earlier, typical areas of conflict include unreasonable schedules, the approval/nonapproval issue, approval standoff, failure to require initial and continuing involvement of major trade contractors, vague and defective updating procedures, failure to require joint updating meetings to force proactive and timely engagement, defective procedures for approval and updating of logic revisions, failure to provide definite methodology for incorporation of logic revisions, failure to provide for definite baseline and methodology for approval and incorporation of time extensions, and submission of early completion schedules. The UFGS has done a good job of dealing with these issues as well. It addresses the unreasonable schedule issue through the review process; addresses approval standoff by requiring that the project not start without approval (as

LEGAL ASPECTS OF SPECIFICATIONS § 4.14A

well through the power of the purse); specifies clear updating procedures; requires joint meetings to update the schedule; provides a protocol for logic revisions; prohibits a litany of devices to game-play the schedule using current software features; provides for a baseline and methodology for incorporating logic revisions and time extension; and addresses early completion schedules in a very successful way through float definitions. The one area that perhaps could be a little clearer is the protocol for time impact analyses and time extensions. What appears to be the standard in the UFGS is use of the updates for the time period in question—here the specification appears to call for evaluating updates both at the beginning and the end of the period to confirm the location of the critical path and to see whether the issue presented was in fact on the critical path and actually delayed contract dates.

CHAPTER 5
RIGHTS AND OBLIGATIONS IN SCHEDULING

§ 5.04 OWNER'S ROLE IN SCHEDULING

[C] Multi-Prime Contracting

Page 139, add at end of subsection:

One decision confirming the duty of an owner to schedule and coordinate the work in a multiple prime setting is *R.W. Granger & Sons, Inc. v. City School District of Albany*, 744 N.Y.S.2d 567, 166 Ed. Law Rep. 744, 2002 N.Y. Slip Op. 05731, 296 A.D.2d 636 (2002). In *Granger*, the New York appeals court considered a multi-prime/multi-phase project where a prime contractor (apparently for the civil work) for a three-phase renovation and addition project at the Albany School of Humanities was terminated for default. Phase II of the project dealt with construction of an addition to the school. Numerous delays extended the date for completion of Phase II from February 7, 1995, and in May 1995 the parties agreed that Phase II was to be substantially complete on June 23, 1995. Although Phase II was completed on June 23, 1995, such that the owner was able to move furniture and materials into the building, the owner terminated the contractor for default for "failure to timely progress the work."

The lower court determined that the termination had been made without cause and awarded the contractor $1,412,745 in damages. The significance of this decision is that it involved a multi-prime contract with separate mechanical, electrical, and plumbing primes. The appeals court found that the decision in favor of *Granger* was justified because the delays were caused *by the failure of the owner to coordinate the work of the various prime contractors and to prepare adequate construction schedules:*

> We affirm. The trial evidence and exhibits are far too voluminous for lengthy recitation here. However, plaintiff's expert engineer, Thomas Fertitta, testified that based upon his "critical path" analysis, the project was delayed for a total of 133 days. Of the 133 days, Fertitta attributed all but 15 days to defendant and its agents by reason of <u>their failure to coordinate the work of the various prime contractors and to prepare adequate construction schedules</u>. These failures, in turn, resulted in the mechanical, electrical and plumbing work interfering with plaintiff's work, thereby causing the complained of delay. [Emphasis added.]

Part II
CLAIM RECOGNITION, PREPARATION, AND PROOF

CHAPTER 8
TIME IMPACT ANALYSIS PROCEDURES

§ 8.11 METHODS FOR MEASURING PRODUCTIVITY LOSS

Page 249, add at end of section:

Two illustrative decisions relating to the issue of proving lost efficiency claims are *Bay Construction Co.*, VABCA No. 5594, 02-1 BCA ¶ 31,795, 2002 WL 442118, and *Fire Security Systems, Inc.*, VABCA No. 5559-63, 02-2 BCA ¶ 31,977, 2002 WL 1979118.

In *Bay*, the VA Board of Contract Appeals considered a claim for lost efficiency supposedly based on a measured mile approach. The testimony of the proffered expert was found to be lacking because it did not even separate trades in developing the "measured mile" presented by the expert:

> Mr. Kim did not prepare the original claim submission using what Appellant referred to as the "measured mile" method; however, he worked on later calculations related to Bay's claim for loss of productivity. (Tr. II/209; R4, tab 10; R4 Supp., tab 23) He defined disruption as "anything that prevents the contractor . . . changes the contractor's intended method of performance, [or] prevents him from doing what he originally anticipated doing in the manner he originally wanted to . . . . [D]isruption often causes the sequence to be shifted, therefore making work being performed out of sequence," and based his opinion as to the Government caused disruption on his critical path analysis. (Tr. II/179, 209; R4, tab 10; R4 Supp., tab 23)
>
> Mr. Kim stated that one of the methods used to measure the impact of disruption was "an industry standard or a Means estimate [Means Estimating Guide]," taking the "should cost" method and applying productivity rates from an industry standard such as Means. He claimed he used that method to do his analysis that shows $62,777.30 in lost productivity. He used "a Means book to calculate the amount of the cost for purposes of lost productivity," and it appeared to him that the amount of time specified in the Means book usually was always less than the durations that Mr. Doerr specified in his schedule. His lost productivity analysis applied what he called "a shift cost estimate" that incorporated the "industry standard method," to calculate $62,777.30 in lost productivity. Bay's original lost productivity claim used what it asserted was a "measured mile calculation" to arrive at $67,637.86 in damages. Bay modified that original claim downward to $50,194. (Tr. II/141, 191, 193-99, 207-09; R4, tab 10; R4 Supp., tabs 22, 23)

When asked to describe the manner in which Bay's performance was disrupted, Mr. Kim referred to his critical path analysis chart and testified that he could see work was "done piecemeal" and "performed out of sequence." He pointed to work that Bay anticipated doing "all at one time" on a particular date and concluded that "as a result of the disruption caused by the supplemental agreement . . . we can see that the work was done piecemeal here and there, here and there." He noted instances where the actual work sequence "flip-flopped" or there was a "change in sequence." Some of the effects of disruption, he opined, might include a loss of momentum and a loss of efficiency. He also referred to a "flattening of the learning curve," and he pointed to areas of his analysis, such as the med-gas work that he said showed a loss of efficiency and "sporadic" work. He concluded "[a]s we can see, because of the effect of the delays, the base line schedule does not compare to the master chart . . . [w]hereas certain tasks were scheduled to be completed prior to others, because of these delays, those time frames were extended and required Bay to do this work and then go back — do one work and then go back to the other, out of sequence." (Tr. II/179-189; R4 Supp., tabs 11 and 51)

Robert L. Clontz, Director of VA's Claims and Risk Management Office, addressed Bay's lost productivity claim. Mr. Clontz has 20 to 25 years of experience reviewing loss of productivity claims and supervises a staff that includes five schedulers and claims analysts. He reviewed Bay's initial lost productivity submission and its revised submission. (Tr. Ill/265; R4, tab 10) In his April 21, 1998 written analysis addressing Bay's original submission, Mr. Clontz noted several discrepancies:

> The loss of productivity analysis presented by the contractor has many errors and does not clearly tie the alleged lost productivity to government actions or inactions. It makes assumptions as if grounded in facts and then arrives at conclusions which are not supported by project records or documents.
>
> Therefore, our review of the Contractor's loss of productivity analysis finds that the Contractor has not clearly demonstrated that the government is liable for any alleged productivity losses. In addition, the Contractor's analysis lacks credibility and is not convincing in [its] attempt to present his alleged losses.
>
> The analysis presented is not a "measured mile" as represented. (R4, tab 41A)

At hearing, Mr. Clontz testified about deficiencies his review of Bay's original application of the "measured mile" method revealed:

> It's represented as being a measured mile analysis. When you get into it, it really doesn't do what would normally be considered a classic measured mile analysis. There are several—besides the numerical problems I found with it and cited in my review, which were documented in my letter, the—there's basically things that as far as the measured mile analysis that appear with it. One of them is that the—in a measured—a classical measured mile analysis, you separate the

different trades that are being—going to be studied. And you separate those trades and determine periods on the job when those trades have periods of performance when they have not been impacted by the alleged government-caused changes or impacts.

And then you compare similar work of that same trade during the alleged or impacted period by the government. And then you compare those two on an hourly basis, and compare the productivity during the period when the trade was impacted by the changes or the government impacts—whatever they were—to the period that's unimpacted. And that gives you a percentage of lost productivity when you do the ratio between the impacted period divided by the productivity per hour during the unimpacted period.

And this analysis doesn't attempt to do that at all. It doesn't separate the trades out. It also doesn't identify the impacted period to any definite government-caused change. It just assumes that the lowest productivity period that they cite through their calculations—right or wrong—is the non-impacted period. They don't tie that period back to when whatever the government-caused change or government-caused impact was going on.

And so there's no connection between not only the trades being separated, but there's no connection between the period when the—what caused the—what period of time during the contract or during the installation of the work, what government cause caused it during what time frame and what work was being done and exactly what trades were being involved. So there's no real comparison. There's no ties that I see there that's been separated to make it a valid lost productivity analysis.

The analysis they presented, as I can tell, mixes both carpenter and laborer trades. It does not separate them out. And it doesn't really indicate the impacted periods.

I found a number of numerical problems in their presentation and analysis. If I could pull out my notes, I could reiterate those. They're in my written analysis. I assume that's been included in the record or not. (Tr. III/265-68)

* * *

In VABCA-5528, Bay claims the Government caused a loss of efficiency and disruption. Loss of productivity or disruption has been defined as the "increased cost of performance caused by a change in the contractor's anticipated or planned working conditions, resources, or manner of performing its work." Michael R. Finke, Claims for Construction Productivity Losses, 26 PUB. CONT. L.J. 311, 313 (1997). Productivity can be affected by many factors that disrupt the efficient performance of work, including multiple changes, interference, delays, alterations in sequencing, suspension and acceleration. These factors may cause a contractor to reassign workers, stack trades and perform work out of sequence, ultimately causing lost productivity and an increase of labor costs. *Id.* at 313-15. A contractor seeking to recover for the impact costs of numerous changes on unchanged work must prove three essential elements: liability, causation, and resultant injury. *Centex Bateson Construction Co.*, VABCA Nos. 4613, 5162-5165, 99-1 BCA ¶ 30,153 at 149,258, *aff'd, Centex Bateson Construction Co. v. West*, 250 F.3d 761 (Fed. Cir. 2000).

Impact costs are additional costs occurring as a result of the loss of productivity; loss of productivity is also termed inefficiency. Thus, impact costs are simply increased labor costs that stem from the disruption to labor productivity resulting from a change in working conditions caused by a contract change. Productivity is inversely proportional to the man-hours necessary to produce a given unit of product. As is self-evident, if productivity declines the number of man-hours of labor to produce a given task will increase. If the number of man-hours increases, labor costs obviously increase.

Id., at 149,257 (citations omitted). Bay has the fundamental responsibility to prove by a preponderance of the evidence that a Government action caused its labor to be less efficient than planned as well as the extent of that impact. *Centex Bateson Construction Company, Inc.*, VABCA Nos. 4613, et al., 99-1 BCA ¶ 20,153; *Dawson*, 93-3 BCA ¶ 26,177; *Triple "A" South*, ASBCA No. 46866, 94-3 BCA ¶ 27,194; *Bechtel National, Inc.*, NASA BCA No. 1186-7, 90-1 BCA ¶ 22,549.

The Appellant wholly failed to present probative evidence of lost productivity. Again, Mr. Kim's charts and summary conclusions that Bay had lost productivity because work was in some instance done out of sequence and piecemeal in some areas fall far short of the proof we expect for such cases. His attempt at quantification, applying two methods to price Bay's alleged damages for what he said was Bay's lost productivity was not compelling for many of the same reasons we articulated in our earlier discussions of his delay and suspension analysis. Bay's lack of contemporaneous project documentation of the impact of the delays and its failure to proffer credible testimony, impeached the overall reliability of its evidence. While Mr. Kim was very willing to assume Government-caused delay and interference, there was very little evidence in the record to back up his assumptions. He had even less professional experience analyzing lost productivity than he had in delay and suspension analysis.

Given the size and complexity of this project, the number and nature of changes reflected in the SAs were not so momentous as to impact the project in the significant and serious ways that Appellant claims. As we recently stated in *Clark Construction Group, Inc.*, "[t]he after-the-fact, conclusory assessments of the project managers or the opinions of its experts are not sufficient substitutes for [the contractor's] underlying obligation to contemporaneously document the severe adverse impact on labor efficiency it now claims resulted from the changes and RFIs." *Clark Construction Group, Inc.*, VABCA No. 5674, 00-1 BCA ¶ 30,870 at 152,413, citing *Fru-Con Construction Corporation v. United States*, 43 Fed. Cl. 306 (1999), *aff'd* 250 F.3d 762 (Fed. Cir. 2000)(Table); *Centex Bateson*, 99-1 BCA ¶ 20,153; *Triple "A" South*, 94-3 BCA ¶ 27,194. We conclude that Bay's evidence failed to provide proof of change to working conditions or loss or productivity. [Emphasis added.]

In Fire Security Systems, VABCA No. 5559-63, 02-2 BCA ¶ 31,977, the VA board considered a claim for delay and lost efficiency arising out of a contract to remove an old system and install a new sprinkler protection system throughout the Harry S. Truman Memorial Veterans Hospital in Columbia, Missouri. The hospital, constructed in the early 1970s, consisted of six stories of occupied patient space, a penthouse, an occupied basement, and a pipe sub-basement.[5]

A major lost efficiency claim by the contractor resulted from the complication of asbestos-containing material (ACM) encountered during the removal and reinstallation project. The VA board, in this decision, recognized the applicability of industry lost efficiency factors (albeit at a lesser percentage than desired by the contractor). It found that measured-mile calculations were not possible under the circumstances of the project, and that an expert put forth by the contractor did not have sufficient support in the record to calculate individual daily delays arising from the ACM complications.

Although the specifications for the *Fire Security Systems* project provided for asbestos to be treated as a "differing site condition," the invitation for bids made no mention of the fact that the VA had already performed a complete assessment of all ACM in the project. Indeed, the VA had taken bids for an earlier potential project to abate the ACM, but had failed to go forward with the work:

> In 1992-93, the VA engaged the firm of Roth Environmental, to perform a complete assessment (the Assessment) of all asbestos containing materials (ACM) present within the hospital building at the Columbia, Missouri VAMC. The individual who actually performed the inspections and authored the reports for Roth Environmental was John Harrington. The VA subsequently issued a solicitation seeking bids for abatement of the ACM within the building. The bids received exceeded the available funds, resulting in the VA's cancellation of the solicitation. (R4, tab 84; Tr. VI/17-19)
>
> In issuing the solicitation that led to the instant Contract, the VA inserted the following General Requirement, paragraph 1.20 in Section 01010 of the Specification
>
> 1.20 ASBESTOS
> A. If, during construction, the contractor suspects the existence of asbestos, other than indicated on the drawings, he will be required to

---

[5] In the realm of how small the world is, one of the authors worked on an omnibus claim for all the contractors arising out of the construction of the original hospital in the early 1970s. The original claim was settled after negotiations with the VA. The original hospital construction suffered from major changed conditions (fractured limestone and complications from an old dump that affected caisson and foundation installation) as well as design deficiencies (throughout the building) due to poor plan preparation by the design team. The author well remembers the pipe sub-basement, the subject of significant asbestos concerns in this renovation project. During the original construction, the plans provided exact locations for utilities to enter the building, unfortunately, they frequently conflicted with concrete beams when the attempt was made to install the utilities in the required locations.

notify the Contracting Officer promptly, and before such conditions are disturbed of the possible presence of asbestos pursuant to the differing site conditions clause.

Other than the language of the clause above, there was no further mention of asbestos, either in the general information and notice to bidders, the drawings or the specifications included within the bid package furnished to all interested bidders. The multi-volume Asbestos Assessment was not mentioned in the solicitation, nor was FSS made aware of its existence prior to bidding. (R4, tabs 299, 300)

During a prebid conference, which Fire Security Systems did not attend, the VA asserted that it had told the prospective bidders about the prior assessment of ACM and its availability. However, there was no mention of this in the minutes to the conference. In fact, the board found that the information should have been provided in the IFB and that the contractor could not be bound by the material in the excluded material:

> Prior to awarding this Contract to FSS, the Government sought bids on a contract for abatement of asbestos at the hospital. Unfortunately, the bids exceeded the available funds and the project was canceled. It also had a consultant, Roth Environmental, prepare a multi-volume Asbestos Assessment of the entire hospital building. That Assessment was available for inspection at the VAMC Safety Office. While prospective bidders who attended the (non-mandatory) pre-bid meeting and walkthrough were made aware of the Assessment, there was no mention of the Assessment in the solicitation itself. Neither was any amendment to the solicitation issued that alerted bidders not present at the pre-bid meeting to the information given by the VA and the issues discussed and questions answered. At the very least, all bidders, whether or not attending a pre-bid meeting, should have been made aware of the Asbestos Assessment, either in the solicitation or by an amendment thereto. Where significant information that could have a bearing on how a contractor will bid and perform a project is not included within the bidding documents, the contractor cannot be bound by the information contained in such excluded materials. *Klefstad Engineering Co. & Blackhawk Heating & Plumbing Co., Inc.*, VACAB No. 602, 68-1 BCA ¶ 6965; cited in *Jack L. Olsen, Inc.*, AGBCA No. 87345-1, 93-2 BCA ¶ 25,767 at 128,217.
>
> This was important information regarding the amount and condition of ACM that was present in the six-story building. <u>Had this information been made available, all potential bidders, including FSS, could themselves have assessed the potential risk to their employees or the difficulty of installing pipe and sprinklers in certain confined areas in close proximity to ACM.</u> Their bids could then be expected to reflect any potential impact on worker productivity. The Appellant was only made aware of the existence of this Assessment at the pre-construction conference—too late to have considered the information in the Assessment in estimating the labor hours necessary to install piping and sprinklers in close proximity to ACM throughout all floors of the building. [Emphasis added.]

TIME IMPACT ANALYSIS PROCEDURES § 8.11

The circumstances of the project did not foster a great deal of confidence between the parties. The VA felt that the contractor used the asbestos issue during performance merely to build a claim. The contractor felt that the VA and its consultant, who had performed the assessment that found significant ACM requiring abatement, were being cavalier and dissembling:

> With respect to the presence of ACM and its effect on the Contractor's workers, Appellant portrays the Government as having a cavalier attitude concerning the safety of the Contractor's employees as well as that of the VA employees and patients at the hospital. For its part, the Government saw the Contractor as overreacting to the mere presence of ACM regardless of its condition, with the ulterior motive of building a claim and pressuring the VA to issue change orders to FSS for abatement of asbestos. Based on the record before the Board, both [parties'] positions are much too extreme. The Government took many responsible measures to guarantee the safety of the Contractor's workers as well as its own personnel and patients and staff of the hospital. As for the Contractor, while we find that its productivity was impacted by the presence of asbestos in certain work areas, we conclude that the impact was far less than claimed. We will discuss these conclusions.
>
> * * *
>
> While the suspected friable asbestos in the overhead spaces sometimes turned out to be nothing more than plaster or gypsum or some other powdery substance—often on the surface of the ceiling tiles, there were some instances where the substance was in fact determined by the VA Safety Specialist to be loose asbestos. In such instances, the responsible VA officials responded by isolating the area and removing the material in accordance with appropriate safety criteria. Then the area would be tested prior to releasing to FSS for further installation work.
>
> <u>The situation with the pipe basement was altogether different from these other experiences, however. There, all four quadrants of this large area with a dirt floor were described in the Asbestos Assessment as virtually saturated with friable asbestos. Its ACTION recommendation that the pipe basement be isolated with restricted access and that the VA "Remove, enclose or encapsulate as soon as possible," had not been followed prior to the award of this Contract</u>. After interpreting the documents as meaning precisely what they said, and conveying their alarm and concern to the VA, <u>both Mr. Hayes and Mr. Knight witnessed a telephone conversation during which the Roth consultant essentially retreated from his original severe assessment under prodding from the VA officials</u>. During the conversation, Mr. Harrington softened his assessment of the condition of the asbestos in the pipe basement, agreeing with the COTR and Safety Officer that the asbestos was actually localized to several areas where discrete portions of insulation had fallen off and landed on the floor. As a result of this experience, the Contractor no longer had any confidence in the assurances of either the VA or its consultant.

> The Board has itself examined the language of the Roth analyses of the pipe basement conditions and simply cannot reconcile the precise descriptions of those conditions ("SEVERELY damaged (99%);" "DISTRIBUTED;" "Friable debris located throughout dirt flooring") with the consultant's "revised" conclusions that the debris was actually located in several discrete piles instead of throughout the dirt floor of every quadrant of the pipe basement. It is small wonder that the Contractor's concerns were magnified as a result of this experience. [Emphasis added.]

Thereafter, the contractor pursued its claim for lost efficiency on the basis of two methodologies. One methodology propounded by contractor personnel, based on the application of three (out of a potential 16) MCA factors, derived lost efficiency of about 30 percent. These included morale and attitude, reassignment of manpower, and dilution of supervision:

> The Contractor's amended claim is in the amount of $143,941. FSS arrived at this amount by calculating a 30% productivity loss factor. It then applied this percentage to what it stated to be the total labor costs for workers (sprinkler pipe-fitters) affected by the presence of asbestos. When the labor cost of $473,470 is divided by 1.30, the resulting $109,262 represents the extra labor cost associated with the presence of ACM. After adding overhead, profit and bond costs, the total claim comes to $143,941. (R4 Supp., tab 534)
>
> Mr. Hayes testified that he utilized the productivity (loss) factors devised by the Mechanical Contractor's Association of America (MCAA) to assist in calculating the impact of the presence or perceived presence of asbestos on the efficiency of the FSS pipefitters. Although there are sixteen factors, the witness focused on three of them as having what he considered to be a severe impact. Factor #2, Morale and Attitude, is described as "Excessive hazard, competition for overtime, over-inspection, multiple contract changes and rework, disruption of labor rhythm and scheduling and poor site conditions." In Mr. Hayes' opinion, several of these conditions applied to the situation in the building. He assigned this factor the severe MCAA rating of 30% inefficiency. Factor #3, Reassignment of Manpower, is described as "Loss occurs with move on, move off men because of unexpected changes, excessive changes or demand made to expedite or reschedule completion of certain work phases, preparation not possible for orderly change." According to Mr. Hayes, the workers had to move from zone to zone which he considered to warrant a severe MCAA rating of 15% inefficiency. The third factor that the witness considered to warrant a severe rating, of 25% inefficiency, was Factor #6, Dilution of Supervision. According to the MCAA, this "Applies to both basic contract and proposed change. Supervision must be diverted to (a) analyze and plan change; (b) stop and re-plan affected work; (c) takeoff order and expedite material and equipment; (d) incorporate change into schedule; (e) instruct foreman and journeymen; (f) supervise work in progress; (g) revise punch list, testing and start-up requirements." Mr. Hayes stated that on many occasions the supervisor (Mr. Knight) had to leave the work area and visit with various

TIME IMPACT ANALYSIS PROCEDURES § 8.11

VA personnel regarding the asbestos problems, creating a severe impact on the crew's efficiency in the superintendent's absence. (Tr. VI/79-88)

The second methodology put forward by the contractor was based on an assessment by the contractor's expert, who had no firsthand knowledge of the specific amounts of lost efficiency experienced daily due to the ACM factor. His assessment was based on daily logs:

> Mr. McLaughlin, Appellant's designated expert witness on loss of efficiency, <u>prepared a report based largely on information contained in the Daily Logs. He had not been present at the job site, nor did he have any first-hand experience with this project</u>. Mr. McLaughlin identified four generally disruptive effects of asbestos, or suspected asbestos, on a contractor's productivity. They are: 1. suspending the work; 2. demobilizing the suspect area; 3. remobilizing the area (after asbestos remediated); 4. impact, that is, even in areas where asbestos is not present. He explained that after asbestos has become a concern to a contractor, he is often more cautious in planning his work and slower and more careful in working in every area. This impacts the Contractor's rate of productivity. In his Report, he first examined all Daily Logs for the base contract pipe installation period from June 22, 1994 through the end of February, 1995. He then assigned one or more of the four disruptive effects to each incident reported in any particular Log. Although the Logs sometimes stated that there was a suspension or a demobilization, he would often assume these impacts even where there was no specific mention. He did this based on his years of experience as a project manager on many construction sites and his ability to estimate the impact of disruptions to work. (Tr. V/167-76)
>
> For instance, on the Log for June 22, 1994, reporting "2 locations of ACM, Zone 4," he assigned two of the disruptive effects, each of two hours on a four-man crew for a total of eight hours multiplied by a fully burdened composite labor rate of $55.00. This came to $440.00 × 2 = $880.00. He considered the initial discovery cause for a suspension of two hours and also that there was another two-hour impact on the same crew. Mr. McLaughlin continued this process for every asbestos-related Log entry, arriving at a total direct impact cost of $22,220. For all other zones where there was no specific mention of asbestos on the Logs, McLaughlin went through each Daily Log and counted the number of workers (assuming a 10 hour day) working in each zone where asbestos was found or suspected. After subtracting out the direct hours already accounted for, he totaled the remaining hours and applied a 25% inefficiency factor for those hours. This total was multiplied by the composite labor rate of $55.00. The resulting total was $71,300. Finally, he computed the labor hours expended in zones where no asbestos was found or suspected and applied a 10% inefficiency factor (the "paranoia" factor). This came to $3,000. The total of the three categories of impact was $96,520. After adding overhead, profit and bond costs, the consultant's price for the overall impact and inefficiency caused by asbestos came to $111,321. Mr. McLaughlin observed that his price was close enough to Appellant's own calculations (using the MCAA

factors) to validate the FSS claim. (R4, Supp., tab 533; Tr. V/176-217) [Emphasis added.]

The board, given these circumstances, made a number of findings with respect to the lost efficiency claim. These included: conclusions that "measured mile" type proof was not applicable to the project in question, as there was no period of undisrupted performance; a finding that the expert witness presentation of individual daily calculations of delay was too speculative and unsupported by the record; a finding that the fact that the contractor actually beat its estimated production rates during actual performance did not bar the contractor from recovering efficiency lost due to the ACM factor; and that the MCAA calculation of lost efficiency required adjustment from 30 percent to 5 percent (for "fear factor"), because the facts of the case did not justify the greater percentage:

> We agree with the VA that the loss of efficiency factors calculated by both Mr. Hayes and Mr. McLaughlin are largely unsupported by the express language reflecting labor efforts in the Daily Logs—language that Mr. Knight stood by as an accurate reflection of each day's events. For example, there is scant mention of the need to demobilize and remobilize. The actual stopping of work occurs only on nine days, usually followed by work in adjacent areas the next day. These impacts are difficult to measure in and of themselves. However, we do agree with Mr. McLaughlin that the frequent discovery of suspected asbestos, whether or not the material proves to be positive for fibers after testing, will ultimately have some negative effect on workers' productivity —something McLaughlin called the "paranoia factor." This is also treated by the MCAA efficiency factors, particularly Number 2, "Morale and Attitude." When the above-ceiling instances of suspected asbestos were combined with the situation in the pipe basement two months into pipe installation there was an impact on worker morale. The contrast between the severe evaluation of asbestos throughout the pipe basement and the dire warnings by the consultant, Mr. Harrington, and the attempted clarification by Mr. Henrickson, only made things worse, regardless of Mr. Henrickson's stated good intentions. Notwithstanding the constant sampling of the ambient air, the Contractor's workers were impacted by the conditions in the pipe basement and the attendant loss of confidence in the VA and its consultant.
>
> General Requirement 1.20 of the Contract clearly states that if the Contractor suspects asbestos while performing its work, it is to "notify the Contracting Officer promptly, and before such conditions are disturbed, of the possible presence of asbestos pursuant to the differing site conditions clause." This is precisely what the Contractor did whenever asbestos was suspected. The fact that most times the suspect substance was other than asbestos does not alter the fact that such discoveries were disruptive in and of themselves. While the Contractor did not attend the scheduled pre-bid conference, there is no reason to believe that such visit would have revealed the extent of ACM that existed in this hospital building. The VA seeks to

downplay the mere existence of ACM on pipes, ducts, valves, etc., so long as it was not damaged and loose. A multi-volume Assessment was prepared and the VA had previously attempted to let a contract for abatement of the hospital's ACM. There obviously was a substantial amount of ACM throughout the building, irrespective of its condition. Certainly, the condition in the pipe basement would amount to a differing site condition by definition of the Contract clause itself. There was nothing on the Contract drawings to indicate the condition reflected in the Assessment. The phrase "other than indicated on the drawings," could reasonably lead one to believe that if the asbestos condition were not shown on the contract drawings, it would be considered a differing site condition. The ACM conditions experienced in this building represent a change in the working conditions that could not reasonably have been anticipated. As such, there was a constructive change to the Contract. *Dark Construction Group, Inc.*, VABCA No. 5674, 00-1 BCA ¶ 30,870.

The Government argues that, because the Contractor actually expended less labor hours than it had estimated in its bid, it has not proven that it was in any way impacted by the presence of asbestos. This ignores the possibility that Appellant may have overestimated the amount of pipe and sprinkler installation effort needed and/or that it worked in an efficient manner. In either case, a contractor in a fixed-price contract is entitled to any labor cost savings that it may experience, just as it is out of luck if it underestimates the amount of effort involved in the contract work. Our Board has recognized that it is somewhere between impractical and impossible to maintain cost records identifying and separating inefficiency costs. For this reason, we have utilized the productivity factors from the MCAA Manual, published by the Mechanical Contractors Association of America, to estimate the extent of impact on labor productivity in the absence of better evidence, such as a "measured mile" analysis. This is appropriate where the record indicates a negative impact on the productivity of a contractor's workforce. *Clark Construction, supra*, at 52, 418-19, citing *Fire Security Systems, Inc.*, VABCA No. 3086, 91-2 BCA ¶ 23,743.

The VA's witnesses testified that the FSS crews were working at the same pace throughout the period of pipe installation. Another witness emphasized that the Contractor had actually achieved greater labor efficiency than it had estimated in its bid. The Government's position that there was no demonstrated inefficiency caused by the asbestos problems begs the question of whether, without the impact of the presence or suspected presence of friable asbestos on the workers, they could have been even more efficient. Since FSS reported suspected asbestos almost as soon as the pipe installation began, there is no "normal" work period by which to measure the impact, thus no useful "measured mile" analysis would be possible for this particular claim. This is why the industry has resorted to the use of productivity factors such as those in the MCAA Manual. While the Daily Logs record very little of the types of impact quantified in the MCAA factors (such as stacking of trades, suspension, etc.), one factor, "Morale and Attitude," seems particularly applicable to the situation that began with discovery of suspect material in the early stage of pipe installation and escalated with the Contractor's reaction to the Roth Analysis of asbestos hazards in the pipe basement. However, considering the amount of ambient air testing regularly performed by the VA, the uniformly favorable results, and the VA's prompt remediation of any areas where asbestos fibers exceeded the allowable limits, we consider the impact on "Morale and Attitude" to have been "minor" and will thus assign a factor of 5% by which to measure the overall impact on worker productivity throughout the course of pipe/sprinkler installation. This is, in our view, comparable to the "paranoia factor" (although of less severity) that was discussed by Appellant's expert, Mr. McLaughlin, in his expert testimony. With respect to the other two MCAA factors that Mr. Hayes considered applicable, we disagree. MCAA factor #3 relating to reassignment of manpower is simply not reflected to any substantial degree in the Daily Logs, which Mr. Knight (their author) considered to accurately record the significant events of each work day. With respect to MCAA factor #6, Dilution of Supervision, Mr. Knight, who was the superintendent during the period in question, testified that his absences were infrequent. He was emphatic in stating that his workmen could be trusted to perform diligently during his absences.

We do not discount the Government's argument that prior to actually designing its pipe runs above the ceiling spaces, FSS had the Assessment available to utilize in order to avoid placing pipe in close proximity to structures containing ACM, most of which were marked to indicate ACM. That is a valid position. However, we are not basing Appellant's recovery on its discomfort in working close to ACM, but on the several instances of suspected and actual asbestos in the overhead areas and in the pipe basement, which served to increase the "fear factor" in its workers.

Chapter 9
APPLYING CPM TECHNIQUES TO CONTRACT CLAIMS

WHERE WE STAND NOW

§ 9.06 A REPORT CARD ON CHOICES FOR CPM PROOF OF DELAY CLAIMS

[E] Chronological and Cumulative Approach/Time Impact Analysis

Page 275, add at end of subsection:

Decisions by the VA board and the Court of Appeals for the Federal Circuit, in *Jimenez, Inc.*, VABCA No. 6351, 2002 WL 31185730, 02-2 BCA ¶ 32,019, VABCA No. 6351, et al. and *P.J. Dick Inc. v. Secretary of Veterans Affairs*, 324 F.3d 1364 (Fed. Cir. 2002), confirm the concept that CPM updates, contemporaneous at the time of the delay, should be used to calculate project delays. In addition, the Court of Federal Appeals in *P.J. Dick* specifically found that monthly updates should be used to calculate the effect of delays on a month-by-month basis under the VA scheduling specification, rather than a longer window of time that might exaggerate the amount due the contractor.

In *Jimenez*, the board considered the project to renovate certain patient wards at a Nashville VA hospital. The contractor departed the project when the VA acted under the "Inspection of Construction" clause to take over performance, notifying the contractor that the VA would correct all remaining defective work. Part of the dispute concerned the contractor's claims for delays.

In *Jimenez*, the contractor claimed that delays to the work on the air conditioning and heating unit (AHU) constituted critical path delays to the project. The contractor had submitted and maintained a CPM during the project. The board found that the contemporaneous schedule updates should be used to locate the critical path and assess delays.[41.1] However, no project delay was found because the AHU work was never on the critical path of the project:

[41.1] This key finding points up the *absolute necessity for Owners to assure that project updates contain correct information* as to starts, finishes, remaining durations, logic, and the location of the critical path. Failure to do so will mean that the owner will have to go to a lot of trouble to show that the update information was wrong and do so with clear evidence that impeaches the contemporaneous updates.

> The Contractor submitted and maintained Critical Path Method (CPM) schedules, the first of which indicated a start date of July 14, 1997, and a completion date of July 14, 1998. The original critical path went through Notice to Proceed, Mobilization, Demo Walls/Ceilings, Electrical R/I Ceiling, Electrical Wire R/I, Panel and Discon, Audio Nurse Call, Pre-punch Inspection, Final Cleanup, Punch List/Demobilization.
>
> The CPM updates submitted through May 31, 1998, indicated the project to be on schedule with the completion date of July 14, 1998. (R4, tab 564) By July 1998, however, the work was only 69% complete. (Tr. 168-69) The August 31, 1998 CPM update, showed the project to be 145 work days, or approximately 7 months, behind schedule, with a project completion date of February 5, 1999. (Tr. 39-40) According to that update, the critical path went through mechanical work on the third floor, not through the AHU in the penthouse. (Tr. 163-66)
>
> Over the next few CPM updates, including the last update in November 1998, the project fell further behind by about a month, with the projected completion date slipping to March 8, 1999. By January 1999, the work was only 90% complete. By November 1999, when performance ended, the work was 98% complete. (R4, tab 513; tr. 170)
>
> The AHU was not on the critical path of the first, or any subsequent, CPM schedule presented by the Contractor during the course of contract performance. . . .
>
> At trial, Appellant's expert argued that the original CPM was defective in numerous details, and that a corrected CPM, with delays due to the AHU inserted therein, demonstrated that the AHU delay was the sole cause of delay in Contract completion. (Tr. 136-38; Exh. A-1)
>
> VA countered that such analysis was faulty as it failed to take into account other critical work remaining at the end of the performance period. According to VA, it was that work, and not the AHU work, that was the primary cause of non-completion. VA's witness identified the critical items as nurse call, fire alarm and medical gas, as well as test and balancing of the AHU. (R4, tab 564; tr. 107-217)
>
> Finally, the Contractor argued at trial that certain items of work on the third floor were tied into the late installation of the AHU, on the theory that the installation of those items depended on having conditioned air. However, this theory is neither supported nor corroborated by any facts in the record. No work was shown to have been delayed due to lack of conditioned air.

In addition, the board found that self-serving analyses, performed after the fact, are of limited value:

> Delay/Suspension Claims
> In addressing delays, each party relied considerably on CPM analysis. VA relied on the Contractor's CPM schedules created, and submitted to VA, during performance of the work. Based on those CPMs, the Contract completion date was never affected by delay in installing the AHU since the AHU was never on the critical path, either because the float was not used

up or because the critical path kept shifting to other work that was being delayed due to other causes.

Appellant, on the other hand, spends considerable time denigrating its own original CPM analyses, for obvious reasons. However, the parties are generally held to the CPMs they created and relied upon during the performance of the work, in the absence of compelling reasons to the contrary. As we stated in *P.J. Dick Incorporated*, VABCA Nos. 5597 et al., 01-2 BCA ¶ 31,647, "we will let the parties 'live or die' by analysis of the CPM to determine the number of days of additional contract performance time," citing *Santa Fe, Inc.*, VABCA No. 2168, 87-3 BCA ¶ 20,104 and *Coffey Construction Company, Inc.*, VABCA Nos. 3361 et al., 93-2 BCA ¶ 25,788.

Appellant seeks to have us rely on its CPM expert, and his newly created CPM analysis, which was prepared during litigation. Not surprisingly, this CPM showed VA-caused delays to the AHU accounting for the entire delay through 1999. Such self-serving analyses, created after project completion and which make adjustments to attain new and revised projected schedules, depending on theoretical contingencies, are of limited value. In *Bay Construction Co.*, VABCA Nos. 5594 et al., 2002 WL 442118 (March 19, 2002), we said:

> [The Contractor's CPM consultant] also attributed all of [it]s time loss and extended performance time to Government changes, delays and suspensions. He ignored or casually dismissed any reference to [the Contractor]'s small crews and lack of progress, and did not appropriately consider any information that was unfavorable to the Appellant. That [the Contractor] was behind schedule was observed by the COTR and noted in almost every monthly progress payment report. Yet, [The Contractor's CPM consultant] downplayed these observations and concluded that his analysis showed the various [Contractor]-caused factors raised by the Government did not in any way impact the critical path. The Appellant did not effectively address various discrepancies in the daily logs and failed to prove several of the key facts upon which it based its case. No subcontractors, who performed significant amounts of the actual work on the job, were called to testify about Government caused delays, and there is no indication any of those subcontractors presented delay or suspension claims.

* * *

> Appellant failed to prove by a preponderance of the evidence any particular time during the Contract where Bay suffered compensable suspension of work solely attributable to the Government's actions or inactions. . . .

The case before us today is strikingly similar. While we find that VA's rejection of the Airtherm AHU did cause some delay in AHU installation, the Contractor has failed to persuade us that this delay caused delay in the overall Contract completion date. Any Government-caused delay in AHU installation was concurrent with Contractor-caused delays in other critical

Contract work.

The Contractor's CPM analyses ignore what was actually occurring throughout the latter months of 1999, i.e., that the Contractor was still working to complete significant Contract work unrelated to the AHU delay, such as the test and balancing of the AHU, and certifications of the nurse call and medical gas systems. In the absence of solely VA-caused delays, the existence of concurrent delays precludes any recovery by the Contractor from the Government for delay. Accordingly, these appeals are denied. [Emphasis added.]

As noted above, in *P.J. Dick* the Court of Federal Appeals specifically found that monthly updates should be used to calculate the effect of delays on a month-by-month basis under the VA scheduling specification, rather than a longer window of time that might exaggerate the amount due the contractor:

> The Secretary and PJD each appeal different aspects of the Board's decision. The Secretary appeals the Board's conclusion granting 201 days of extension for the "combined directives" delay. The dispute on this question is whether the language of the contract requires the Board to analyze the effect of each change separately. . . .
>
> II. Although we review the Board's interpretation of a contract *de novo*, the Board's interpretation "is accorded careful consideration due to the board's considerable experience in construing government contracts." *Wickham Contracting Co. v. Fischer*, 12 F.3d 1574, 1577 (Fed. Cir. 1994) (citation omitted). The relevant provision of the contract reads: "The Contracting Officer's determination as to the total number of days of contract extension *will be* based upon the *current* computer-produced calendar-dated schedule for the *time period in question* and all other relevant information." Specification § 01311.1.13(A) (emphasis added). The Secretary agrees with the Board's conclusion that the "time period in question" is "the date an action or activity occurred on which a time extension is based." The Secretary argues only that the Board erred in its subsequent determination that the "time period in question" for all six of the changes included in the "combined directives" was November 1995—the date the DVA issued the first of those change orders. We agree.
>
> <u>We conclude that the language of the contract required the Board to analyze the changes of the "combined directives" separately utilizing the most recent monthly update of the "computer-produced calendar-dated schedule."</u> The express language of the contract establishes that the "current" schedule "will be" the basis for determining the extent of the delay. By using "will" the contract indicates that this is the sole method of calculating the delay. The <u>Board circumvented this language by crediting litigation arguments that the six unrelated changes issued over ten months had a unitary effect, making the "time period in question"</u> the date the DVA issued the first change order. <u>This was error because the language of the contract requires the use of the "current" computer schedule as the basis for making such a determination. In other words, regardless of what the testimony</u>

showed, under the contract, the only way of determining the effect of the changes was to analyze each of them using the current computer schedule. Thus, if the changes did have a unitary effect, it had to be demonstrated by the computer model, not the testimony PJD presented.

We therefore reverse the Board's determination that the "combined directives" should all be analyzed utilizing the October 1995 schedule update—the update most current as of November 1995—and remand for a damages analysis in accordance with this opinion. On remand the Board should determine whether PJD's delay claims that it found were not controlling because of the "combined directive" delay (the underground conduit and the radiology and cardiology claims) become controlling as a result of any reduction in the "combined directive" delay and analyze them accordingly. (Footnote omitted) [Emphasis added.]

[F] Window Analysis

Page 275, add at end of subsection:

The decisions by the VA board and the Court of Appeals for the Federal Circuit in *Jimenez, Inc.*, VABCA No. 6351, 2002 WL 31185730, 02-2 BCA ¶ 32,019, VABCA No. 6351, et al. and *P.J. Dick Inc. v. Secretary of Veterans Affairs*, 324 F.3d 1364 (Fed. Cir. 2002), confirm the concept that CPM updates, contemporaneous at the time of the delay, should be used to calculate project delays. In addition, the Court of Federal Appeals, in *P.J. Dick*, specifically found that monthly updates should be used to calculate the effect of delays on a month-by-month basis under the VA scheduling specification, rather than a longer window of time that might exaggerate the amount due the contractor. See discussion of both cases in § **9.06[E]** of this supplement.

HOW WE GOT THERE

§ 9.08 HOW CPM TECHNIQUES HAVE EVOLVED—A DETAILED REVIEW OF MAJOR DEVELOPMENTS IN CPM ANALYSIS SINCE 1974

[A] CPM Acknowledged as Preferred Method for Proving Delays

Page 290, add to note 53:

R.W. Granger & Sons, Inc. v. City Sch. Dis. of Albany, 296 A.D.2d 636, 744 N.Y.S.2d 567, 166 Ed. Law Rep. 744, 2002 N.Y. Slip Op. 05731 (2002); RPR & Assocs., Inc. v. University of North Carolina-Chapel Hill, 153 N.C. App. 342, 570 S.E.2d 510 (2002); Slidell, Inc. v. Millennium Inorganic Chems., Inc., 2002 WL 649086 (U.S. Dist. Ct., D. Minn., Apr. 17, 2002)

§ 9.08[D]

Page 296, add at end of subsection:

State decisions from 2002 reflect the fact that CPM is the preferred method for proving project delays on complicated projects. In *RPR & Associates v. University of North Carolina-Chapel Hill*, 153 N.C. App. 342, 570 S.E.2d 510 (2002), the Court of Appeals of North Carolina looked to the testimony of a CPM expert as justifying the grant of 347 days of compensable delay. *See also R.W. Granger & Sons v. City School District of Albany*, 296 A.D.2d 636, 744 N.Y.S.2d 567, 166 Ed. Law Rep. 744 (2002) in which a New York appeals court relied on critical path analysis evidence in upholding a decision that a termination (allegedly for failure to timely progress the work) had been made without cause.

[D] Requirement for Contemporaneous Baseline in Measuring Quantum of Delay

Page 332, add at end of subsection:

The decisions by the VA board and the Court of Appeals for the Federal Circuit in *Jimenez, Inc.*, VABCA No. 6351, 2002 WL 31185730, 02-2 BCA ¶ 32,019, VABCA No. 6351, et al. and *P.J. Dick Inc. v. Secretary of Veterans Affairs*, 324 F.3d 1364 (Fed. Cir. 2002), confirm the concept that CPM updates, contemporaneous at the time of the delay, should be used to calculate project delays. In addition, the court in *P.J. Dick* specifically found that monthly updates should be used to calculate the effect of delays on a month-by-month basis under the VA scheduling specification, rather than a longer window of time that might exaggerate the amount due the contractor. See discussion of both cases in **§ 9.06[E]** in this supplement.

[G] Key Issues Involving Concurrent Delay and Extended Duration Claims

[2] Willingness of Courts to Segregate/Apportion Concurrent Delays Between Critical and Noncritical Delays Based on CPM Principles

Page 366, add at end of subsection:

State and federal decisions from 2002 (including the recent landmark *PCL* decision) addressed the issues of concurrent delays and apportionment of damages.

The first state decision, *RPR & Associates, Inc. v. University of North Carolina-Chapel Hill*, 153 N.C. App. 342, 570 S.E.2d 510 (2002), considered a claim by the contractor in connection with construction of an alumni center. The court made two interesting findings. First, it accepted CPM proof as to construction delay on the project but denied inefficiency (and apparently delay damages) for the masonry contractor. With respect to the claim for masonry damages, the court specifically reaffirmed the principle that when both parties contribute to the delay, neither can recover damages for breach of contract, unless there is *proof of clear apportionment of delay and expense to each party*. Relevant portions of the decision stated:

> Defendant next argues that the finding by the trial court that plaintiff suffered damages totaling $138,800.00 due to a delay on the project of 347 days is unsupported by the evidence. Defendant asserts that the trial court neglected to deduct from its total of 347 days a time extension of forty-eight days granted to plaintiff by a series of change orders, as well as a time period of eighty days previously awarded to plaintiff by the State Office of Construction. We disagree.
>
> Plaintiff presented extensive evidence at trial on the cause and effect of construction delay. Mr. William W. Gurry ("Gurry"), an expert in the analysis of construction delay and critical path methodology of construction scheduling, testified in detail concerning the construction delays caused by defendant. Gurry testified that, according to his calculations, the project "was 391 days late beyond contract completion[,]" a figure which "include[d] a 44 day time extension." Thus, contrary to defendant's assertions, the evidence before the trial court, and the trial court's findings concerning the delay, took into account the time extensions granted to plaintiff. Moreover, the trial court explicitly recognized that the State Office of Construction had previously awarded plaintiff damages, but found that defendant "refused to pay any portion of that award of the State Office of Construction." The trial court therefore included these time extensions in its award. We conclude that the trial court's award to plaintiff of damages suffered due to delay of the project is supported by the evidence and does not constitute a double recovery for plaintiff. We therefore overrule defendant's final assignment of error. We now examine the issues presented by plaintiff on appeal.

* * *

A. Masonry Claim
[12][13] Plaintiff asserts that the trial court erred in concluding that plaintiff had presented insufficient evidence of the specific damages it incurred in connection with the masonry phase of construction. In its judgment, the trial court found that

> RPR's budget for the masonry work, including materials and subcontract labor to install the masonry and appurtenances, was $669,064.00, which is found to be reasonable. RPR's actual cost for this work was $1,280,268.00. RPR's budget amount is found to be reasonable. <u>RPR has been unable to prove to the court by the greater weight of the evidence how much of this additional masonry expense which was actually incurred by RPR was due to the conduct of UNC</u>. Some, but not all of these additional costs, likely arose out of estimating errors. <u>Although</u>

> it is clear on this masonry claim that RPR suffered damages through owner caused inefficiencies, the amount of such actual damages has not been proven with the degree of specificity required by law. Therefore, the court rules that the Plaintiff cannot receive any monetary recovery for this claim.

Plaintiff argues that the trial court's failure to award damages on its masonry claim arises from the trial court's misapprehension of the law concerning speculative damages. Plaintiff correctly notes that, " 'where the plaintiff can prove the fact of damage, but not the extent of it, the reasonable certainty rule as it is now applied in most courts does not require proof of damages with mathematical precision.' " *Bolton Corp. v. T.A. Loving Co.*, 94 N.C. App. 392, 405, 380 S.E.2d 796, 805 (1989) (quoting *Dobbs, Remedies* § 3.3 (1973)), *disc. review denied*, 325 N.C. 545, 385 S.E.2d 496 (1989). Plaintiff contends that it produced sufficient evidence to support an award for damages on the masonry claim, and that the trial court erred in failing to make such an award. We disagree.

Contrary to plaintiff's assertions, it is clear that the trial court's denial of its masonry claim was based on plaintiff's failure to present sufficient evidence as to the cause of the damages rather than the extent of such damages. As recited above, the trial court found that

> RPR has been unable to prove to the court by the greater weight of the evidence how much of this additional masonry expense which was actually incurred by RPR was due to the conduct of UNC. Some, but not all of these additional costs, likely arose out of estimating errors.

It is well established that, for breach of an executory contract, the plaintiff has the burden of presenting sufficient evidence of damages "as can be ascertained and measured with reasonable certainty." *Biemann & Rowell Co. v. Donohoe Cos.*, 147 N.C. App. 239, 245, 556 S.E.2d 1, 5 (2001). "Moreover, where both parties contribute to the delay, neither can recover damages, unless there is proof of clear apportionment of the delay and expense attributable to each party." *Id.* In the instant case, the trial court found that plaintiff had failed to sustain its burden on the issue of apportionment of damages on the masonry claim and declined to award any monetary damages for such. The trial court's findings were based on competent evidence, and we conclude that the trial court did not err in failing to award damages for plaintiff's masonry claim. See *Biemann*, 147 N.C. App. at 246, 556 S.E.2d at 6 (holding that the trial court did not err in failing to award the plaintiff damages for its construction claim where the plaintiff "failed to properly establish responsibility for its additional costs"). We therefore overrule this assignment of error. [Emphasis added.]

In *Alcan Electrical & Engineering Co., Inc. v. Samaritan Hospital*, 109 Wash. App. 1072 (2002), the Washington appeals court was concerned with a hospital construction project. Moen was the prime contractor, Apollo the mechanical contractor, and Alcan the electrical contractor. The project finished late with attendant liquidated damages. The issue on appeal was the validity of the apportionment by the trial court between two subcontractors relative to their responsibility for a 201-day delay of the project. Apollo had installed nonconforming pipe and Alcan had failed to submit fire alarm drawings to the fire marshal in a timely manner.

Moen, the prime, wanted to assess both subs with full liquidated damages for the same period. However, the trial court and the appeals court (citing Illinois authority) found that the *trier of fact could apportion delay damages* between the parties using a large measure of "responsible and informed discretion." The court stated:

> The project was substantially completed on December 17, 1992—201 days after the agreed completion date of May 27.
>
> Claiming it had not been paid under the terms of its contract, Alcan sued Moen. Moen answered that any amount owing was subject to offsets because of Alcan's delay of the project that triggered the assessment of liquidated damages. Moen also filed a counterclaim against Alcan for breach of contract and a cross claim against Samaritan for breach of contract.
>
> The court determined the entire 201-day delay was attributable to Moen and its subcontractors. Samaritan was therefore entitled to $180,900 in liquidated damages.
>
> The court found the 201-day delay was the result of <u>Apollo's unauthorized installation of nonconforming pipe, as well as Alcan's failure to submit fire alarm shop drawings to the Fire Marshall in a timely manner</u>. Apollo's work on the project should have been done by July 8, 1991, but was not completed until January 4, 1992. <u>The court accordingly determined that Apollo's installation of the wrong pipe delayed the project 170 days</u>.
>
> Even though Alcan's work also should have been completed by July 8, 1991, <u>its work was not substantially completed until after February 4, 1992. The court found Alcan's untimely submission of fire alarm shop drawings caused a 31-day delay</u>.
>
> The court determined that under the subcontract, Alcan was liable to Moen for liquidated damages assessed against it for the 31-day delay of the project attributable to Alcan. The court also held that Apollo was similarly liable to Moen for liquidated damages assessed against it for Apollo's 170-day delay of the project.
>
> As to Moen and Alcan, the net result after resolution of their various claims against each other was that Moen owed Alcan $25,235 for its work on the project. The court also awarded Alcan statutory costs. This appeal follows.
>
> Moen claims the court erred by holding Alcan was only responsible for 31 days of the delay. It is undisputed that although the project completion date was May 27, 1992, substantial completion of the project actually occurred on December 17, 1992—201 days late. It is also undisputed that both Apollo and Alcan were the subcontractors responsible for the delay. <u>What Moen disputes is the apportionment of their delay by the trial court. Moen asserts that the two subcontractors caused a concurrent delay and are therefore both liable for liquidated damages for the same period of time.</u>

Generally, a party to a contract cannot recover liquidated damages for a breach to which he has contributed and there can be no apportionment of liquidated damages when both parties are at fault. *Baldwin v. Nat'l Safe Depository Corp.*, 40 Wn. App. 69, 72, 697 P.2d 587, *review denied*, 104 Wn. 2d 1002 (1985). The reason for this rule is the difficulty in proving who is responsible for what damages. *Id.* But there are certain circumstances when apportionment is proper. *Id.* In Baldwin, the court permitted apportionment because the jury was presented with an adequate basis to allocate the contractual measure of damages to the respective parties. *Id.* at 73.

Moen claims that both Alcan and Apollo should have been held to be jointly and severally liable for the entire delay. However, it cites no authority in support of this claim. Indeed, other than citing cases that it admits are factually distinguishable, Moen provides no other supporting legal argument. We have not been directed to any authority in Washington or any other jurisdiction that holds joint and several liability is proper in this situation and we decline to so hold.

Moen also takes issue with the court's apportionment of the delay between Alcan and Apollo. It argues that Alcan was responsible for more than 31 days of the delay. No Washington case specifically addresses how to apportion liquidated damages when two subcontractors cause a concurrent delay. But Illinois has addressed the question and found that "the issue of apportioning damages in a case of mutual delay is a question of fact." *Pathman Constr. Co. v. Hi-Way Elec. Co.*, 65 Ill. App. 3d 480, 488, 382 N.E.2d 453, 460 (1978). The amount of the delay attributable to each party is a question that must be resolved by the trier of fact. *Id.* This approach is similar to that in Washington for awarding damages when more than one factor is responsible for the damages:

> [W]here the amount of damage is not susceptible of exact apportionment between the defendant's fault and other factors contributing to the loss, absolute certainty is not required. The trier of fact must exercise a large measure of responsible and informed discretion where the fact of damage is proved.

Long v. T-H Trucking Co., 4 Wn. App. 922, 927, 486 P.2d 300 (1971); see also *Alpine Indus., Inc. v. Gohl*, 30 Wn. App. 750, 755, 637 P.2d 998, 645 P.2d 737 (1981), *review denied*, 97 Wn. 2d 1013 (1982). We find the Illinois court's resolution persuasive in answering the question at hand. Determining how to apportion the delay is an issue that should be left to the discretion of the trier of fact.

The trial court, in so acting, apportioned the delay between the subcontractors. It found Apollo was responsible for 170 days of the delay. The evidence adequately supports this finding. [Emphasis added.]

The third state court decision, *Gladwynne Construction Co. v. Mayor & City Council of Baltimore*, 147 Md. App. 149, 807 A.2d 1141 (2002), concerned a project to renovate several science laboratories and classrooms at Baltimore Polytechnic Institute, a famous high school in the city. The contract included significant work to replace utility lines under a concrete slab. The project, which was to have taken 180 days, was not completed for another 300 days after the original completion date. The project involved major changes to remedy design deficiencies and a major transformation of the scope of the work when it was discovered that the utility crawlspace to house the replacement utility lines did not exist. During performance, the contractor was never notified that it was responsible for any of the delays to the project. Not until trial did the city assert the position that Gladwynne was responsible for concurrent delays. At that time, the city took the position that the *Acme/Blinderman* line of cases prohibits recovery, because concurrent delays could not be apportioned.

The court discussed the facts of the delay claim in the appeal of the lower court's ruling:

> Appellant asserts that it was delayed by the City at least through December 1998 or January 1999, because "the City redesigned the Project via change orders in an attempt to remedy its defective plans and specifications." According to appellant, "the City continued to issue change orders through December, 1998, and Gladwynne continued to work on those change orders through January, 1999." Therefore, appellant disagrees with the circuit court's determination that the delays attributable to the City only extended appellant's performance through September 11, 1998. Appellant argues:
>
>> The evidence adduced at trial clearly showed that the schedule around which the City builds its Brief was, along with the architect's very design, rendered completely meaningless by the eventual recognition that contrary to the architect's drawings, there was no utility crawlspace. That defining event severely impacted all of Gladwynne's original work. Added to this was the fact that during the time that Gladwynne was attempting to surmount the utility problem, the City added 54 change orders for various other reasons.[ ]
>>
>> To hang one's hat, therefore, upon the failure to meet a meaningless submittal schedule when the very nature of the job has been fundamentally altered is to engage in the worst form of Monday morning quarterbacking. This is particularly true where, as here, the quarterback is the one who misdesigned the Project in the first place.
>>
>> What Mr. Sider, or for that matter Mr. Weeks and Mr. Cohen, did not do was point to one item of work which Gladwynne could have performed but did not. Mr. Sider admits that he never performed any analysis whatsoever which showed that any days were lost due to delays by Gladwynne.
>
> * * *
>
> Mr. Weeks, for his part, admits that when he made his after-the-fact assessment that Gladwynne should have been completed by May 30, 1998, he was taking into account work which was neither requested nor performed until at least *September 2, 1998.* Although the City's own witness conclusively established the complete baselessness of the City's position, the City persists in arguing that work which had not

<u>yet come into existence should somehow have been completed by May 30, 1998</u>.

Further, Gladwynne contends that "the City raised for the first time at trial allegations of performance problems by Gladwynne and then argued that those generalized grievances somehow coalesced into a concurrent delay on the part of Gladwynne." In its view, "there is absolutely no evidence that any item of work performed by Gladwynne could have been accomplished at an earlier time." Among other things, appellant relies on the following testimony of Behrle:

> Well, what happened was, there was no-first off, we got a notice to proceed on September 2nd. We really couldn't start until the end of September because there was asbestos that needed, that was removed by the school or DPW or somebody, but it was not in our contract. So, we had to wait for that.
>
> Once we waited for that, we got on the site and nobody could find the crawl space under [classroom] 29. . . .
>
> * * *
>
> [W]e expended approximately five to six weeks of looking for a crawl space that didn't exist. . . . We're basically at a standstill. There's nothing we can do until we get this resolved.

* * *

Gladwynne also points out that because the crawlspace did not exist, it had to order a different type of pipe, which did not arrive until January 19, 1998, resulting in a four and a half month delay. Moreover, appellant explains that, "since entire floors were now being trenched, instead of merely receiving two 4 inch penetrations, no other work could be started until the trenches were filled on or about February 18, 1998." Consequently, the work was delayed by another month. Appellant explains:

> As a result of the trenching in Room 29, Gladwynne had to flash patch the entire floor prior to installation of the vinyl. Only after that was completed, in early May 1998, could Gladwynne begin to install cabinetry. It took until the middle of July to finish the cabinet installation due to two unforeseen asbestos abatements as well as having to stop work while the City mishandled various window leaks. Then, and only then, could Gladwynne measure and place the order for the manufacture of the countertops. Installation of the countertops was completed in mid-August, 1998, at which time Gladwynne was able to install the faucets, electrical devices, gas tops and the pipe chases which the City added midway through the Project. During the time that Gladwynne was accomplishing these original and changed tasks, the City added more electrical change orders.

Further, appellant notes that the estimate of completion contained in the progress meeting notes of May 5, 1998, took into account only eleven of forty-four change orders, of which just six had been completed at that time.

Additionally, it claims that the City counted $127,500 of delivered but uninstalled cabinets as completed work. Therefore, Behrle testified that the Project's actual percentage of completion at the time was only 63%.

While urging us to accept the 93% completion figure, the <u>City does not refute that the percentage of completion did not include thirty-three out of forty-four change orders, and did not take into account that $127,000 worth of cabinetry was not yet installed</u>. Nevertheless, the City maintains that appellant should have been able to finish "the remaining 7% of the project over the next three weeks." The City states:

> As it turned out, the Appellant needed from May 5, 1998 to August 11, 1998 to reach 98% completion. It took Gladwynne more than three months to complete five percent of the work. It then took the Appellant another one month to complete the remaining two percent of the work before the substantial completion date.

The City also contends that it was responsible for delays only through May 30, 1998, because by that date Gladwynne "had completed more than 90% of the project and had received from the City $430,400 of the total contract amount of $497,000."

As we indicated, in asserting that the Project was 93% complete by May 5, 1998, the City did not consider the change orders and uninstalled cabinets. Moreover, the City does not explain why, given those omissions, the Project was really 93% completed. <u>Even if only 7% of the Project remained to be completed by that time, however, the City gives no explanation as to why appellant could have been finished in three weeks</u>. For example, if appellant were awaiting the delivery of the duriron pipes, as was the case earlier in the Project, it could not necessarily have finished the work within three weeks. <u>Without knowing what remained to be finished and its status, the fact that only 7% of the work had to be completed does not mean that it necessarily could have been accomplished in a discrete period of time</u>.

<u>The City presented conclusory testimony that appellant's work progressed too slowly and inefficiently</u> . . . . Appellant, on the other hand, presented factual evidence indicating that change orders were still being issued as late as December 1998. Clearly, appellant could not have completed the Project while change orders were still forthcoming.

It appears to us that appellee has tacitly acknowledged in its brief that, at least through November 1998, the delay was not attributable to appellant. Instead, the City seems to challenge appellant's effort to recover through December 1998 or January 1999. We quote from the City's brief:

> Even now, Gladwynne is achieving to be paid for a period of time from September 11, 1998 to December 31, 1998. Counsel for the appellant has written that "the undisputed evidence was that Gladwynne remained on the job through January 1999 . . . ." However, Mr. Behrle testified that the renovation work at the high school was approximately finished in November 1998. He added that he was replacing the project at the high school in November 1998. Gladwynne's superin-

tendent was not at the job site for the high school on a full time basis in November 1998. The trial court reasonably found that Gladwynne should not receive any damages for this period after September 11, 1998, the date the parties agree that substantial completion of the project occurred. As Mr. Sider testified, he only went to the site on two occasions after the punch list inspection and substantial completion in September 1998.

* * *

Gladwynne is attempting to obtain damages from November 1998 to January 1999 for a period of time when no one from the company regularly worked on the project at the high school. Punch list items were being worked on by the Appellant as of September 11, 1998 when the project was substantially completed.

As we noted, the court found that appellant was entitled to recover extended field costs due to delays occasioned by the City, but only for 195 days, representing the period from February 28, 1998, to September 11, 1998. We conclude that the court erred in limiting the period of delay for which field costs were compensable to the period from February 28, 1998 to September 11, 1998. Therefore, we shall vacate the court's judgment and remand for further proceedings as to the length of delay for which appellant is entitled to compensation for extended field costs. [Emphasis added.]

The court next found that, on the law, the contractor's proof was sufficient to establish the city as the sole cause of delay:

In its cross-appeal, the City contends that the trial judge erred in awarding any damages to appellant. Appellee asserts that "[t]here is absolutely no basis for the Appellant's claim for delay damages." A contractor cannot recover "where the delays are 'concurrent or intertwined' and the contractor has not met its burden of separating its delays from those chargeable to the [City]." *Blinderman Constr. Co. v. United States*, 695 F.2d 552, 559 (Fed. Cir. 1982). Appellee asserts that the burden of separating the "submittal delays in comparison with [the] construction schedule" was on the appellant, and appellant failed to meet that burden. In other words, appellee asserts that both parties contributed to the delay, and appellant had the burden to apportion the delay and expense attributable to each party. The City adds:

In the instant case it is clear that the trial court did not resolve the contractor's delay in the project correctly. A concurrent delay by Gladwynne meant that the company had to separate its delay from the government's delay. There was no such separation of which party was responsible for what portion of the delay.

* * *

The burden is on the Appellant to show the separate delays and damages caused by the City. This burden was not met by the Appellant;

therefore, it was incorrect for damages to be awarded based on the record.

Gladwynne responds that:

(a) the City did not even argue, let alone establish, that one item of work could have been performed at an earlier date, (b) the City issued Change Orders through December, 1998, and (c) the documents which the City alleges were submitted in an untimely fashion by Gladwynne were no longer required due to the missing utility crawlspace, and thus no delay could possibly have resulted.

The Judge's comment that Gladwynne did not have enough people to do the job does not reflect a finding that the City presented substantial evidence of concurrent delay. Had [the trial judge] so ruled, it would have been reversible error. The only evidence presented by the City was in the form of witnesses who said, in essence, that they thought that Gladwynne should have had more men, and that there were periods of inactivity. That was all.

The City presented absolutely no evidence as to when the inactivity, or lack of manpower, occurred, or what work was available. Gladwynne, for its part, freely admitted that it was inactive when, for instance, the utility problem, or the owner's abatement of asbestos, or the owner's failure to stop leaking windows near the cabinetry, prevented it from working. Indeed, the crux of Gladwynne's complaint was that the city through incompetent design and redesign forced its contractor into sustained periods of inactivity or unproductivity. And it bears repeating that while the City found much fault after Gladwynne brought suit; there was not one mention of Gladwynne having insufficient forces or areas of available work which were not being prosecuted during the Project.

We are satisfied that the decision of the lower court was supported by sufficient evidence. Indeed, appellant presented the lower court with ample evidence of separate and distinct causes of the contract delays attributable to the City. These causes included change orders issued by the City, as well as the missing crawlspace. Given this evidence, we see no reason to reject the lower court's decision to award damages to appellant. [Emphasis added.]

The most significant recent decision relating to apportionment is *PCL Construction Services, Inc. v. United States*, 53 Fed. Cl. 479 (2002), written by Judge Horn of the U.S. Court of Federal Claims. This decision considered the issue of assessment of liquidated damages by the government when the contractor had been terminated for default, on a project to construct a visitor center and parking garage at Hoover Dam.

This decision was *significant in the first instance because it addressed the issue of burden of proof*. The U.S. Court of Federal Claims found that *once the government had met its initial burden by showing that the contract performance requirements were not substantially met by the contract completion date, and that the period for which the assessment was made was proper, the burden of going forward shifted to the contractor* to show that any delays were excusable:

> In *Sauer Inc. v. Danzig*, 224 F.3d 1340 (Fed. Cir. 2000), the United States Court of Appeals for the Federal Circuit stated generally: "[A] party asserting that liquidated damages were improperly assessed bears the burden of showing the extent of the excusable delay to which it is entitled." 224 F.3d at 1347 (citing *Dean Constr. Co. v. United States,* 188 Ct. Cl. 62, 66-68, 411 F.2d 1238, 1240-41 (1969); *N. Va. Elec. Co. v. United States*, 230 Ct. Cl. 722, 723 (1982); *In re Cent. Ohio Bldg. Co.*, P.S.B.C.A. No. 2742, 92-1 B.C.A. (CCH) ¶ 24,399, at 121,824, 1991 WL 187546 (1991)). In *Central Ohio Building Co.*, P.S.B.C.A. No. 2742, 92-1 B.C.A. (CCH) ¶ 24,399, at 121,824, 1991 WL 187546, a case cited favorably by the Federal Circuit in *Sauer Inc. v. Danzig*, 224 F.3d at 1347, the Postal Service Board of Contract Appeals provided a more detailed explanation of the burden of proof with regard to a government claim for liquidated damages. According to the Board, with regard to a liquidated damages claim, the government has "the ultimate burden of persuasion as well the initial burden of going forward to show that the contract was not completed by the agreed contract completion date and that liquidated damages were due and owing." *In re Cent. Ohio Building Co.*, P.S.B.C.A. No. 2742, 92-1 B.C.A. (CCH) ¶ 24,399, at 121,824, 1991 WL 187546. The government may meet its initial burden by showing that "the contract performance requirements were not substantially completed by the contract completion date and that the period for which the assessment was made was proper." *Id*. Once the government satisfies its initial burden, the burden of going forward shifts to the contractor "to show that any delays were excusable and that it should be relieved of all or part of the assessment." *Id*.

Next, however, the court in PCL noted that this *general rule concerning burden of proof would not apply in circumstances in which the government contributed to the delay in the completion of the contract*:

> The general rule expressed in *Sauer* and *Central Ohio Building Co.*, that, once the government has met its initial burden of going forward, the contractor must prove excusable delays to be relieved of all or part of the liquidated damages assessed, has not been applied, however, when the government has contributed to the delay of the completion of the contract. In *United States v. United Engineering & Constructing Co.*, 234 U.S. 236, 242, 49 Ct. Cl. 689, 34 S. Ct. 843, 58 L. Ed. 1294 (1914), the United States Supreme Court held that in order to enforce a liquidated damages clause, the government "must not prevent the performance of the contract within the stipulated time[.]" When performance of the contract is delayed by the government and the contractor, "the rule of the original contract cannot be insisted upon, and liquidated damages measured thereby are waived." *Id*. [Emphasis added.]

Judge Horn, in *PCL, then confronted the apparent anomaly between the Acme rule of not apportioning concurrent delays and Sauer-type rulings that allow apportionment when clear proof of apportionment is provided.*[256.1] The judge noted federal cases following both principles:

> Likewise, in *Acme Process Equipment v. United States*, 171 Ct. Cl. 324, 347 F.2d 509 (1965), *rev'd on other grounds*, 385 U.S. 138, 87 S. Ct. 350, 17 L. Ed. 2d 249 (1966), *reh'g denied*, 385 U.S. 1032, 87 S. Ct. 738, 17 L. Ed. 2d 680 (1967), the United States Court of Claims specifically addressed the situation in which the government attempts to recover liquidated damages in contracts during the performance of which concurrent delay occurred. The court held that " '[w]here delays are caused by both parties to the contract the court will not attempt to apportion them, but will simply hold that the provisions of the contract with reference to liquidated damages will be annulled.' " 171 Ct. Cl. at 367, 347 F.2d at 535 (quoting *Schmoll v. United States*, 91 Ct. Cl. 1, 28, 1940 WL 4133 (1940) and citing *United States v. United Eng'g & Constructing Co.*, 234 U.S. 236, 242, 49 Ct. Cl. 689, 34 S. Ct. 843, 58 L. Ed. 1294 (1914); *Vogt Bros. Mfg. Co. v. United States*, 160 Ct. Cl. 687, 709, 1963 WL 8571 (1963); *Commerce Int'l Co. v. United States*, 167 Ct. Cl. 529, 543, 338 F.2d 81, 90 (1964)); *accord Fortec Constructors v. United States*, 8 Cl. Ct. 490, 508 (1985), *aff'd*, 804 F.2d 141 (Fed. Cir. 1986); *Prestex, Inc. v. United States*, 3 Cl. Ct. 373, 382 (1983), *aff'd*, 746 F. 2d 1489 (Fed. Cir. 1984) (table); *In re Bildon, Inc.*, A.S.B.C.A. No. 46,937, 95-1 B.C.A. (CCH) ¶ 27,562, at 137, 366, 1995 WL 113489 (1995); *In re Gaffny Corp.*, A.S.B.C.A. No. 37,639, 94-1 B.C.A. (CCH) ¶ 26,522, at 132,010, 1993 WL 493326 (1993).

* * *

> Some courts and boards, however, have criticized the rule in *Acme Process Equipment*, also known as the "rule against apportionment," as too harsh and outdated. *See, e.g., E.C. Ernst, Inc. v. Manhattan Constr. Co.*, 551 F.2d 1026, 1038-39 (5th Cir.), *modified*, 559 F.2d 268 (5th Cir. 1977), *cert. denied*, 434 U.S. 1067, 98 S. Ct. 1246, 55 L. Ed. 2d 769 (1978); *In re Santa Fe, Inc.*, V.A.B.C.A. No. 1943, 84-2 B.C.A. (CCH) ¶ 17,341, at 86,409, 1984 WL 13360 (1984). Thus, some courts and boards have attempted to apportion concurrent delay in assessing liquidated damages. *E.C. Ernst, Inc. v. Manhattan Constr. Co.*, 551 F.2d at 1038-39; *United States ex rel. Thorleif Larsen and Son, Inc. v. B.R. Abbot Constr. Co.*, 466 F.2d 712, 714 (7th Cir. 1972); *In re J.W. Creech, Inc.*, A.S.B.C.A. No. 45,454, 94-1 B.C.A. (CCH) ¶ 26,459, at 131,662, 1993 WL 625480 (1993); *In re Consol. Constr., Inc.*, G.S.B.C.A. No. 8871, 88-2 B.C.A. (CCH) ¶ 20,811, at 105,209, 1988 WL

[256.1] Significantly, in *Sauer* the court looked to CPM proof to distinguish between critical and noncritical delays. In fact, in *Sauer*-type decisions—so-called clear proof of apportionment decisions—the courts or finders of fact are making specific findings of causation by one party or another of critical path delays by that party. It is submitted that this is a finding of causation of critical path delay, not apportionment.

63386 (1988); *In re Santa Fe, Inc.*, V.A.B.C.A. No.1943, 84-2 B.C.A. (CCH) ¶ 17,341, at 86,409; *In re Midstate Constructors, Inc.*, P.S.B.C.A. No. 913, 81-1 B.C.A. (CCH) ¶ 14,898, at 73,702, 1981 WL 6937 (1981). In *E.C. Ernst, Inc. v. Manhattan Construction Co.*, 551 F.2d at 1038-39, the United States Court of Appeals for the Fifth Circuit offered its reasoning for permitting the apportionment of fault in liquidated damages situations when there existed concurrent delay. The court explained:

> The opposing rule [the rule against apportionment] is an old one whose underlying policies do not remain in full force. One of the dominant reasons underlying it is early judicial hostility to the use of privately agreed upon contract damage remedies. *See, e.g., Mosler Safe Co. v. Maiden Lane Safe Deposit Co.*, 199 N.Y. 479, 93 N.E. 81 (1910):
>
>> While such an agreement has not the harshness of a penalty, it is, nevertheless, in its nature, such that its enforcement, where the party claiming the right to enforce has, in part, been the cause of delay, would be unjust.
>
> Today, given the increasing complexity of contractual relationships, liquidated damage provisions have obtained firm judicial and legislative support. *See, e.g., Otinger* [*v. Water Works & Sanitary Sewer Board*, 278 Ala. 213, 177 So. 2d 320 (1965)]; Ala.Code tit. 7A, § 2-718 (1966 Recomp.). As long as the owner's own delay is not incurred in bad faith, it is not unjust to allow proportional fault to govern recovery. Generally, owners do not benefit from delays that they incur. Another reason cited in support of the rule is that proving apportionment is simply too difficult. We do not disagree with the difficulty of the task, but recovery should not be barred in every case by a rule of law that precludes examination of the evidence.

Id. (footnotes omitted).

Judge Horn then considered the status of affairs in the Federal Circuit. Although he found that *Acme* had not been directly overruled by *Sauer* and similar other decisions,[256.2] he did recognize that *both rules continued to coexist* and **that critical path techniques were used to apportion delays:**

> The status of the rule against apportionment in the United States Court of Appeals for the Federal Circuit is unsettled. In *Acme Process Equipment v. United States*, 171 Ct. Cl. 324, 347 F.2d at 535, the Court of Claims stated and followed the rule against apportionment. In Sauer Inc. v. Danzig, 224 F.3d at 1347, decided after *Acme Process Equipment*, however, the Federal Circuit upheld a decision from the Armed Services Board of Contract Appeals apportioning delay for the purpose of assessing liquidated damages. *Sauer* involved a contract for the construction of the interior of a building

---

[256.2] Judge Horn noted that *Sauer* was a decision only by a three-judge panel and not a decision by the full court, en banc.

at a submarine base. *Id.* at 1341. During performance of the contract by the plaintiff, Sauer Inc., another contractor was installing cranes inside of the building. *Id.* at 1342. In addition, during performance of part of the contract, the Navy stored a large crane in the building. *Id.* at 1343. Sauer did not complete the contract on time and the government assessed liquidated damages for nine days. *Id.* Sauer filed an appeal with the ASBCA seeking damages due to government caused delay and disruption and the remission of the liquidated damages assessed by the government. *Id.* <u>Both Sauer and the government presented critical-path-management experts.</u> *Id.* at 1344. Each party argued that the other party was responsible for at least a portion of the delay. The Board found that Sauer only was entitled to an additional contract extension of two days, due to the storage of the large crane during the performance of the contract. *Id.* Consequently, the board granted a "commensurate remission of liquidated damages." *Id.*

At the United States Court of Appeals for the Federal Circuit, Sauer argued that the Board should have recognized a longer period of delay and, thus, should have remitted a larger portion of the liquidated damages. *Id.* at 1347. The Federal Circuit rejected the contractor's argument, stating:

> <u>As a general rule, a party asserting that liquidated damages were improperly assessed bears the burden of showing the extent of the excusable delay to which it is entitled.</u> See *Dean Constr. Co. v. United States*, 188 Ct. Cl. 62, 411 F.2d 1238, 1240-41 (1969) (affirming a Board finding that a contractor had failed to meet its burden); *Northern Va. Elec. Co. v. United States*, 230 Ct. Cl. 722, 723 (1982); *Central Ohio Bldg. Co.*, PSBCA No. 2742, 92-1 B.C.A. (CCH) ¶ 24,399, at 121,824, 1991 WL 187546 (Aug. 30, 1991). <u>We have affirmed the Board's finding that Sauer proved only two days of excusable delay</u>. As a result, Sauer has not shown that it is entitled to a remission of liquidated damages greater than the remission already granted by the Board.
>
> Sauer cites two of this court's cases for the proposition that it was the Navy's burden to establish that Sauer was responsible for the delay in performance, but those cases are inapposite. In both *William F. Klingensmith, Inc. v. United States*, 731 F.2d 805 (Fed. Cir. 1984), and *Blinderman Construction Co. v. United States*, 695 F.2d 552 (Fed. Cir. 1982), the government's fault for delays had been established, and the court applied the rule that "[w]here both parties contribute to a delay neither can recover damage, unless there is in the proof a clear apportionment of the delay and the expense attributable to each party." *Coath & Goss, Inc. v. United States*, 101 Ct. Cl. 702, 714-15, 1944 WL 3694 (1944); *see Klingensmith*, 731 F.2d at 809; *Blinderman*, 695 F.2d at 559. In this case, the Board found that Sauer failed to show more than two days of government-caused delay; those cases are therefore inapplicable.

Id. Thus, unlike the rule against apportionment, which would annul a liquidated damages provision in a concurrent delay situation, *Sauer* awarded the government liquidated damages for delay, even though delay by the government had been found on the contract. *Id*. The rule espoused in *Sauer*, however, would only apportion damages when there "is in the proof a clear apportionment of the delay and the expense attributable to each party." *Id*. (quoting *Coath & Goss, Inc. v. United States*, 101 Ct. Cl. at 714-15).

Regardless of the apparent discrepancy between the rule against apportionment, as described in *Acme Process Equipment*, and the clear apportionment rule, described in *Sauer*, the two rules have coexisted in the United States Court of Claims, the United States Claims Court, and the United States Court of Federal Claims, as well as the United States Court of Appeals for the Federal Circuit, for many years. The rule against apportionment was adopted by the Court of Claims in 1940 in the case of *Schmoll v. United States*, 91 Ct. Cl. 1, 28, 1940 WL 4133 (1940), which based its ruling on an even earlier United States Supreme Court case, *United States v. United Engineering & Constructing Co.*, 234 U.S. 236, 242, 49 Ct. Cl. 689, 34 S. Ct. 843, 58 L. Ed. 1294 (1914). The "clear apportionment" rule cited by *Sauer* dates back to *Coath & Goss, Inc. v. United States*, 101 Ct. Cl. 702, 714-15, 1944 WL 3694 (1944). Prior to *Sauer*, however, the clear apportionment rule generally was applied to situations in which the contractor was attempting to recover for delays for which it was not responsible, not to situations in which the government was seeking to recover liquidated damages. *See, e.g., William F. Klingensmith, Inc. v. United States*, 731 F.2d at 805; *Blinderman Constr. Co. v. United States*, 695 F.2d at 553; *Coath & Goss, Inc. v. United States*, 101 Ct. Cl. at 714.

In considering whether *Sauer* overruled *Acme Process Equipment*, replacing the rule against apportionment with the clear apportionment rule in the liquidated damages context, the court notes that opinions from the United States Court of Claims serve as binding precedent until overturned by the United States Court of Appeals for the Federal Circuit, en banc, the United States Supreme Court, or intervening statutory change. *See Bankers Trust N.Y. Corp. v. United States*, 225 F.3d 1368, 1373 (Fed. Cir.) (citing *South Corp. v. United States*, 690 F.2d 1368, 1370-71 (Fed. Cir. 1982)), *reh'g and reh'g en banc denied* (2000); *Middleton v. Dep't of Defense*, 185 F.3d 1374, 1379 n.2 (Fed. Cir. 1999). *Sauer* was a ruling from a three judge panel, not the Federal Circuit en banc. Thus, the rule against apportionment would appear to remain viable in the Federal Circuit. Moreover, there is insufficient proof to find that *Sauer* clearly overruled *Acme Process Equipment* because the court in *Sauer* did not include a discussion of the rule against apportionment, nor cite to any of the cases discussing the rule. *Sauer Inc. v. Danzig*, 224 F.3d at 1347. [Emphasis added.]

In fact, the Court of Federal Claims might have considered other means to explain any purported difference between the *Acme* and *Sauer* lines of cases, as follows:

- When two concurrent critical path delays by the two different parties are present at the same time, the court will not apportion delay damages between the parties.

- When two delays occur at the same time (apparent concurrent delays) but one delay is critical and the other is not, and it is possible to isolate critical path delays to the responsibility of one party, delay damages may be assessed (against the critical-path-delay party).

Additional guidance is contained in the *PCL* decision. The court looked to the use of critical path principles and the lack of adequate proof by the claiming party (the government) that critical path delays were solely caused by the contractor to justify the assessment of liquidated damages against the terminated contractor at the Hoover Dam project. Significantly, the court looked to admissions by the government's own scheduling expert of critical path delays by the government (as well as the parties' failure to keep the CPM schedule current to reflect delays as they occurred) to rule against the assessment of liquidated damages:[256.3]

[256.3] However, the court also found that the contractor, PCL, had failed in its effort to claim and prove delay damages, due to the use of a total-cost-type delay claim. PCL did not provide a CPM analysis, but rather summary inadequate and unsupported proof:

> In short, PCL's hindrance/delay claim is presented as a total cost claim. PCL has not presented an analysis to demonstrate that delays it encountered were due to government hindrance or that, in fact, such hindrance extended project completion, because PCL apparently has not performed and certainly has presented no in-depth critical path analysis.
> PCL has never submitted a detailed delay/impact claim to the court. PCL has argued that a delay analysis of this project is either unnecessary, impossible, or not relevant, but that the government caused delays are part of their claims of "severely defective" drawings , cardinal change, hindrance, and breach of contract.
>
> * * *
>
> PCL never provided USBR or this court with a critical path analysis of the alleged government-caused hindrance and its effect upon the critical path of this project. Indeed, PCL appears never to have prepared and certainly never to have offered, a legitimate critical path analysis, and has even chose to reject and to ignore the "summary-level delay analysis" by Petersen Consulting that it did have prepared.
> *PCL Constr. Servs., Inc.v. United States* 47 Fed. Cl. at 800-02. With respect to liquidated damages, plaintiff attempts to rely on the "summary level as-planned and as-built retrospective analysis" (SLSA) which was prepared by Peterson Consulting for plaintiff, but which plaintiff chose not to submit at the trial, and which was rejected as incorrect by James Bennet, president of PCL Enterprises, during his testimony at the trial. The Peterson SLSA, however, was introduced at trial by the government. In its analysis, the Peterson SLSA stated:
>
>> Utilizing the adjusted as-planned schedule as the baseline for our analysis, summary roll-up activities were developed which represent an adjusted as-planned critical path sequence of work for both the Visitor Center and the Parking Structure. Actual dates were obtained from the project records for these summary level roll-up activities and a comparison was made to the adjusted as-planned schedule resulting in the identification of delayed start and extended duration variances.
>
> The Peterson SLSA found that the government was responsible for 18.8 months of project delay, leaving three months of unconceded project delays attributable to

Most strikingly, at the trial, the defendant's schedule expert determined and established that the government contributed to the delay of both the Parking Structure and the Visitor's Center. With regard to the Parking Structure, defendant's expert found, for example, that government changes contributed to the delay in commencing work on the Level 3A foundations, delay in commencing work on the Level 3A Beams and Slabs, delay in commencing work on the Level 4A Beams and Slabs, delay in commencing work on the Level 4A Columns and Walls, delay in commencing work on the Level 5A Beams and Slabs, delay in commencing work on the Level 2 Columns and Walls, delay in commencing work on the Level 4 Beams and Slabs, delay in commencing work on the Level 4 Columns and Walls, and delay in commencing work on the Level 5 Beams and Slabs. With regard to the Visitor Center, for example, the defendant's expert found that government changes contributed to the delay in commencing work on the excavation of the Theater Level Plaza of the Visitor Center, delay in commencing work on the construction of Shaft B, delay in commencing work on the Theater Level concrete, delay in commencing work on the V-cut structural steel, delay in commencing work on the framing and drywall of the Visitor Center, and delay in the completion of framing, drywall, electrical and architectural finishes on the theater level of the Visitor Center. Another example of the delays by the government with regard to the Parking Structure is the problem encountered in the excavation of the backslope, which led to the delay in commencing work on the Level 3A foundation. . . .

In its post-trial opinion, the court found that PCL's own delays and difficulties in its excavation operations contributed to the delay involving the backslope and, thus, that the government's actions with regard to the backslope did not amount to a breach of contract. *Id.* at 804. PCL did not submit a claim for delay with regard to the backslope. *Id.* at 800. The government's own expert report, however, conceded "that the backslope was in fact a delay event on the as-built critical path."

PCL. Furthermore, the Peterson SLSA concluded hat the three months of PCL "unconceded" project delay was concurrent with the government caused delay and was therefore determined to be a period of "non-compensable, excusable delays."

Although the government submitted the Peterson SLSA into evidence, it also presented sufficient evidence to attack its credibility. First, although plaintiff's schedule expert, Joseph Kellogg, was an advisor in the preparation of the Peterson SLSA, Mr. Kellogg chose not to rely on the Peterson SLSA in discussing the government's hindrances relative to the plaintiff's breach of contract claim. It appears that Mr. Kellogg did not trust the report, prepared by his company with his advice. Moreover, Mr. Kellogg testified that during preparation of the Peterson SLSA, several key documents were either missing or overlooked which could have influenced the conclusion of the report. Moreover, the report was prepared by a Martin Jenkins, who was not called as a witness at trial, and whose competence was not presented to te court or subjected to cross-examination. <u>Finally, James Bennet, President of PCL</u> Enterprises during the time of contract performance, who himself was a civil engineer and, according to PCL, "since 1959, has had broad, in-depth experience constructing all types of structures," <u>testified that with regard to the SLSA, "it's obvious that Peterson is worng.</u>" Therefore, the court finds that it is unable to rely on the Peterson SLSA for a clear apportionment of delay. [Emphais added.]

* * *

Although the court has found that the government did not delay the construction of the project to the extent plaintiff claims, and, therefore, did not breach the contract, based on the evidence adduced at trial, it is clear that the government did contribute to the delay. <u>Throughout the litigation of this case, defendant has conceded that the government was responsible for at least a portion of the delay in contract performance</u> that occurred in the construction of the Parking Structure and Visitor Center. In addition, the <u>defendant's expert testified that the government contributed to the delay on the project</u>. Finally, the evidence presented at trial, and discussed in the court's September 20, 2000 post-trial opinion, <u>presented specific incidents in which the government delayed the construction of the project</u>. Under the rule against apportionment, as described in *Acme Process Equipment*, the court, therefore, should not attempt to apportion damages in this situation. Instead, the <u>government's actions result in the annulment of the liquidated damages provision of the contract</u>.

Even if the court were to forego <u>the rule against apportionment, however, in favor of the clear apportionment rule, as described in *Sauer*, the court also would reject defendant's claim for liquidated damages because, based on the trial record</u>, including testimony and exhibits before the court, <u>it is impossible to apportion damages in this case due to the nature of the plaintiff's claims and the evidence submitted</u>, or not submitted, by the parties. In <u>determining whether there is a clear apportionment of delay it is useful to recall some of the basic rules on the proof regarding delay</u>. As was stated in the court's September, 2000 opinion, **one established way to document delay is through the use of Critical Path Method (CPM) schedules and an analysis of the effects, if any, of government-caused events upon the critical path of the project.** However, in order to properly demonstrate delay to a project, the CPM schedule must be kept current to reflect any delays as they occur. *Fortec Constructors v. United States*, 8 Cl. Ct. at 505. "The required nexus between the government delay and a contractor's failure to complete performance at some unspecified earlier date cannot be shown merely by hypothetical, after-the-fact projection." *Interstate Gen. Gov't Contractors, Inc. v. West*, 12 F.3d 1053, 1060 (Fed. Cir. 1993). Part of one's understanding that an activity belongs on the critical path of a project is also an understanding of how that activity affects the other activities. *Wilner v. United States*, 26 Cl. Ct. 260, 262-63 (1992), *rev'd on other grounds*, 24 F.3d 1397 (Fed. Cir. 1994) (en banc); *see also Mega Constr. Co. v. United States*, 29 Fed. Cl. 396, 424 (1993). "A general statement that disruption or impact occurred, absent any showing through use of updated CPM schedules, logs or credible and specific data or testimony, will not suffice to meet the plaintiff's burden." *Preston-Brady Co.*, V.A.B.C.A. Nos. 1892, 1991, 2555, 87-1 B.C.A. (CCH) ¶ 19,649 at 99,520, 1987 WL 41248 (1987).

Neither party has submitted evidence which relates, with sufficient credibility, how the changes and delays affected other activities on the project and, thus, would allow the court to clearly apportion the delay present in the case. [Emphasis added.]

The fact that Judge Horn and the United States Court of Federal Claims continued to recognize the right of a party to recover when proof established distinctions between critical and noncritical delays during the same time frame was detailed in *Manuel Brothers, Inc. v. United States*, 55 Fed. Cl. 8 (2002), decided on December 23, 2002 (a few months after *PCL*). In *Manuel*, the court considered whether a contractor could recover delay damages on a contract with the FAA to install fiber optic cable at the Dallas Fort Worth airport, There, *Judge Horn recognized the right of the contractor to recover when CPM proof segregated critical and noncritical delays occurring at the same time. However, as noted in the decision, the proof offered by the contractor and its expert was not adequate to actually segregate between such delays to prove that the government was the sole proximate cause of delay to the project*:

> A contractor seeking compensation for alleged government-caused delay must establish the following:
>
> (1) whether and to what extent any part of the contractor's work was unreasonably delayed by the [government's] failure to provide access to the [work site]; (2) whether any unreasonable delays caused by the [government] were concurrent with or separate from delays due to the subcontractor's shortage of labor or other delays chargeable to the contractor; and (3) whether the contractor is entitled to a time extension and/or a recovery of damages and if so, how much.
>
> *Blinderman Constr. Co., Inc. v. United States*, 695 F.2d at 559; *see also W.M. Schlosser, Inc. v. United States*, 50 Fed. Cl. 147, 152 (2001); *Coastal Indus., Inc. v. United States*, 32 Fed. Cl. 368, 372 (1994); *Commercial Contractors, Inc. v. United States*, 29 Fed. Cl. 654, 662 (1993).
>
> The burden of establishing these factors falls squarely upon the contractor. *William F. Klingensmith, Inc. v. United States*, 731 F.2d 805, 809 (Fed. Cir. 1984); *Avedon Corp. v. United States*, 15 Cl. Ct. 648, 653 (1988). Moreover, "[o]nly if the delay was caused solely by the government will the contractor be entitled to both an extension of time within which to perform, and recovery of excess costs associated with the delay." *Weaver-Bailey Contractors, Inc. v. United States*, 19 Cl. Ct. 474, 476 (1990) (emphasis in original) citing *William F. Klingensmith, Inc. v. United States*, 731 F.2d at 809), *reconsid. denied*, 20 Cl. Ct. 158 (1990); *G.M. Shupe, Inc. v. United States*, 5 Cl. Ct. 662, 700 (1984); *see also Blinderman Constr. Co. v. United States*, 695 F.2d at 559. The contractor must show that the government was the "sole proximate cause" of the delay and that no concurrent cause would have equally delayed the contract, regardless of the government's action or inaction. *Merritt-Chapman & Scott Corp. v. United States*, 208 Ct. Cl. 639, 650, 528 F.2d 1392, 1397-98 (1976); *Avedon Corp. v. United States*, 15 Cl. Ct. at 653, 659 (recovery denied "because concurrent delays rendered the [government-caused] delay ... irrelevant"). Moreover, "the court [will] award delay damages only for the unreasonable portion of a government-caused delay." *Mega Constr. Co., Inc. v. United States*, 29 Fed. Cl. 396, 425 (1993) (quoting *Wilner v. United States*, 26 Cl. Ct. 260, 263 (1992), *rev'd on other*

grounds, 24 F.3d 1397 (Fed. Cir. 1994) (en banc)).

If both parties contribute to a delay, neither can recover damages from the other, "unless there is in the proof a clear apportionment of the delay and expense attributable to each party." *William F. Klingensmith, Inc. v. United States*, 731 F.2d at 809 (quoting *Blinderman Constr. Co. v. United States*, 695 F.2d at 559).

MBI claims that the critical path of the project was directly affected by the alleged differing site conditions of the clay and rock, by the alleged breach of the implied duty to cooperate as a result of limited escort availability which limited MBI's access to the project site, and by the additional time required for the location of unknown or misplaced utilities. The CO and the court have found the government liable for locating additional and unknown utilities encountered by MBI. The CO compensated the plaintiff for additional and unknown utilities, although plaintiff now claims delay damages for these additional and unknown utilities. The plaintiff has not shown, however, that the defendant is liable for the alleged differing site conditions of clay and rock or for the alleged governmental breach of the implied duty to cooperate through the interference with access to the work areas.

The government cannot be found liable for delay damages associated with encountering the additional utilities because the plaintiff has failed to present evidence at trial or through its expert witnesses to apportion the delay associated with the additional utilities from the uncompensable delay associated with site access and working in the clay soils.

* * *

The inability of MBI to separate the alleged differing causes of delay was further emphasized by the plaintiff's expert, Mr. Robert Vail. Mr. Vail is the founder and president of the Vail Network Company. Although Mr. Vail does not hold a degree in engineering, he has spent twenty-four years in the construction industry, most recently forming his own consulting company to serve the construction industry "by helping owners, contractors, architects/engineers to plan, organize, control and implement their construction processes." Mr. Vail testified that he reviewed the documents related to this project and rendered an opinion as to "whether Manuel Brothers could have completed this job per the original schedule that they had submitted, and also to look and see if they had incurred additional costs that may have come about because of any changes to the job." Mr. Vail produced a report detailing the alleged damages suffered by the plaintiff at the DFWA south loop ductbank project.

Mr. Vail's expert testimony and report did not separate the alleged delays attributable to the clay and rain, the availability of escorts, or the additional utilities. Regarding the clay soils and the weather experienced by MBI on the project, Mr. Vail testified that the contractor is responsible for the costs associated with abnormal weather. When asked whether the abnormal [weather] on the project cost MBI a fair amount of time and money, Mr. Vail replied, "I believe it did, yes, but I've not been able to make the distinction between the time lost to weather, the time lost to soils, utilities or escorts to—I don't have a precise number for what that would be, but I would presume that would be the case, yes." [Emphasis added.]

The last federal decision is a VA board ruling, *Fire Security Systems, Inc.*, VABCA No. 5559-63, 02-2 BCA ¶ 31,977, 2002 WL 1979118. With the *Fire Security Systems* decision, the VA board has taken a step backward with a ruling that may give the VA temporary advantage in asserting concurrent delays, but may harm the VA and owners in the long run due to the logic it propounds. Specifically, the VA board in this decision took the position that if any substantial base contract work remains after the recognized contract completion date, it must be viewed as critical, absent proof by the contractor that it would have done the work sooner had not the owner delays been present. Thus the VA board, per the reasoning in this decision, is no longer looking at critical path calculations for delays after the official contract completion; instead, it is using bar charts prepared by the VA showing that substantial base contract work remained.

On this basis, the VA Board found that concurrent delays were present after the contract completion date in *Fire Security Systems,* even though there was proof of long periods of inactivity on the base contract work paths. The VA board is, by this ruling, placing an additional requirement on the contractor to show affirmatively that it could have done the base contract work sooner.

[3] Ability of Parties to Use Additional Float—Parties Not Required to "Hurry Up and Wait" or "Slavishly Follow" Out-of-Date Schedule

Page 371, add at end of subsection:

The VA board's decision in *Fire Security Systems, Inc.*, VABCA No. 5559-63, 2002 WL 1979118, 02-2 BCA ¶ 31,977, appears to be at odds with a consistent line of cases running from *Weaver Bailey* to *MCI* to the 1997 *Cogefar Impressit* decision. That line of cases concerns the nature and quality of float, as well as the significance of work performed after the current contract completion date. In *Fire Security Systems*, the VA board held that the burden of proof is on the contractor to show that base contract work performed after the contract completion date could or would have been performed sooner, absent owner delays.

It will be recalled that the *Weaver Bailey* line of cases *recognizes the right of the parties to take advantage of float created in the schedule as a result of another party's or delays other events* (such as strikes or unusually severe weather). In this sense, cases have noted that the contractor is not required to "slavishly follow" the original schedule when project delays occur. In other words, a contractor or an owner can reschedule activities to take into account actual project progress and not "hurry up and wait."

Similarly, existing authority recognizes the fact that the critical path does not stop at the date of the latest official contract completion date, even though a project has gone negative, there is still a critical path. Authority cited in

§ 9.08[K] references the fact that on a negative-float project, we look to the activities with the highest negative float to find the critical path or paths.[265.1]

Now turn to the language of the *Fire Security System* ruling. First, the decision notes that the contractor offered *Gulf Contracting*-type, time impact analysis proof of five periods of owner delay on a chronological and cumulative basis. Next, the VA defended by showing a bar chart of base contract work performed after the adjusted contract date. Finally, there is the board ruling concerning the new requirement that the contractor show that it would have performed the base contract work sooner:

> The Appellant claims various costs associated with an alleged 188 calendar days of delay to its critical path activities that it asserts to have been caused solely by the actions or omissions of the Government.
>
> * * *
>
> The Appellant's Expert Testimony
> The Appellant's scheduling consultant, Mr. McLaughlin, performed a Time Impact Analysis. He identified five time impacts on performance of this Contract. Time Impact No. 1 was the Late Start of Shop Drawings, which he attributed to the dispute over the AutoCad drawings furnished by the Government. In his analysis, this caused FSS to begin its shop drawings 21 calendar days later than planned. Time Impact No. 2 was the Late Finish of Approve Shop Drawings, allegedly caused by the Government's insistence that the Contractor comply with the specifications calling for Schedule 10 piping instead of the non-compliant thin wall piping that the Contractor repeatedly submitted for approval. Notwithstanding that the Contract at Section 15500, paragraph 2.1A required "Schedule 10 [piping] per NFPA 13," and without any explanation for his conclusion, Appellant's expert characterized the 55 calendar days of delay as attributable to "defective specifications (i.e. Section 15500)." When the Government finally agreed to allow a deviation from the specifications in return for the Contractor's extended warranty on the substituted thin wall piping, the parties executed bilateral Supplemental Agreement (SA) #3. This operated as a complete accord and satisfaction releasing both parties from any liability attributable to the piping change, including delay or suspension damages, up to the time of SA #3. Time Impact No. 3 was the Contractor's Early Start of Fabricate and Deliver, which recovered the 21 days previously lost over the delayed start of the shop drawings and thus offset that delay. Thus, taken together,

---

[265.1] By contrast, if we follow the *Fire Security* holding to its logical conclusion, it would seem to tell us that when the shoe is on the owner's other foot—that is, when the owner issues change orders after the contract completion date—the owner has the affirmative duty to show that such change orders are not critical and could have been performed sooner. To state it another way, if we have a project that is −180 days and the owner issues changes for 30 days of delay to activities that are −100, under the *Fire Security* ruling these would be presumed to be critical path delays. Thus, any delays to activities with negative float (whether or not they represented the highest negative float) would be presumed to be critical and constitute concurrent delay at a minimum.

the first three time impacts identified by Mr. McLaughlin are effectively neutral with respect to Appellant's entitlement to any extended performance time. (R4, tab 533, part III; Tr. VIII/264; Tr. VIII/75-78)

<u>Time Impact No. 4</u>, although given the label of Late Finish of Install Off Hour Zones Sprinkler Piping, actually relates entirely to pipe/sprinkler installation in Zone 3, the dietetic kitchen. <u>Mr. McLaughlin attributes 300 calendar days of delay to the critical path to what he concludes was the Contractor's justified refusal to install piping above the kitchen ceiling "due to the presence of asbestos containing material."</u> In testifying, he stated that this situation, together with the VA's issuance of Supplemental Agreement #17, amounted to a defective specification, thus rendering all time lost from the planned start of sprinkler installation until the completion of SA #17 (allowing piping installation below the kitchen ceiling) solely attributable to a Government-caused suspension. (R4, tab 533, Part III, Tr. VIII/295)

The FSS expert's Time Impact No 5 was designated Early Finish of Punch List, Testing, Cleanup. In his analysis, Mr. McLaughlin concluded that the Contractor had actually recovered 112 calendar days of the 300 days attributable to Time Impact No. 4, for a net 188 calendar days of compensable delay damages. He concluded that the VA achieved beneficial occupancy on November 20, 1995, although punch list work extended into 1996. In his view, "[t]he extended punch list duration is not relevant to entitlement determination for delay damages such as extended home office overhead." (R4, tab 533, Part III)

<u>Mr. McLaughlin testified that, while other work was sporadically being done during the delay associated with the kitchen piping installation, all of these other activities had considerable float and did not control the critical path. Only if any of these other activities extended beyond the end of the kitchen-associated delay period, could they become critical to project completion. In his view, kitchen piping/sprinkler installation was the critical controlling activity</u> from Spring through mid-November of 1995. (Tr. VII/231, 284-91)

Mr. McLaughlin's view that the Government was solely responsible for the kitchen sprinkler piping delays was based on the fact that "a change order was issued, and it is very clear that the design was changed, and it is very clear that the specification was not that of Fire Security." He did not indicate any in-depth understanding of the circumstances leading to the VA's decision to allow a change in the previously-approved design—which design was that of his own client, Fire Security. When asked if it was determined by the Board that FSS, and not the VA, had created the necessity for issuance of the kitchen piping design change, he admitted that the Contractor would be responsible for the 188 days of delay. (Tr. VIII/291, 289-90)

The Government's Expert Testimony
Mr. Gymory, the Government's scheduling expert, conducted an in-depth review of all of the Contract documents, including the Contractor's as-planned schedule, correspondence, certified payrolls and Daily Logs. Having done this, he <u>prepared a fully documented as-built bar chart depicting the duration of every identifiable Contract activity from issuance of Notice to</u>

Proceed on December 27, 1993 through completion of the punch list work in late summer of 1996. (R4, tabs 366, 367)

This <u>as-built bar chart shows seven separate activities extending beyond the Contract's extended completion date</u> of May 12, 1995. . . . In Mr. Gymory's opinion all of these ongoing activities beyond the Contract's completion date were critical to project completion and thus were concurrent with any delays experienced in connection with dietetic kitchen work. (R4, tab 366, 367)

The Appellant's scheduling expert <u>was critical of Mr. Gymory's position that all substantive work remaining to be done after the extended completion date had passed became critical and therefore concurrent</u>. In Mr. McLaughlin's view: "Until the controlling delay is resolved, no other delay can have any other influence on the end of the project." (Tr. VIII/269-70)

In his analysis, Mr. Gymory initially conceded that the Government was responsible for forty calendar days of delay where the Daily Logs simply stated "No work on sprinklers due to ACM in remaining areas." These entries begin on May 2, 1995 and end on June 14, 1995, with the following notation: "Survey areas where piping is to be removed/replaced in Zones 1, 2, 4, 5 & 7 with Mike Atchley & John S_____. Possible ACM debris located in Rooms B-01Q, B-17, A-102 & A-54. Areas to be cleaned by VA prior to work." However, during his testimony Mr. Gymory revised his position, observing that the period in question was concurrent with delays to several base Contract activities (as depicted on his as-built progress chart) for which the Government was not responsible. Mr. Gymory concluded that Appellant is due no delay damages for that period, since the ACM would only have affected the sprinkler installation work—not the other activities that could have been worked on during the same period. (R4, tabs 366, 367, 290, Tr. VIII/179-81)

* * *

VABCA-5583: DISCUSSION & DECISION

The Appellant's scheduling expert based his client's entitlement to delay damages entirely upon the sprinkler installation in the dietetic kitchen. He was of the opinion that this work was the only critical path activity through November, 1995. Consistent with that position, the Board has examined all relevant facts of record concerning this work in the kitchen. For reasons to be discussed, we conclude that it was the Appellant, not the Government, who unreasonably delayed installation of sprinkler piping in the dietetic kitchen.

The Government witnesses, particularly Safety Officer Henrickson, credibly testified that the area above the kitchen was far more expansive than any other area of the hospital save for the auditorium. The Contractor had access to the Asbestos Assessment of every area of the hospital prior to designing the routing of its piping above the kitchen ceiling. It submitted its shop drawings showing the placement of the piping above the kitchen ceiling and they were approved. The constant ambient air sampling conducted by the Safety Office, the results of which were conveyed to the Contractor, showed that there was no airborne asbestos that exceeded the applicable OSHA standard. The condition of the ACM insulating the duct work was described by the Safety Officer as well-adhered with no evidence of any damage. There was no technical or contractual basis for the Contractor's adamant refusal to install the sprinkler piping exactly as it had designed in the approved shop drawings.

The conclusion by Appellant's scheduling expert that SA #17 was issued to correct the VA's "defective specification" is without factual basis. While it is true that the CO ultimately did agree not only to let FSS proceed with a [sic] an alternate installation below the ceiling and to actually pay for the "privilege," she could just as easily have followed through on her repeated threats to terminate the Contract for default. We have found, however, that the longer the problem remained unresolved, the more concerned the VA became over losing its accreditation if the sprinkler work was not completed prior to the next inspection by the JCAHO committee. In the CO's own words, this was the impetus for her decision to issue SA #17. She was under pressure, much of it caused by the Contractor, who seems to have taken advantage of the situation. Under these circumstances, we do not consider that change order to operate as an irrebutable presumption of Government responsibility for the situation preceding its issuance.

Once the decision was made to change the design there is no evidence whatsoever that the Government caused the work to be delayed until October/November of 1995. As before, FSS submitted sprinkler pipe, this time plastic, that failed to comply with the prior sprinkler pipe deviation that the Contractor had itself precipitated (SA #3). This time, however, the VA refused to further relax the specifications. Insisting on steel pipe, the VA, through its A/E, took the initiative and confirmed that the manufacturer of the desired plastic DecoShield soffit material, could provide the soffit in a size that would accommodate steel pipe, contrary to the position of FSS.

We also disagree with the Appellant's expert concerning Mr. Gymory's testimony concerning the concurrent delays to contract completion. While it is logical that during the original (or contractually extended) performance period, any work on parallel paths with significant amounts of float will not become critical so long as critical path work is delayed, these characterizations become meaningless once the Contract's completion date has been reached. Once past that point, common sense dictates that any substantive work remaining becomes critical to Contract completion. In other words, even had the delay in kitchen sprinkler installation never occurred, the Government's scheduling expert has graphically illustrated at least seven other substantive items that remained incomplete after the Contract's extended completion date. Of these items, three were base Contract work: fire alarm installation (electronic)—not completed until November 18, 1995; signage—not completed until the week of December 1, 1995; and door and frame installation in rooms C05 and C05A—not completed until the week of January 10, 1996. There is no evidence whatsoever that the Government caused any delay in completion of these three basic elements of the Contract. While it is clear from Mr. Gymory's as-built progress chart that there were extremely long periods with no work shown on each of these activities' parallel paths, we will not presume that the Contractor could and would have performed these activities earlier had the kitchen sprinkler piping work not been delayed. Proof rather than presumption is a part of the Contractor's burden. The burden cannot be met by educated guesses or conclusions, no matter the qualifications of the expert offering them. Hard verifiable evidence of how and why these activities were not completed sooner must be presented. This was not done. [Emphasis added.]

[K] Denial of Automatic Time Extensions for Changes After Completion Date

Page 377, add at end of subsection:

See full discussion in **§ 9.08[G][3]** of this supplement.

[M] Presumptions from CPM Approvals and Time Modifications

Page 394, add at end of subsection:

Two decisions that bear on the issue of presumptions from CPM approvals and time modifications are *P.J. Dick Inc. v. Secretary of Veterans Affairs*, 324 F.3d 1364 (Fed. Cir. 2003) and *Cable & Computer Technology, Inc.*, ASBCA No. 47420, 03-1 BCA ¶ 32,237, 2003 WL 1640324.

In *P.J. Dick*, the Court of Federal Claims considered the effect of a stipulation between the parties within the context of an extended-duration-type *Eichleay* claim. Here, *even though the contractor had not shown* at the trial board hearing that the *government delays had required it to be on standby* during government-caused delay, *the court of appeals found that a stipulation between the parties obviated the need for this proof. Per the stipulation, the contractor was "required to only prove entitlement under the contract's suspension of work (SOW) clause to establish entitlement to all types of damages, including unabsorbed home office overhead"* The decision stated:

> The interpretation of the parties' stipulation, like any contract, is a question of law which we review *de novo. See Kearns v. Chrysler Corp.*, 32 F.3d 1541, 1545 (Fed. Cir. 1994) (reviewing a district court's interpretation of a litigation stipulation de novo because it was essentially a contract); *see also Wickham*, 12 F.3d at 1577. The relevant language of the parties' "Stipulation on Quantum" reads:
>
>> [F]or any days of delay for which it is determined that [PJD] is entitled to compensation under the Suspension of Work Clause [which is the subject of] this appeal, [PJD's] recovery shall be calculated by multiplying that number of days by the following daily rates without the need for future proof of costs or damages [going on to include daily rates for field and home office overhead].
>
> The Board, however, concluded that the stipulation related solely to quantum and thus PJD was still required to demonstrate entitlement to Eichleay

damages. PJD argues that the stipulation only requires it to show entitlement to damages under the Suspension of Work contract clause. We agree with PJD's interpretation.

We conclude that the stipulation did obviate the need for PJD to separately prove facts demonstrating entitlement to Eichleay damages beyond showing its right to recover for delays compensable under the SOW clause. The language of the stipulation establishes a single condition precedent to PJD's receipt of the enumerated damages: entitlement to damages under the SOW clause. Entitlement to recovery under the LOW clause requires proof entirely different, and less demanding, than that required to show entitlement to Eichleay damages. *Compare P.J. Dick, Inc.*, 2001 WL 1219552, 2001 VA BCA LEXIS 12, at *120 ("PJD must provide proof meeting a four-part test to establish its entitlement to recover an equitable adjustment under the suspension of work clause. First, there must be a delay of unreasonable length extending the Contract completion time. Second, the delay must have been proximately caused by the VA's action or inaction. Third, the delay resulted in some injury and fourth, there is no delay concurrent with the suspension that is the fault of PJD."), *with All State Boiler*, 146 F.3d at 1373 ("We have adopted two prerequisites to application of the Eichleay formula to recover unabsorbed overhead . . . (1) that the contractor be on standby and (2) that the contractor be unable to take on other work." (internal quotation marks omitted)). Establishing a right to recover under the SOW clause—and, thus, to the stipulated damages including home office overhead—therefore requires no separate proof of entitlement to Eichleay damages (as is required in the normal case).

In addition, there are two indications in the record that the parties originally intended the stipulation to be interpreted in just such a manner. This is relevant as "the parties' contemporaneous construction of an agreement, before it has become the subject of a dispute, is entitled to great weight in its interpretation." *Blinderman Constr. Co., Inc. v. United States*, 695 F.2d 552, 558 (Fed. Cir. 1982). First, although the Eichleay case law explicitly places the burden to prove standby on the contractor, before the Board PJD "provided neither evidence nor allegation that it was on standby." Given its clear burden of proof, it is unlikely that PJD would have chosen not to submit any evidence whatsoever showing it was on standby unless it believed the stipulation relieved it of that burden. Second, in its post-hearing briefing (drafted by the signer of the stipulation), the DVA presented the following: "Based on the foregoing, Respondent is entitled to compensation for 11 calendar days of delay under the Suspension of Work Clause. Based on the stipulated quantum, [PJD] is entitled to the following daily rates [going on to recite the stipulated daily rates for both field and home office overhead]." It is apparent that, absent a gross mistake, the drafter of the post-hearing brief, like PJD, understood that under the stipulation the contractor had only to prove entitlement to damages under the less exacting tests of the SOW clause. (Footnotes omitted.)

In *Cable & Computer Technology, Inc.*, ASBCA No. 47420, 03-1 BCA ¶ 32,237, the board addressed issues created by time extensions given in modifications for changes/defective specifications after the period of delay had already occurred. The court made two significant rulings. First, the court found a rebuttable presumption, in the contractor's favor, of project delay (of the type previously espoused in the *McMullen* line of cases) arising from time granted for changes in a modification; second, the court found that, as to a portion of the overall delay, of 452 days the government had rebutted the presumption as to 181 days. The 181 days were then found to constitute concurrent delay:

> 3. Delay
> Recoverable performance costs include those caused by delay, and the contractor bears the burden of proving that performance delay resulted from defective specifications. See, e.g., *Laburnum Construction Corp. v. United States*, 325 F.2d 451 (Ct. Cl. 1963). We found that, due to the defective specifications, appellant's performance was adversely affected during the following general time periods: (a) NIIF Interface for SAFENET I and II—November 1989 through February 1991; (b) CSR Definition—November 1989 through September 1991; (c) Board Physical Definition—December 1989 through July 1990; (d) Futurebus+ Clock Synchronization—November 1989 through July 1990; (e) SAFENET Power Budget—November 1989 through April 1990; (f) SAFENET Time Synchronization—November 1989 through October 1991. However, this record does not enable us to determine with anything resembling precision the delay to overall contract performance from any of the individual claim items.
>
> The Government issuance of contract modifications extending the period of performance indicates that the Government recognizes that the overall project was delayed to the extent of the time extensions and constitutes an administrative determination that the delay was not due to the fault or negligence of the contractor. It also raises a presumption, subject to rebuttal, that the Government was responsible for the delay. *Gottfried Corporation*, ASBCA No. 51041, 98-2 BCA ¶ 30,063; *Robert S. McMullan & Son, Inc.*, ASBCA No. 19023, 76-1 BCA ¶ 11,728. This presumption is especially strong where the time extensions are granted after the delay has occurred. *Papathomas*, ASBCA No. 49512, 50895, 97-2 BCA ¶ 29,317 at 145,780.
>
> <u>We have found here that the Navy issued contract Modification Nos. P00004 and P00005 extending the time for contract performance from the original contract delivery date of 12 October 1990 to 22 January 1992, a total of 467 days. Those modifications, in effect, constituted a recognition that the contract was delayed by 467 days, without the fault or negligence of CCT, and create a presumption that the Government was responsible for the delay. In this case, as in Papathomas, supra, the presumption is strong, as those contract modifications were issued after the delay was experienced.</u> We conclude that there is a presumption that the performance delay which the Government recognized in its issuance of Modification Nos. P00004 and P00005 was the responsibility of the Government and that, with the exception of our conclusions regarding concurrent delay below, the Government has not rebutted that presumption. Therefore, in the absence of concurrent delay, which we discuss below, the Government is responsi-

ble for compensable delay from 12 October 1990 to 7 January 1992, a total of 452 days.

4. Concurrent Delay

A contractor seeking to recover compensable delay has the burden of demonstrating that any Government caused delays were not concurrent with delay for which the contractor is responsible. *Donohoe Construction Co.*, ASBCA Nos. 47310, 47312, 99-1 BCA ¶ 30,387 at 150,190; see also *Sauer, Inc. v. Danzig*, 224 F.3d 1340, 1348 (Fed. Cir. 2000). The contractor is not entitled to recover the costs of delay incurred during the period of concurrency. *Commerce International Co. v. United States*, 338 F.2d 81 (Ct. Cl. 1964).

Here, we have concluded that there is a presumption that the Government was responsible for the delay. However, we also conclude that our record reflects that, to the extent described below, that presumption has been rebutted. We have found that CCT's subcontract with Unisys was not executed until 1 May 1990. Although our findings also reflect that Unisys was performing some work for CCT under a purchase order issued on 19 December 1989, we do not have evidence of the nature and extent of that work. We have also found that, on 8 March 1990, CCT advised the Navy that it would not make a presentation to the SAFENET Working Group meeting on 22 March 1990 because it was still in negotiations with three potential subcontractors for the NGCR SAFENET requirements. We have found that CCT, by letter dated 8 June 1990 reflecting its presentation during its 30-31 May 1990 program review, advised that subcontract negotiations with Unisys had caused a 4-6 week "schedule impact." Further, our findings reflect that Mr. Andersen of Unisys did not attend any interoperability meetings on behalf of CCT until the fourth meeting on 24 May 1990, after award of the 1 May 1990 purchase order from CCT to Unisys. We conclude that the, at best, limited participation by Unisys in early contract performance was a cause of delay for which CCT bears responsibility, and that the period of that concurrent delay was generally from November 1989 until 1 May 1990, a total of 181 days. [Emphasis added].

Page 414, add new section at end of chapter:

§ 9.11 FAILURE TO PROVIDE ACCEPTABLE NETWORK ANALYSIS SCHEDULE AS MATERIAL BREACH OF CONTRACT JUSTIFYING TERMINATION/RELEVANCE OF DEFECTIVE SCHEDULES TO DEFAULT TERMINATIONS

Case authority on major projects recognizes the importance of acceptable schedules being prepared by the contractor. This authority thus recognizes the significance of defective schedules in justifying default termination. In fact, the decision in *Stone & Webster*, 279 B.R. 748 (Bankr. D. Del. 2002), found that the failure to provide an acceptable schedule was a material breach of contract justifying termination for default on its own.

Turning to recent authority concerning the role that defective schedules can play in justifying and opposing default termination, we look to *R.W. Granger*

& Sons, Inc. v. City School District of Albany, 296 A.D.2d 636, 744 N.Y.S.2d 567, 166 Ed. Law Rep. 744, 2002 N.Y. Slip Op. 05731 (2002); and *Fraya,* ASBCA No. 52222, 2002 WL 31008637, 02-2 BCA ¶ 31,975.

In *Granger*, the New York appeals court considered a case in which a prime contractor (apparently for the civil work) for a three-phase renovation and addition project at the Albany School of Humanities was terminated for default. Phase II of the project dealt with construction of an addition to the school. Numerous delays extended the date for completion of Phase II from February 7, 1995; in May 1995, the parties agreed that Phase II was to be substantially complete on June 23, 1995. Although Phase II was completed on June 23, 1995, such that the owner was able to move furniture and materials into the building, the owner terminated the contractor for default for "failure to timely progress the work."

The lower court determined that the termination had been made without cause and awarded the contractor $1,412,745 in damages. What is significant about this decision is that it involved a multi-prime contract with separate mechanical, electrical, and plumbing primes. The appeals court found that the decision in favor of Granger was justified because the delays were *caused by the owner's failure to coordinate the work of the various prime contractors and to prepare adequate construction schedules:*

> We affirm. The trial evidence and exhibits are far too voluminous for lengthy recitation here. However, plaintiff's expert engineer, Thomas Fertitta, testified that based upon his "critical path" analysis, the project was delayed for a total of 133 days. Of the 133 days, Fertitta attributed all but 15 days to defendant and its agents by reason of their failure to coordinate the work of the various prime contractors and to prepare adequate construction schedules. These failures, in turn, resulted in the mechanical, electrical and plumbing work interfering with plaintiff's work, thereby causing the complained of delay.

In *Fraya*, the Armed Services Board considered a contract to renovate the interior of a classified facility in Puerto Rico for the Navy, including replacement of the raised computer access flooring; new finishes; repair and replacement of the existing mechanical system, ductwork, and air control systems; upgrade of the electrical system; new lighting, and so on. Because the facility had to stay in operation, the procurement called for phasing of the work and for numerous submittals, including network analysis schedules. The network analysis schedule was to be used by the contractor for "planning, organizing and directing the work, reporting progress, and requesting payment for work accomplished."

The contractor made no progress on the work on the required schedule during the first phase of the project. Not until a cure notice was sent did the contractor first assert that a hurricane had delayed its efforts. When the schedule was finally submitted, it was defective, in that it ignored required phasing of the project, ignored sequencing of trades into predecessor/successor relationships (showing numerous trades as one continuous operation), and ignored the status of the project at the time of submission of the schedule:

> 49. Even though Fraya was supposed to submit its Network Analysis Schedule on 8 November 1998, Fraya did not submit the schedule until 16 February 1999 (tr. 187, 189). . . .
>
> 50. Camacho reviewed Fraya's Network Analysis Schedule and in a memorandum dated 19 February 1999 to AROICC Garcia, recommended disapproval and resubmission of the schedule. The memorandum identified 17 specific deficiencies. It indicated that Fraya had totally disregarded the phasing requirement of the contract. It also identified work (e.g., mercury, asbestos and lead abatement, fire alarm, mechanical, lighting fixture, and electrical wiring) Fraya erroneously believed could be done in one continuous operation. The memorandum indicated that the schedule was not current—showing work starting in October 1998, and finishing on 5 November 1999, one month past the contract completion date. Presumably, Fraya added 30 days to the project to account for the effects of the hurricane, but the schedule did not indicate what submittals were delayed by the hurricane and to what extent they were delayed. The schedule did not break out the activities into their submittal, procurement and work stages. (R4, tab 26, Enclosure 3, tab 154; tr. 70, 186, 194)
>
> 51. Fraya's Network Analysis Schedule did not reflect the status of the work as of the date of submission (16 February 1999). It indicated mobilization to have taken place back on 14 October 1998. Except for the delivery of trailers to the site, however, no mobilization had actually taken place. The Network Analysis Schedule showed Fraya planned to take 387 days (from 14 October 1998 to 5 November 1999) to complete the contract. Even assuming that Fraya was entitled to the 30-day time extension it claimed, there were only 262 days (16 February 1999 to 5 November 1999) remaining on the contract as of 16 February 1999. <u>The schedule did not show how Fraya was going to "recuperate" to complete the contract within that time</u>. (See R4, tab 26, Enclosure 3; tr. 232-33)
>
> 52. AROICC Garcia testified that after he reviewed Fraya's Network Analysis Schedule, he was certain that Fraya would not be able to finish the project on time because Fraya had shown "<u>an obvious failure to understand the work, itself, because the phasing is inherent to the work</u>." Moreover, he believed that since the project was already five months late, the project would be at least five months late if it had to be properly phased. (Tr. 74) [Emphasis added.]

Thereafter, the Navy terminated the contractor for default. Significantly, the board, in upholding this action, looked to the contractor's failure to provide an acceptable schedule and agreed with the Navy's expert that there was no reasonable likelihood that the contractor could complete the contract within the milestone dates:

Phasing without overlapping was a key ingredient of the contract. <u>Fraya's inability to perform in accordance with this requirement was made clear when it submitted its Network Analysis Schedule which totally ignored the phasing requirement</u> (finding 50). Ignoring this plain requirement was indicative of Fraya's lack of diligence in performing its contract. <u>Without an approved schedule, we agree with the Navy expert's assessment that "there was not a reasonable likelihood at the time of the default termination that Fraya could have completed the contract effort within any of the milestone dates</u> . . . even if the milestone dates had been extended by 30 days" (see finding 60). See *Discount Co., Inc. v. United State*s, 554 F.2d 435 (Ct. Cl. 1977), *cert. denied*, 434 U.S. 938 (1977) (the default clause did not require a finding that completion within the contract's time limitations was impossible, but only that the Government could not be assured of timely completion).

We conclude that the Navy has made out a prima facie case that termination of Fraya's contract for failure to make progress and for failure to perform within the specified time was justified. [Emphasis added.]

By far the most significant case in this regard is *Stone & Webster*, 279 B.R. 748 (Bankr. D. Del. 2002), in which one of the bases for terminating the contractor for default was its failure to provide an acceptable schedule. This case concerned a project to decommission the Wiscasset nuclear power plant for Maine Yankee Atomic Power Company, Stone and Webster was the contractor on the $252 million contract. Under the contract, Stone and Webster was required to address issues of construction, engineering, health, physics, and radioactive waste cleanup.

The specifications for the Wiscasset project required the development of a network analysis system using the P-3 (Primavera) program:

> As explained by Raymond Burke and James Garvey, section 11.9 requires SWEC to provide the schedule using a scheduling software package called P-3. It must also update the schedule to show progress thereunder. The schedule must delineate the project's execution, logical constraints on project tasks, durations for tasks, project milestones, and beginning and completion dates for each task. It must also include dates for licensing activities, interfaces with subcontractors, arrival of personnel, etc. The completion date for physical work was to be April 2004, and the completion date for license termination was to be September 2004. Pursuant to section 11.9.3.3, the schedule was to be submitted to Maine Yankee within 90 days of the contract's execution and was subject to Maine Yankee's approval. SWEC was also to report progress and project status to Maine Yankee, which used the schedule as a project management device. If SWEC deviated from the critical path logic of the schedule or missed a project milestone by more than 20 days, the Agreement requires SWEC to set forth a revised schedule indicating new logic and a plan for recovering the lost time. Moreover, if SWEC is projected to exceed the completion date by more than 6 months, Maine Yankee could take over the project and take reasonable measures to attempt to implement the schedule at SWEC's expense.

Maine Yankee had the right to terminate for cause under Section 11.2 of the specifications *"if [SWEC] fails to substantially perform under the Contract Documents or if [SWEC]* **materially breaches** *any of the terms of the Contract Documents."*

During performance, problems with Stone and Webster's execution of the work began in early 1999. The problems were grouped in three categories: "(i) financial issues at SWEC, whereby SWEC was unable to pay its bills or its subcontractors; (ii) SWEC's failure to develop an adequate project schedule; and (iii) SWEC's failure to make adequate progress on the project."

The initial project manager for the contractor, Chuck Lepisto, per the testimony of Maine Yankee, had problems in coordinating and executing the work and in the areas of licensing and permitting.

Maine Yankee further determined that the schedule submitted by Stone and Webster was inadequate, incomplete, and not resource loaded:

> Burke reports that as of December 1999, there was still not an approved schedule. The schedules that SWEC had submitted were not resource loaded to include the costs of labor, supplies, etc. Moreover, the schedules were incomplete. To remedy this, SWEC and Maine Yankee employees met in workshops. Burke explained that the workshops were designed to provide SWEC with a better understanding of the complexity and details of the project. After the workshops, Burke states, the number of tasks in the schedule nearly doubled and the completion date of the project was pushed from April, 2004 to sometime in 2005. [Emphasis added.]

During performance, Jerry Kane was called upon by Stone and Webster to replace Mr. Lepisto. Significantly, Mr. Kane agreed that the prior project manager had been in way over his head; that the prior project manager had felt that engineering, scheduling, cost, health, licensing, and the like were secondary to the construction effort; and that the project had been run in a haphazard manner, with work schedules being made up at morning meetings:

> Kane's testimony confirms that under Lepisto's leadership, the project was having numerous problems. He noted that Lepisto had "never run a large fixed price contract [involving liquidated damages on a schedule and] was way over his head." Kane explained that the Maine Yankee project was not merely a construction project; it involved licensing, engineering, health, physics, and radioactive waste clean-up. While Lepisto was a "good construction site manager," he had never been involved with a project of this complexity and scale. Kane also explained that the Maine Yankee proposal bid had been prepared by Lepisto and "sold" to the Stone & Webster management "on the premise that it was purely a deconstruction—a construction job in reverse, and that there was very little technical content."
>
> On or about December 6, 1999, Jim Callahan, the Senior Vice President of the Boston Office of SWINC, received a call from Maine Yankee's Michael Meisner, who asked Callahan to remove Lepisto. Callahan called

upon Kane, who was "the most senior person and most experienced person in running large projects" that SWEC had, to immediately take over the project manager position of the Maine Yankee project. Kane went on to testify that when he arrived, he found that SWEC was significantly over-budget in man hours spent with regard to the schedule, that the organization of the project was "dysfunctional," that it had overspent the entire project contingency, and that it had failed to take into account SWEC's obligations to comply with Maine regulations. Kane further explained that when he arrived on site, he found that the project was "dysfunctionally organized" in that "it was organized by a construction person who felt that all of the other aspects of the project, including cost and scheduling, engineering, contracts, health, physics, RAD waste, licensing, were secondary to the construction effort." <u>The project was being run only by Lepisto and one manager of construction, without giving proper consideration to management of the numerous technical functions of the project</u>. As a result,

> <u>the project was being run in a haphazard manner in that schedules were made at the morning meeting</u>. One of the construction superintendents would say I didn't get that job done yesterday and then say alright, the job that was scheduled today we won't do, we'll finish the one yesterday, or even worse, the job that was supposed to start today, somebody would say I didn't have the materials or I'm not ready to start the job or didn't have the work permit or whatever and he, <u>the construction manager, literally would reach out two, three, four weeks ahead in the schedule, pick a task and say alright, we'll do this one today, and we weren't ready, we didn't have work packages, we didn't have permits, we didn't have sketches, we didn't have a plan</u>.

Kane also reported that due to these problems, the relationship with Maine Yankee was "horrible at best." [Emphasis added.]

Kane, after taking charge of the project, sought in early 2000 to complete a fully integrated detailed project schedule and obtain approval of it. However, the testimony of Maine Yankee was that even after Mr. Kane's arrival on the project, defective schedules were submitted by Stone and Webster:

> It had <u>open ends, inconsistent logic, and failed to identify all of the scope of the work</u>. Moreover, he said, the updated versions of the schedule were inaccurate because they continued to show that the project was on track for on time completion, due to an "<u>inappropriate mandatory restraint</u>" that fixed that date in the schedule, instead of letting it logically float base on the completion of all the necessary tasks. [Emphasis added.]

Although the parties pursued joint workshops in efforts to obtain an adequate schedule, Maine Yankee ultimately terminated Stone and Webster for default.

The court considered whether Maine Yankee had properly terminated Stone and Webster for default, under Article 11.2 of the contract, due to its failure to perform. This inquiry specifically addressed *whether the failure to develop an acceptable project schedule was a material breach and grounds for the termination. The court answered in the affirmative.*

In making this determination, the court found *that the development of the comprehensive project schedule was a major substantive requirement of the contract; that the project schedule was required to be based on true logic and avoid misleading imposed dates; and that the schedules always contained logic problems, were not resource loaded, lacked work activities, and included false logic:*

> b. *Failure to Develop an Acceptable Project Schedule*
> [4] Numerous witnesses for both sides stressed the importance of a detailed project schedule for effectively managing projects of this size and complexity. It is also clear that the development of a comprehensive project schedule was a major substantive requirement of the Agreement. As stated by Norton in his March 16, 2000 letter to Kane, an acceptable schedule ensures that "the project can move forward with the proper tools to support logical decision making and problem identification." Section 11.9 of the Amended RFP sets forth detailed specifications for SWEC's development of a schedule that reflected each task necessary to complete the work and, including all licensing and permitting tasks, and their associated resource requirements. Under the Agreement, the project schedule was required to be based on "true logic," include the projected completion dates for tasks and the overall project, and avoid "misleading imposed dates."
>
> The parties do not dispute that during the time that SWEC was the contractor on the Maine Yankee project, SWEC never developed a project schedule that was accepted and approved by Maine Yankee. They only dispute which of the parties was to blame for this failure. Maine Yankee points to the fact that SWEC never developed an acceptable project schedule as proof that SWEC breached its obligations under the Agreement, while SWEC maintains that the reason a schedule was never agreed upon is because Maine Yankee unreasonably rejected countless SWEC schedules, making it impossible for SWEC to comply with its contractual obligation.
>
> SWEC argues that the record, particularly the testimony of Boyea, demonstrates Maine Yankee's project schedule requirements were ill-defined and capriciously applied and that every time SWEC sought to resolve the scheduling problems, and was assured by Maine Yankee that only one more change was required, Maine Yankee would come up with new hurdles and issues. SWEC also points to the relative success of its workshop program in gaining piecemeal approval of all but one portion of the schedule, the ISFSI. **[FN18]**
>
>> **FN18.** SWEC asserts that approval of the ISFSI schedule was stalled by the inability to identify a start date for certain ISFSI construction, which resulted from a lawsuit filed by Maine Yankee against the State of Maine over regulation of radiological issues at the site. The impasse over the ISFSI start date was resolved in early May, after termination.
>
> In response, Maine Yankee points out that, despite SWEC's machinations

to the contrary, no schedule that SWEC had submitted—including the resubmitted schedules for which SWEC purportedly had satisfied two particular conditions for approval—ever fully complied with the requirements of Section 11.9. Maine Yankee also underscores that Garvey testified that <u>even as late as May 2000, after the workshops, the schedule still contained logic problems that masked the fact that the project was close to nine months behind, was not resource loaded, and lacked a number of work activities, including licensing and permitting tasks</u>. Maine Yankee also notes that even after termination SWEC continued to add required detail to the schedule and that Maine Yankee itself had to add a significant amount of detail, particularly in the areas of ISFSI, RCRA closure, and concrete disposal, after it took responsibility for the schedule in connection with its choice to self-perform.

<u>It is clear that Maine Yankee demanded great attention to detail in the schedule, when reviewing the SWEC schedule submissions for approval. However, Maine Yankee was entitled to demand that</u>, in order to gain its approval, SWEC's schedule strictly comply with the many requirements of section 11.9 of the Agreement. Aside from the fact that Maine Yankee was within its rights to demand compliance with the schedule, <u>it was also reasonable to do so in light of some of the problems on the work site that stemmed from problems with the schedule. For example, witnesses described a number of occasions where activities were performed before requisite permits were obtained</u>. SWEC had problems meeting its obligations in connection with licensing and permitting issues throughout the project.

<u>No evidence shows that Maine Yankee demanded anything of SWEC but strict compliance with SWEC's obligations under the scheduling provisions of the Agreement</u>. Despite the anecdotal evidence regarding Maine Yankee's unreasonableness, no witness for SWEC could confirm that the schedules it submitted for approval ever included the level of detail required by the Agreement.

<u>Early schedules</u> that SWEC submitted did not include all of the licensing and permitting tasks, [were] not <u>resource-loaded, and included false logic</u>. The new SWEC project management team headed by Kane recognized these shortcomings and implemented a series of workshops beginning in January 2000 in hopes of getting an approved schedule. While it is clear that the workshop program did help the parties to get on the same page on scheduling matters, it did not bring SWEC into compliance with section 11.9. <u>Despite SWEC's efforts, the final SWEC schedule still did not include all work activities</u>, particularly in the area of licensing and permitting, <u>and lacked sufficient details</u>. The consistent inability of SWEC to develop the schedule in this area can be attributed in part to the original mismanagement of Lepisto and in part to SWEC's inexperience with State of Maine regulatory issues.

<u>Moreover, when the details were later added to the schedule, the updated schedule did not reflect the true completion date for the project of July 7, 2005, due to an inappropriate logical constraint that fixed the completion date to the original project irrespective of scheduling logic that compelled a later completion date</u>. While there is contradicting testimony about how

this inappropriate constraint was entered into the schedule, the court cannot credit Boyea's speculation that this was the fault of either Maine Yankee or a technical computer problem. Such evidence does not convince the court that it was Maine Yankee's fault that the constraint was entered. Under the Agreement, the ultimate responsibility for the schedule lay with SWEC.

Developing a schedule to the level of detail required by the Agreement for a project as complicated as the Maine Yankee decommissioning was truly a herculean task. Despite SWEC's efforts, it was a task that SWEC never completed. While the record indicates that but for SWEC's financial problems and impending bankruptcy, it is unlikely that Maine Yankee would have terminated SWEC based on the schedule issues alone, <u>Maine Yankee was technically within its rights to terminate the Agreement for cause due to inadequacies in the schedule</u>. [Emphasis added.]

CHAPTER 10
STANDARDS OF PROOF FOR CONTRACTOR TIME DELAY CLAIMS

Page 451, add new section at end of chapter:

§ 10.08 NEGATIVE INFERENCES DRAWN FROM CLAIMANT'S FAILURE TO CALL WITNESSES WITH ACTUAL KNOWLEDGE OF PROJECT

A VA Board of Contract Appeals decision disregarded the testimony of an expert witness as to an extended duration claim. In this case the claimant failed to call any witnesses who knew anything about what had happened on the project (and failed to show that the expert had performed sufficient and adequate research to remedy this failure). The board decision, *Bay Construction Co.*, VABCA No. 5594 et al., 02-1 BCA ¶ 31,795, 2002 WL 442118, detailed the negative inferences to be drawn in these circumstances, as well as the line of authority previously establishing this principle:

> The Appellant called Mr. Kim, a Bay project manager, as its primary witness, and most of its arguments are premised on the opinions and estimates provided by Mr. Kim. We note at the outset of this discussion that the Appellant failed to elicit the testimony of Mr. Doerr, who had actual knowledge of how this project was planned, scheduled, or staffed; Mr. Yu, who supervised on-site work during the project; or, Mr. Lee, who as one of Bay's owners, managed the VA project, and interfaced with the VA. Bay also failed to call any witnesses who had interacted with CO Prescott or COTR Katanics, who were present throughout this Contract and who raised various concerns about Bay's lack of progress. <u>Essentially, Bay failed to produce any witnesses who actually knew or understood what was happening at the time Phase I work was being performed. In these circumstances, we drew the negative inference that, if so questioned, those witnesses would not have provided testimony helpful to the Appellant</u> and would not have substantiated these claims. *Centex Bateson Construction Co.*, VABCA Nos. 4613, 5162-5165, 99-1 BCA ¶ 30,153 at 149,258, *aff'd*, *Centex Bateson Construction Co. v. West*, 250 F.3d 761 (Fed. Cir. 2000); *Dawson Construction Company, Inc.*, VABCA Nos. 3306, et al., 93-3 BCA ¶ 26,177, *aff'd sub nom Dawson Construction Company v. Brown*, 34 F.3d 1080 (Fed. Cir. 1994) (Table); *Blount, Inc.*, VABCA No. 3236, 93-1 BCA ¶ 25,474. [Emphasis added.]

CHAPTER 11

SCHEDULING INDUSTRY CRISIS—"ROTTEN BANANAS IN SOFTWARE PARADISE" OR "THE RETURN TO THE UNCERTAINTY OF THE BAR CHART"

§ 11.03 ROTTEN BANANAS IN SOFTWARE PARADISE

Page 465, add at end of section:

See § **9.11** for a discussion of *Stone and Webster*, 279 B.R. 748 (Bankr. D. Del. 2002), in which the court held that an owner was entitled to terminate a contractor for default on a major project because of the contractor's failure to provide an acceptable schedule. The schedule failed to include resource loading, contained open ends and incorrect logic, and imposed constraints.

CHAPTER 12

CALCULATING CONTRACTOR'S DAMAGES FOR DELAY, DISRUPTION, AND LOSS OF EFFICIENCY

§ 12.14 THE SAGA OF *EICHLEAY* CONTINUES

Page 542, add at end of section:

The Maryland Court of Special Appeals, that state's intermediate appellate court, approved use of the *Eichleay* formula in *Gladwynne Construction Co. v. Mayor & City Council of Baltimore*, 147 Md. App. 149, 807 A.2d 1141 (2002). This case concerned a project to renovate several science laboratories and classrooms at a Baltimore High School, including significant work to replace utility lines under a concrete slab. The project, which was to have taken 180 days, was not completed for another 300 days after the original completion date. The project was delayed by changes to remedy design deficiencies and a major transformation of the scope of the work when it was discovered that the utility crawlspace to house the replacement utility lines did not exist.

The contractor had claimed delay damages, including damages for extended home office overhead based on *Eichleay*, for 245 days of the extended performance period. The trial court found that 195 days of delay were attributable to the owner, but awarded the contractor only extended field costs, ruling "that Ikely [sic] as a formula does not apply in this case based on the contract, circumstances and factors of evidence that were submitted in this case." 807 A.2d at 1156. The trial court did not specify which particular element of the *Eichleay* formula was not satisfied.

On appeal, the court first noted that it had found no reported Maryland case that had expressly adopted the *Eichleay* formula. Citing with approval federal case law, however, the court found that it appeared the contractor had presented evidence to satisfy the *Eichleay* formula for at least a portion of the total delay. Because the trial court had failed to identify which element of *Eichleay* it believed had not been satisfied, the judgment of the trial court was vacated and the case was remanded for further proceedings on overhead delay damages. 807 A.2d at 1161.

Bay Construction Co., VABCA No. 5594 et al., 02-1 BCA ¶ 31,795, concerned a contract to perform demolition and renovation at a VA medical center in San Francisco. The contractor alleged that the government had delayed its performance by 304 days and claimed it was entitled to recover its extended home office overhead calculated utilizing the *Eichleay* formula. The board first noted that the contractor had incorrectly used the terms *delay* and *suspension* interchangeably, and also that it had failed to prove that the suspensions it claimed were unreasonable. The board went on to deny the claim for *Eichleay* damages, finding the contractor had failed to prove that it had been on "standby":

> The Court has made it clear that, in order to recover Eichleay costs, a contractor must meet two tests. First, a contractor must be on "standby"; in other words, the contractor's work on a project must be suspended for an uncertain duration due to a SOW [suspension of work] and the contractor can be required to return to work immediately at any time. The second test that must be met is that the contractor was unable to take on other "replacement" work during the period from the beginning of the suspension to the end of the contract. All State Boiler, Inc. v. West, 146 F.3d 1368-1373; Melka Marine, Inc. v. United States, 187 F.3d 1370 (Fed. Cir. 1999).

(Citing *P.J. Dick*, 2001 WL 1219552, at 50.)

> We find that the Appellant wholly failed to address a critical element for recovery of unabsorbed home office overhead or "Eichleay" damages, that being, it was forced it to be on "standby" because of Government caused delay and suspension. Other than Mr. Kim's prompted and ungrounded conclusion that Bay did not know "the actual duration of the delays or when they would end . . . it would be impossible to determine—to calculate when this job would end, and thereby, be able to get another project," we heard nothing about Bay being on "standby." Even if we had found delay and suspension had occurred, Bay would still not be entitled to recover Eichleay damages because it failed to establish that it was on "standby."

02-1 BCA at 157047. *See also Cable & Computer Technology, Inc.*, ASBCA No. 47420, 03-1 BCA ¶ 32,237 (*Eichleay* claim denied because contractor failed to prove its forces were on standby.)

In *Charles G. Williams Construction, Inc. v. White*, 326 F.3d 1376 (Fed. Cir. 2003), a government contractor was awarded a fixed-price contract to renovate a government building. The work was to be done in two phases. The government, however, failed to vacate the portion of the building as required by the contract, causing substantial delays in the contractor's Phase I performance. Also, the government issued a large number of change orders, many of which increased the price of the contract. The government ultimately terminated for convenience the contractor's work on the second phase. The contractor completed the first phase 93 days after its extended completion date.

The contractor filed a claim to recover *Eichleay* damages for unabsorbed home office overhead costs with respect to the alleged period of extended contract performance. The Armed Services Board of Contract Appeals originally denied the claim for unabsorbed office overhead, relying solely on an auditor's report stating that the overhead for the entire period of extended contract performance had been fully absorbed by the base contract, contract modifications and other projects. In 2001, the Federal Circuit vacated the board's original decision, holding that the board did not fulfill its function of determining whether the contractor had proven the "standby" test for *Eichleay* damages. 271 F.3d 1055 (2001). On remand, the board again denied the contractor's *Eichleay* claim, finding that the contractor had not proven that it was on standby because it had not shown that performance of the work was suspended or significantly interrupted during the period in dispute. The board based this decision on the auditor's report and testimony, the daily reports, the scope of the contract modifications, and other data. In addition, the board accepted the auditor's testimony that the contractor continued to work on the project during the time of the contract and did not have any reduction in its flow of direct costs. The contractor did not present any evidence showing that on any particular day, it was unable to do any work at all on the contract, but still was required to remain able to resume work on short notice. Moreover, there was no evidence that the government directed the contractor to remain on call. The contractor's representative had testified that, to his knowledge, the only prerequisite to an *Eichleay* formula recovery was a government-caused delay.

On appeal to the Federal Circuit for a second time, the court held that merely showing that the government caused the delay is not enough. *Eichleay* damages are used to compensate a contractor for its indirect costs that cannot be allocated to a particular contract for the period during which the government made contractual performance impossible, while requiring the contractor to remain available to resume performance on short notice. If the contractor is able to continue performing the contract, although not in the same way as it had anticipated, it can allocate a *portion* of its indirect costs to that contract. Accordingly, the Federal Circuit affirmed the board's decision holding that the contractor could not recover *Eichleay* damages because it had not met its burden of proving that it had been required to stand by.

In *Nicon, Inc. v. United States*, 331 F.3d 878 (Fed. Cir. 2003), the contractor sought damages for unabsorbed home office overhead resulting from a delay period between award of the government contract and the government's termination for convenience. The contractor was awarded a contract with the Department of the Army to repair a dorm facility on March 30, 1998. Subsequently, a disappointed bidder filed a bid protest, which suspended action on the contract before any repair work was commenced. The bid protest was dismissed on July 15, 1998, but the government never directed the contractor to proceed with the contract. Eventually, the government terminated the contract for convenience on January 12, 1999. A period of 288 days had elapsed from the time of contract award to the time of termination for convenience.

After the convenience termination, the contractor submitted a settlement proposal to the government, seeking direct costs, overhead, profit, and unabsorbed home office overhead for the time period between contract award and termination. Because the contractor never began performance, it used a modified version of the *Eichleay* formula to calculate its unabsorbed home office overhead damages. The contracting officer denied the contractor's claim for unabsorbed overhead. The contractor filed suit to recover the unabsorbed overhead damages, but the Court of Federal Claims (COFC) granted the government's summary judgment motion and the contractor appealed.

The Federal Circuit vacated the COFC decision granting summary judgment for the government and remanded. The appeals court agreed that the contractor could not use the *Eichleay* formula to recover its unabsorbed overhead, because that formula is not applicable when performance never started. Typically, in cases applying the *Eichleay* formula, performance of the contract occurs or resumes after a government-caused delay. Here, however, the government terminated the contract after a long delay, and the contractor never began performance of the contract. Thus, there were no actual contract billings or any days of performance to use in the formula.

The contractor proposed that the court substitute constructive figures based on assumptions that the contract would have been completed within the time required by the contract and that the contractor would have received the full amount of the contractual billings. The court held that constructive figures could not be substituted into the formula, and noted that *Eichleay* was limited to situations in which performance had begun and was suspended by the government. When performance has not yet occurred, it is impossible to determine the length of time by which the government's delay would have extended performance.

Although the Federal Circuit disallowed recovery of unabsorbed overhead damages under *Eichleay*, it instructed the court below to determine whether Nicon was entitled to recover these damages as part of its termination settlement by "some other method of allocation." This was contrary to the Federal Circuit's longstanding position that the *Eichleay* formula is the only acceptable method for computing unabsorbed overhead. The court continued, however, that its holding was narrow and that a contractor seeking unabsorbed overhead damages as part of a termination-for-convenience settlement must still show that: (1) before the government terminated the contract, there was a period of government-caused delay of uncertain duration; (2) the contractor itself played no role in the delay and the delay was not the fault of someone or something beyond the government's control; and (3) the contractor was on standby and unable to take on other work.

In *P.J. Dick Inc. v. Principi*, 324 F.3d 1364 (Fed. Cir. 2003), the Department of Veterans Affairs (DVA) entered into a fixed-cost contract with the contractor to construct an addition to the DVA Medical Center in Ann Arbor, Michigan. During the contract, the government caused various delays by issuing more than 400 change orders. These modifications caused the DVA to extend the contract completion date by 107 days and increased the contract price by 5 percent. Also, the contractor reserved its right to seek additional impact and suspension costs. Ultimately, the contract was completed 260 days after the original contract completion date and 153 days after the revised date. The contractor submitted claims for relief as a result of the delays. The contracting officer denied the claims, and the contractor appealed to the Veterans Affairs Board of Contract Appeals (VABCA). The board granted the contractor a time extension of 260 days, of which 65 days were due under the suspension of work (SOW) clause. The board denied *Eichleay* damages, however, because the contractor did not show that it had been on standby.

In affirming the board's decision with respect to the *Eichleay* damages issue, the Federal Circuit agreed that the contractor had not proven that it had been on standby. The court provided a thorough analysis for evaluating a contractor's claim for *Eichleay* damages. The court summarized this analysis as follows:

> A court evaluating a contractor's claim for *Eichleay* damages should ask the following questions: (1) was there a government-caused delay that was not concurrent with another delay caused by some other source; (2) did the contractor demonstrate that it incurred additional overhead (i.e., was the original time frame for completion extended or did the contractor satisfy the *Interstate* three-part test); (3) did the government CO issue a suspension or other order expressly putting the contractor on standby; (4) if not, can the contractor prove there was a delay of indefinite duration during which it could not bill substantial amounts of work on the contract and at the end of which it was required to be able to return to work on the contract at full speed and immediately; (5) can the government satisfy its burden of production showing that it was not impractical for the contractor to take on replacement work (i.e., a new contract) and thereby mitigate its damages; and (6) if the government meets its burden of production, can the contractor satisfy its burden of persuasion that it was impractical for it to obtain sufficient replacement work. Only where the above exacting requirements can be satisfied will a contractor be entitled to *Eichleay* damages.

In this case, the *Eichleay* damages issue hinged on the requirement that the contractor show that a suspension occurred on all or most of the work on the contract; that is, that the contractor was on standby. The court noted that there was no evidence that the contractor's direct billings were less than they would have been absent the suspensions, and said that the contractor's direct billings during the delay periods could not be deemed "minor." The court found that the contractor was able to perform substantial amounts of the work on the contract during the suspension periods, and therefore the contractor was not on standby.

The court's ruling applied only to the days of delay not granted under the SOW clause. With regard to the 65 days granted under the SOW clause, prior to the board hearing, the parties had entered into a stipulation as to the amount of damages recoverable under the SOW clause (including extended home office overhead). Interpreting that agreement, the Federal Circuit held that the stipulation only required the contractor to show entitlement to damages under the SOW clause. By showing entitlement to damages under the SOW clause, the contractor was entitled to all types of damages, including unabsorbed home office overhead. In other words, with regard to the 65 days of delay under the SOW clause, the stipulation obviated the need for the contractor to prove that it had been on standby.

§ 12.16 LOSS OF EFFICIENCY

Page 553, add at end of section:

More recent decisions relating to the issue of proof of lost efficiency claims include *Bay Construction Co.*, VABCA No. 5594, 02-1 BCA ¶ 31,795, 2002 WL 442118; and *Fire Security Systems, Inc.*, VABCA No. 5559-63, 02-2 BCA ¶ 31,977, 2002 WL 1979118. See discussions of both cases in **§ 8.11** of this supplement.

CHAPTER 13
CALCULATING OWNER'S DAMAGES FOR DELAY

§ 13.03 LIQUIDATED VERSUS ACTUAL DAMAGES

[A] Lack of Actual Damages

Page 562, add at end of subsection:

Other, more recent state and federal decisions confirm longstanding principles related to liquidated damages. First, in *Lummus Global Amazonas, S.A. v. Aguaytia Energy del Peru*, 2002 WL 31401996 (S.D. Tex. 2002), a federal court upheld an arbitration award of liquidated damages (in a case involving New York law) for most delays asserted by the owner, where the panel had applied a so-called "total time" analysis test:

> The panel noted that LGA had conceded that it had to "[e]stablish a causal link between the claimed Company Delay and its inability to progress the work necessary to achieve the particular contract milestone for which it seeks a Target Schedule Adjustment." (Aguaytia Ex. 6, p. 4). The panel cited to New York law and rules. (*Id.*, p. 12) (citing CUSHMAN & MEYERS, CONSTRUCTION LAW HANDBOOK, § 23.01[D], p. 825 (Aspen Law 1999)). LGA agrees that the panel correctly stated the applicable New York law on concurrent delay and that the panel correctly applied the law when it granted LGA a twenty-seven day extension of the First Completion Date based on a shared responsibility for a pressure control valve that was not timely installed. LGA argues that except as to this one area, the panel failed to apply New York law on concurrent delay and instead applied a more stringent federal law standard that uses a "total time" analysis.
>
> Under a "total time" analysis, LGA had to prove the following elements: a causal connection between Aguaytia's improper conduct and a specific amount of delay; that other methods (other than the one prohibited by Aguaytia) to achieve the same result were not available; or that such methods, if used, would have been unavailing. (Docket Entry No. 36, Ex. A, p. 8) (citing *WRB Corp. et al. v. United States*, 183 Ct. Cl. 409, 427 (Ct. Cl. 1968)).
>
> The panel specifically addressed five areas that LGA asserted as "Company Delays": Aguaytia's denial of right of way access to LGA; Aguaytia's announced plan to shut down two wells; Aguaytia's inspectors' refusal to allow LGA to use tack welds to close pipe ends, resulting in dirty

pipes that slowed LGA's pipe cleaning; Aguaytia's failure to control inlet pressure of gas into the plant; and Aguaytia's rejection of LGA's pipeline tests. The record reveals that the arbitration panel considered each of these arguments and found that LGA had failed to show a Company Delay by the project owner, Aguaytia, as defined in Section 13.01(a) of the Agreement. The record supports these findings.

As to the claim of failure to provide access to the right of way, the panel found that Aguaytia had not breached any obligation under the parties' "early start agreement" or under the Agreement itself to make right-of-way access available before a certain date. The panel also concluded that LGA did not show that its inability to have right of way access before that date was a "critical path delay." The panel did not, as LGA contends, apply federal law to this issue. Instead, the panel examined the Agreement provisions on access; heard the disputed evidence as to the effect of obstructed right of way access; and concluded that LGA had not met the contractual criteria for a "Company Delay" that would trigger the application of the concurrent delay rule. (Docket Entry No. 36, Ex. A, pp. 5). Federal case law involving a "total time" analysis played no role in the panel's decision on this issue.

The panel cited federal case law, and referred to a "total time" analysis, as to only two of the "Company Delay" claims. The panel did not cite federal law, or refer to a "total time" analysis, in analyzing the right of way access delay claim; the claim of delay from Aguaytia's planned shutdown of two wells; or the claim of delay from the failure to control inlet pressure of gas into the plant. The panel did cite federal cases and law, and refer to a "total time" analysis, in its decision on LGA's claim that Aguaytia's refusal to allow tack welded end caps on open sections of pipeline caused dirt and debris to gather in the pipelines and delayed the pipeline cleaning work. The panel also referred to a "total time" analysis in discussing LGA's claim of delay arising from Aguaytia's rejection of certain tests LGA performed. A review of the record reveals that in neither section of the award did the panel manifestly disregard controlling New York law.

Further, in *William F. Klingensmith, Inc.*, ASBCA No. 52028, 2002 WL 31546517, 03-1 BCA ¶ 32,072, the Board of Contract Appeals considered a motion for summary judgment by the contractor to set aside the assessment of liquidated damages when the government assessed liquidated damages for five phases and for a final phase. The arguments of the contractor included the following:

WFK's remaining assertions in its motion fall into three categories as listed above in outline form in our prefatory remarks: (1) delay by HHS, not contractor delay, was the cause of late performance, (2) the LDs are an unenforceable penalty, and (3) LDs were withheld during a so-called "final phase" during which no contractual basis exists for the assessment of LDs. Some of appellant's assertions present affirmative defenses for which WFK has the burden of coming forward with or pointing to competent and credible evidence for support of each element of its defenses or to show an absence of evidence supporting the nonmovant's case. *Celotex Corp. v. Catrett*, 477

U.S. 317, 323-25 (1986); *DJ Mfg. Corp. v. United States*, 86 F.3d 1130, 1135 (Fed. Cir. 1996); Idela Constr. Co., ASBCA No. 45070, 01-2 BCA ¶ 31,437 at 155,257; *Elam Woods Constr. Co.*, ASBCA No. 52448, 01-1 BCA ¶ 31,305 at 154,545, aff'd on recon., 02-1 BCA ¶ 31,658.

The court in *Klingensmith* found that the liquidated damages set did not constitute an unenforceable penalty (because the propriety of liquidated damages is evaluated at the time of award); that deletion of the requirement for a CPM from the contract (due to a lack of confidence in the contractor) did not stop the contractor from putting forward its own schedule analysis of delay; and that liquidated damages will be enforced so long as the damages are hard to measure and the amount is not disproportionate. *However, it also found that the assessment of liquidated damages for a final phase* (where none had been set forth in the contract) *was inappropriate*:

Unenforceable Penalty
a. Space Rental Costs
Appellant challenges the LDs rate as an unenforceable penalty because it is based in part on rental costs that HHS allegedly never incurred. According to appellant, the contract specified that HHS would occupy the entire building while the project was being performed.

* * *

Concerning LDs generally, the focus of an inquiry concerning the propriety of an LDs rate is at the time of contract award, not LDs assessment. HHS need not actually incur the rental costs as a condition precedent to recovery of LDs. *U.S. Floors, Inc.*, ASBCA No. 45915, 94-2 BCA ¶ 26,636 at 132,486.

The LDs rate was calculated prior to award, was included in the solicitation, and WFK agreed to the resulting contract terms (Statement of Facts 1, 3). The contractor claims that "[e]ven when viewed from the time the contract was formed, the [LDs] provided in the contract did not constitute a reasonable attempt by the NIH to forecast any actual delay damages" (app. mot at 2). Appellant has thus far brought forth no credible evidence of impropriety in the LDs amount at the time of its calculation. Appellant's assertions are not evidence.

For its part, HHS has presented some evidence that rental costs were projected based on expected space needs that were to be met by rental of alternative space on account of the contract work (Statement of Facts 3, 9). WFK disputes that; however, in at least one instance, appellant asserts that the Government vacated certain space in anticipation of phase 4 of the project (app. requests for admission, ¶ 179).

Appellant misconstrues the contract as it relates to the potential for delay on account of occupancy of the buildings by HHS. Further, WFK has made no showing that the LDs rate is a penalty. Therefore, we are not convinced that appellant is entitled to summary judgment.

b. CPM Deletion

The contractor contends that deletion of the contractual requirement for a CPM made it "impossible to determine revised completion dates after the incorporation of numerous change orders and PDLs." According to WFK, by eliminating the requirement for submission by appellant of the CPM to HHS, the Government "waived any claim to [LDs]." (App. mot. at 2, 4; app. mot suppl. at 2, 7) No legal authority is cited in support of the waiver claims.

The HHS PO came to have no confidence in WFK's CPM as a project management tool. Therefore, the parties genuinely dispute the ongoing utility of the CPM. <u>Further, whether the CPM or some other form of schedule continued in use by the contractor is a factual issue that cannot be determined from this preliminary record (by deleting the CPM requirement, HHS did not preclude appellant from using whatever scheduling, time, and resource management technique it wished, whether a CPM, a bar chart, or some other methodology)</u>. (Statement of Facts 6) <u>As we stated above, neither party has yet shown any delay analysis or related evidence that would tend to support the contractor's statements concerning the practicability of analyzing alleged performance delays.</u>

Waiver of LDs also was discussed above. Facts related to the effect of the deletion of the CPM requirement from the contract are genuinely disputed. We are not convinced that appellant is entitled to judgment as a matter of law on the issue of waiver.

c. No Reasonable Expectation by Government of Suffering Delay Damages

* * *

To prevail, appellant must show that " 'the contested [LDs] bear no reasonable relation to the probable loss that [HHS] was likely to have suffered from a delay in performance' . . . a [LDs] clause will not be set aside unless the contractor presents credible evidence that the rate was disproportionately high to the reasonably anticipated damages." *U.S. Floors, Inc., id.* quoting *Jennie-O Foods, Inc. v. United States*, 217 Ct. Cl. 314, 338, 580 F.2d 400, 414 (1978).

When damages are uncertain or difficult to measure, a [LDs] clause will be enforced as long as 'the amount stipulated for is not so extravagant, or disproportionate to the amount of property loss, as to show that compensation was not the object aimed at or as to imply fraud, mistake, circumvention or oppression' . . . .

[The burden of challenging a LDs provision] is an exacting one, because when damages are uncertain or hard to measure, it naturally follows that it is difficult to conclude that a particular [LDs] amount or rate is an unreasonable projection of what those damages might be. . . .

DJ Mfg., 86 F.3d at 1133-34 (and cases cited), quoting *Wise v. United States*, 249 U.S. 361, 365 (1919). For the reasons discussed above under space rental costs, we are not convinced that WFK is entitled to judgment as a matter of law concerning the propriety of the LDs rates. Therefore, summary judgment is not appropriate.

Final Phase LDs

* * *

Each of five phases, together covering much but not all of the work under the contract, has a rate for LDs for failure timely to finish that phase only. The contract does not include LDs for contract completion as a whole or for any final phase. <u>The Government has pointed to no contract provision that specifies a final phase</u>. That term appears to have been used for the first time in the COFD. It is clear that the COFD attempts to incorporate into phase 5 the 59-day period of the overall performance period that follows after the conclusion of phase 5. The Government has pointed to no evidence that shows phase 5 work underway after 11 July 1997. (Statement of Facts 3-4, 16-17)

* * *

The facts concerning whether LDs may be assessed for a so-called final phase, as such, are not disputed as there is no provision in the contract for a final phase. Therefore, LDs may not be assessed for a separate final phase. It is clear that some work is specified by the contract to occur after the completion of phase 5. Activities specifically called out in the contract to be performed after completion of phase 5 cannot, alone, be the subject of LDs. (Statement of Facts 3-5)

The Government contention that certain work must be accomplished for the project as a whole to be considered substantially complete has no bearing on assessment of LDs during phases 1-5. Logic notwithstanding, if the Government thought that LDs were important for overall substantial completion, it would or should have specified such in the contract. It did not. LDs may not be assessed for any activity not within one of the phases for which LDs were specified in the contract, even if non-completion of those activities leaves the project less than substantially complete. Each LDs assessment for each separate phase, as defined by the contract, stands or [falls] on its own. *U.S. Floors*, 94-2 BCA at 132,487.

Appellant is entitled to summary judgment on the issue of whether LDs may be withheld for a 59-day so-called "Final Phase" after substantial completion of phase 5 of the contract work. The Government must return to appellant the amount withheld on that basis. [Emphasis added].

[B] Prohibition Against Penalty

Page 563, add at end of subsection:

See entire discussion in § 13.03[A] of this supplement.

CHAPTER 15

LEGAL DECISIONS AFFECTING EXPERTS—EXPERT'S ROLE IN PREPARING AND DEFENDING SCHEDULE CLAIMS

LEGAL DECISIONS

§ 15.02 WHY SOME EXPERTS HAVE FAILED—HAS THE PROPER FOUNDATION BEEN LAID?

Page 642, add at end of section:

Three decisions in the last year have provided guidance for scheduling experts in the age of *Daubert*. These include *Sherman R. Smoot Corp.*, ASBCA No. 52,261, 03-1 BCA ¶ 32,197, 2003 WL 715270; *Lake Michigan Contractors, Inc. v. Manitowoc Co., Inc.*, 225 F. Supp. 2d 791 (W.D. Mich. 2002); and *Bay Construction Co.*, VABCA No. 5594, 02-1 BCA ¶ 31,795, 2002 WL 442118.

The *Smoot* decision is particularly relevant to *Daubert* issues because it concerned a direct challenge under Federal Rule of Evidence 702 to the admission of a scheduling expert's testimony. The case here concerned a $19 million contract to perform a construction project at the Washington Navy Yard, with typical claims for changes, suspensions, and delays.

In this matter, the contractor at the hearing *moved to exclude* the testimony of the government's proposed scheduling delay expert, *on the basis that the expert's purported expertise did not fit the facts of the instant litigation.* The key argument from the contractor was that the proposed government expert, although knowledgeable as to certain types of schedules (e.g., CPM/PERT in manufacturing) had little knowledge as to construction scheduling or its relevant principles (such as excusable or compensable delay). The hearing judge agreed; this was affirmed by the full panel of three judges in its final decision. The relevant portions of the decision include the following:

> 26. On 7 November 2001, Smoot moved to exclude the testimony and written report (ex. G-55) of proposed Government expert witness, Dr. Paul Kauffmann, who had prepared a CPM schedule analysis (tr. 1517). Smoot asserted that Dr. Kauffmann was not qualified as an expert in construction CPM schedule analysis. Dr. Kauffmann's curriculum vitae sets forth his aca-

demic experience at Pennsylvania State University, Christian Brothers University, and Old Dominion University; his bachelor and master's degrees in mechanical engineering from Virginia Polytechnic Institute and State University, and his doctorate in industrial engineering from Pennsylvania State University; his industrial experience at Philip Morris USA; his recent consulting and research; his publications and papers and technical reports; and his professional licenses and societies (app. mot., ex. D). <u>In his pre-hearing deposition, Dr. Kauffmann stated that he lacked education and experience in construction, his study and teaching of PERT/CPM analysis were in manufacturing and production, not construction, he had not prepared a construction schedule, he had not used the terms "excusable" and "compensable" delay in dealings with contractors, and he was not an expert in "concurrency"</u> (ex. A-72 at 7-9, 14-18, 33-35, 38-39, 54,91).

27. At the hearing, after receiving argument on Dr. Kauffmann's qualifications and reviewing his curriculum vitae, deposition transcript and proposed expert report, the presiding judge granted Smoot's motion to exclude from evidence the testimony and written report of Dr. Kauffmann in this appeal and ASBCA Nos. 52173, 53049 and 53246. <u>The reason for so ruling was that Dr. Kauffmann's qualifications in construction CPM generation, adjustment and analysis were "quite thin" if not non-existent</u>, and major portions of his written report relied upon schedule information in a compact disk received in evidence as appellant's ex. A-87, but which the Board could not access to verify the dates of such schedules.

* * *

On 7 November 2001, Smoot moved to exclude the testimony and written report of respondent's proposed expert witness Dr. Paul Kauffmann, contending that he was not qualified as an expert in construction CPM schedule analysis (finding 26), and could not assist the trier of fact to understand the evidence or to determine a fact in issue, pursuant to Rule 702, Federal Rules of Evidence (FRE). <u>Smoot cited several federal circuit and district court decisions for the rule that, in accordance with Rule 702, a trial court should exclude expert testimony when the witness's expertise does not "fit" the facts of the instant litigation, in this appeal, construction CPM schedule analysis.</u>

* * *

Respondent argues that "[i]n a clearly erroneous ruling, the Board refused to allow Respondent's expert, Prof. Kauffmann, to testify regarding the alleged impact on the CPM schedule" (Gov't br. at 93). Smoot's briefs are silent on this issue. In accordance with Board practice, when a party challenges an evidentiary ruling in its post-hearing brief, the panel will review it. We do so here.

Dr. Kauffmann's curriculum vitae sets forth his academic experience at Old Dominion University, Christian Brothers University, and Pennsylvania State University, his bachelor and master's degrees in mechanical engineering and PhD in industrial engineering; his industrial experience at Philip Morris USA; his recent consulting and research; his publications and papers and technical reports; and his professional licenses and societies. Dr. Kauffmann indicated that he lacked education and experience in construction, and his study and teaching of PERT/CPM analysis were in manufacturing and production, not construction, he had not prepared a construction schedule, he had not used the terms "excusable" and "compensable" delay in dealings with contractors, and he was not an expert in "concurrency" (finding 26).

<u>The panel concludes that Dr. Kauffmann is not qualified to testify as an expert in construction CPM schedule analysis and affirms the exclusion of his testimony and report on that basis</u>. We do not reach the issue of failure to provide supporting schedule data in an accessible disk. [Emphasis added.]

The *Lake Michigan Contractors, Inc.*, 225 F. Supp. 2d 791 (W.D. Mich. 2002), decision also addressed *Daubert*-type challenges, in a Michigan federal court decision under Rule 702. The controversy concerned whether the contractor (Manitowoc and Bay State Constructors) on a T&M-type agreement had overcharged the owner, Lake Michigan Contractors (LMC), by failing to adhere to the schedule, failing to perform the work in an enclosed facility, and failing to perform the work in a timely, cost-effective manner. This decision is significant in evaluating both scheduling and lost-efficiency experts.

This decision addressed a request for a *motion in limine* to determine whether a number of conclusions by a proposed expert—concerning overcharging, rework, premature moving of dredge to an outdoor location, the effect of rain on the outdoor construction location, and poor contractor efficiency—would be admitted into evidence. Here, *the court initially found that the expert was qualified under Rule 702* to express opinions, but *then found that the offered testimony was totally unreliable and excludable, as it was not grounded in the facts*, represented mere speculation rather than facts in the case, and could not be explained (other than the expert saying that it represented his professional opinion).

In the *Lake Michigan* decision, the court considered the testimony of LMC's expert, Willis. Material from the decision giving guidance on the use of experts includes: a discussion of the relevance inquiry required under Rule 702,—which states that the testimony must "fit the case"; a discussion of the gatekeeper reliability requirement under Rule 702, in which the court confronted the issue of whether the testimony and opinions are sufficiently reliable as to be helpful to the trier of fact (e.g., more than "credentials and a subjective opinion" and "expert's testimony that 'it is so'" is required[31.1]); and a discussion of the reliability requirement under Rule 702 that the expert opinions sufficiently account for the facts of the case (e.g., general observations about what should normal-

---

[31.1] For example, the reliability of an expert's conclusion on a calculation of lost efficiency cannot be tested if he cannot explain from the facts of the case how he arrived at his lost efficiency figure.

ly occur in the course of a shipbuilding project are not relevant when a "normal production planning effort" using critical path principles was not possible, in a case where "LMC controlled the process and essentially spoon-fed BSC its work orders on a daily basis"). The court discussed these matters as follows:

> The Court first addresses the relevance inquiry because identifying the factual issues in contention will enable the Court to hone in on the permissible areas of expert testimony. To be relevant the expert's testimony must "fit" the case, or, in other words, be tied to the facts closely enough to be of use to the trier of fact in resolving the issues in contention. *Daubert*, 509 U.S. at 591-92, 113 S. Ct. 2786. The "fit" in this case is informed by the Court's recent Opinion and Order on the parties' cross motions for summary judgment. Pursuant to the Court's rulings in that Order and the parties' admissions cited in the Opinion, the following facts are established as a matter of law: (1) in November 1999 the parties entered into an agreement pursuant to which BSC would construct the hull of the Dredge for $1.00 per pound and the deckhouse for $1.15 per pound; (2) in January 2000 the parties converted the agreement to a T & M agreement for all work[,] which continued in effect through September 2000 when BSC completed its work on the Dredge; (3) BSC's Price Schedule supplied the rates, terms, and conditions for the T & M agreement; (4) the parties never reached a not-to-exceed agreement; and (5) LMC's defective coatings claim was untimely under the terms of the Price Schedule. With these facts defining the parameters of the case, the only issues in contention are those set forth in the complaint, namely, whether BSC breached the T & M agreement by: (1) failing to adhere to a schedule; (2) failing to construct the Dredge entirely within the covered fabrication shop; and (3) failing to perform the work in a timely, cost effective manner. (Compl. 5.)
>
> <u>Willis' opinions and conclusions in his Initial Report meet the "fit" requirement because they pertain to the issues in dispute</u>. Whether BSC properly billed LMC under the Price Schedule, whether BSC charged LMC for BSC-responsible rework, whether LMC incurred extra costs because of the early move-out of the Dredge from the covered fabrication shop, and whether the hours billed by BSC properly reflect the level of efficiency (or inefficiency) BSC achieved on the project would all be proper areas of expert testimony.
>
> <u>In contrast to his Initial Report, much of Willis' Supplemental Report fails to meet the "fit" requirement because Willis relies upon facts or assumptions having nothing at all to do with this case</u>. In fact, portions of the Supplemental Report are so far afield that one familiar with the facts in this case would be compelled to wonder after reading the report whether it was prepared for a different case. For instance, Willis concludes on his own that the parties initially agreed that BSC would construct the hull and the deckhouse for a fixed amount of $1,266,200, in spite of admissions by LMC and BSC that they initially agreed on $1.00 and $1.15 per pound for the hull and deckhouse, respectively. <u>Willis also ignores admissions by both parties</u>

that the agreement was converted to a T & M basis in January 2000 when he renders an unfounded and inadmissible legal conclusion that there is "no document or other evidence of any agreement by the parties regarding any form of Time and Materials (T & M) contract for work on the Dredge." (Supplemental Report at 4.) Other portions of the Supplemental Report do not fit with the facts of the case because the Court has made certain rulings as a matter of law.

* * *

In considering whether Willis' testimony and opinions are sufficiently reliable to be helpful to the trier of fact, the Court finds guidance in the following statement from the advisory committee's notes to the 2000 amendment to Rule 702:

> Nothing in this amendment is intended to suggest that experience alone—or experience in conjunction with other knowledge, skill, training or education—may not provide a sufficient foundation for expert testimony. To the contrary, the text of Rule 702 expressly contemplates that an expert may be qualified on the basis of experience. In certain fields, experience is the predominant, if not sole, basis for a great deal of reliable expert testimony.
>
> If the witness is relying solely or primarily on experience, then the witness must explain how that experience leads to the conclusion reached, why that experience is a sufficient basis for the opinion, and how that experience is reliably applied to the facts. The trial court's gatekeeping function requires more than simply "taking the expert's word for it."

Fed. R. Evid. 702, advisory committee's note (citations omitted). Applying these principles, the Court will examine each area of Willis' testimony for reliability. As a preliminary matter, however, it should be noted that BSC does not dispute that Willis is qualified to testify as an expert witness about such matters as shipbuilding practices and factors affecting shipbuilding efficiency. Willis has over 50 years of experience in the shipbuilding industry at various levels of responsibility, including 13 years as a civilian employee with the United States Navy and 12 years of experience with Newport News Shipbuilding, during 6 of which he has served as the director of contracts with responsibility for administering all government and commercial contracts (except repair). (Willis Summary Curriculum Vitae, Initial Report Ex. 1.) In addition, Willis developed the method of analyzing shipyard efficiency which serves as the model for NAVSEA, the United States Navy's disruption analysis methodology. (Willis Aff. 10, 21, Pl.'s Br. Opp'n Ex. 1.) Based upon his qualifications, Willis is qualified to opine on the matters set forth in the Initial Report.

1. BSC Labor Rates

. . . At the hearing, Willis testified that he was mistaken in this portion of his report because he misunderstood how the composite labor rate of $36 was calculated. (5/7/02 Hr'g Tr. at 44–45.) In fact, Willis testified that he had retracted "[e]very bit" of his opinion in paragraph 3.a. (*Id.* at 46.)

Therefore, Willis' conclusions regarding BSC's labor rates in paragraph 3.a. of his Initial Report are unreliable and, therefore, inadmissible.

2. BSC-Responsible Rework

[3] In paragraph 3.b., Willis concludes that BSC is responsible for various items that were required to be reworked. LMC was charged for the additional work. Willis obtained information regarding these items from LMC representatives and opined that 132 straight-time hours of labor and $150 in material was required to complete the rework. Applying a 3.7% overtime rate and adding production support materials of $204 plus BSC's 15% material markup, Willis determined that LMC is entitled to a credit of $5,303. <u>Although BSC did not raise a specific objection regarding this portion of the report, the Court concludes that this portion of the report should be excluded because, while Willis is certainly competent to make such a calculation, he fails to set forth the factual basis and methodology he used to arrive at 132 hours.</u>

3. Extra Work and Costs Resulting from Early Move-Out

[4] In paragraph 3.c. of his Initial Report, Willis discusses the effects of BSC's decision to move the Dredge out of the covered fabrication shop to the graving dock in May 2000, prior to completion of the Dredge. LMC alleges that BSC breached the agreement by failing to complete the Dredge in the covered shop. Willis states that "good shipyard practice would require that the Dredge's hull, deckhouses, exterior platforms, hatches, coamings, foundations for the A-Frame and deck equipment, and other similar work be completed before leaving the Fab Shop." (Initial Report at 9.) Willis estimates at the time of the move, the hull, deckhouses, and associated weather-sensitive work was approximately 75% complete. (*Id.* at 10.) Willis divides the effect of the early move-out into four categories: (1) direct impact of early move-out; (2) weather-related efficiency losses; (3) added protection and clean-up due to rain days; and (4) added cleaning/coating caused by water intrusion. (*Id.* at 10-13.)

With regard to the first category, direct impact of the early move-out, Willis concludes that from May 10-15, 2000, when production was shut down, the Dredge was moved, and production was resumed, BSC was at most 50% efficient. According to Willis, efficiency was lost because BSC's workers were required to shut down their work for most of that time and had to remobilize once the Dredge was into place in the graving dock. Willis opines that the move resulted in 350 extra hours being charged to LMC at a total cost of $12,748. <u>At the hearing, Willis elaborated on the process he used to determine the 50% efficiency rate</u>:

> I went back and looked at the process that was followed, talked to the people on the scene, and evaluated the—as I started to—it's described to the best of my ability on page 10, subparagraph (i), where substantial extra labor was incurred because the work had to be shut down. They had to demobilize the work force, get the support facilities off the dredge, and remove the dredge from the facility, transport it down to the floating dock, and then transfer it again to the dry dock. During that period of time, the production workers that had been working on

the dredge were not able to continue their normal processes. So they had to go somewhere else and come back to the dredge. And that, in my view, certainly introduces inefficiency.

. . . So Bay Shipbuilding had said during that period of time that it charged 705 manhours to the dredge. And so I assumed that meant 705 manhours had been worked on the dredge. <u>And working them under those inefficiency conditions, it's my professional opinion that you would not achieve more than 50 percent of the efficiency.</u> (5/7/02 Hr'g Tr. at 48-49.)

<u>The basic premise of Willis' opinion is sound: interruptions reduce work efficiency.</u> That premise is a truism for any task, be it a simple household chore, a summary judgment brief, or an opinion on a motion in limine to exclude expert testimony. There is also a factual basis for Willis' opinion because there is no dispute that the move interrupted work being performed by BSC workers and that some of the 705 hours spent on the Dredge during the five-day period involved demobilizing—removing and disconnecting lines, removing materials and putting away tools, and cataloging drawings and other documents— and remobilizing. <u>Finally, as noted above, Willis' experience, by itself, is sufficient to allow him to testify as an expert.</u> *United States v. Kunzman*, 54 F.3d 1522, 1530 (10th Cir. 1995). <u>However, none of this means that the Court is required to accept Willis' testimony because he is an expert and says "it is so."</u> See *Viterbo v. Dow Chem. Co.*, 826 F.2d 420, 424 (5th Cir. 1987) ("<u>Without more than credentials and a subjective opinion, an expert's testimony that 'it is so' is not admissible.</u>"). <u>In other words, Rule 702 does not allow the Court to take Willis merely at his word, but rather requires an examination of both the "sufficiency of the testimony's basis" and "the application of a methodology to the facts" to ensure some degree of reliability.</u> Rudd v. Gen. Motors Corp., 127 F. Supp. 2d 1330, 1336 (M.D. Ala. 2001).

With regard to the basis of his opinion, <u>Willis simply assumed that all 705 hours spent on the Dredge involved work that was necessarily interrupted by the move.</u> There is <u>no indication that Willis took into account</u> whether any of the <u>hours spent on the Dredge were related to the move itself</u>—work which was not interrupted and which would have been required at some point even if all work was completed in the covered shop—<u>or whether the move affected the efficiency of some trades more than others, for example</u>, electricians versus painters or welders versus general shop workers. <u>Nor did Willis provide a breakdown of what was occurring on the Dredge at the time of the move and how many of the 705 hours were allocable to those specific jobs. Because Willis did not consider these factors, the basis for his conclusions is insufficient.</u> A more significant factor undermining the reliability of Willis' conclusion, however, is <u>his inability to explain how he reached his 50% efficiency figure.</u> In effect, <u>Willis cannot be cross-examined on his conclusion and he admitted as much at the hearing.</u> (5/7/02 Hr'g Tr. at 50-51.) As the Supreme Court has observed, an expert should be able to explain the link between the facts and the result:

[C]onclusions and methodology are not entirely distinct from one another. Trained experts commonly extrapolate from existing data. But nothing in either *Daubert* or the Federal Rules of Evidence requires a district court to admit opinion evidence that is connected to existing data only by the *ipse dixit* of the expert. A court may conclude that there is simply too great an analytical gap between the data and the opinion proffered.

Gen. Elec. Co. v. Joiner, 522 U.S. 136, 146, 118 S. Ct. 512, 519, 139 L.Ed.2d 508 (1997). That is precisely the case here. Because Willis cannot explain how he arrived at the 50% figure, as opposed to, say 45% or 65%, there is no way to test his opinion through cross-examination. In short, "there is simply too great an analytical gap." *Id.*

[5] Willis next concludes that BSC suffered a 50% reduction in efficiency on each day there was rain between May 13 and June 30, 2000. [Footnote omitted.] Willis determined the number of rain days based upon United States Coast Guard records and the memories of LMC on-site representatives. Based upon his 50% efficiency figure, Willis determines that BSC charged LMC for 950 hours which produced no progress because of the rain, totaling $34,504. (Initial Report at 12.) The Court <u>concludes that Willis' opinions and conclusions on this issue are unreliable and inadmissible. Willis admitted at the hearing that he had no idea when it rained on the days with reported rain.</u> (5/7/02 Hr'g Tr. at 57–58.) Thus, as demonstrated by the hypothetical posed by the Court at the hearing, if it rained from 3:00 p.m. to 4:00 p.m., a worker whose shift was from 8:00 a.m. to 4:00 p.m. would be prevented from working only one hour. (*Id.* at 57.) Yet, Willis failed to explain how he allowed for such a scenario in reaching his conclusions. Instead, it appears that <u>he simply assumed that BSC's efficiency was no more than 50% on any day when there was rain even if the rain had only a slight impact on the work</u>. Willis' opinion is <u>also unreliable because he did not account for differences in rain volume</u> and the impact that rain might have had on the types of work to be performed. (*Id.* at 54.)

Willis <u>next estimates that on each rain day during May and June, BSC expended 16 hours for protective measures and 24 hours for clean-up after the rain stopped</u>. Willis determines that BSC charged LMC for a total of 640 hours, or $22,072, that would not have been required if the Dredge had been completed in the covered fabrication shop. (Initial Report at *12*.) This opinion is unreliable for many of the same reasons the weather-related efficiency opinion is unreliable. <u>Willis' opinion is really no more than speculation based upon assumed conditions that may or may have not been present</u>. . . . Finally, the opinion is inadmissible because Willis fails to explain how [he] reached his conclusion that 16 hours of work for protective measures and 24 hours of clean-up were required for each rain day.

The final element of early move-out charges is added cleaning/coating work required because of water intrusion. . . . Willis' opinion is based upon his personal observation of many of the affected areas, interviews with LMC's on-site representatives, and his experience in the shipyard industry. Although Willis' personal observations and interviews with LMC representatives provide a sufficient factual basis for his opinion, his conclusion suffers from the same infirmity as the others, namely, lack of any explanation of how he arrived at the 1,200 hour figure, other than by relying on his experience. Thus, this opinion is not admissible.

* * *

The Court concludes that Willis' opinions regarding BSC's efficiency are unreliable for several reasons. First, Willis' opinions do not sufficiently account for the specific facts of this case. That is, while Willis makes general observations about what should normally occur in the course of a shipbuilding project, he does not tailor those considerations to what actually occurred between the parties. For example, one of the factors in Willis' inefficiency calculus was BSC's failure to perform its normal production planning and scheduling effort. Willis states that this failure contributed to wasted hours as a result of miscommunications between workers in different BSC production groups and work being done out-of-sequence. However, this was not a normal situation in which BSC was able to apply its "normal production planning effort." LMC never provided BSC with a detailed set of plans and specifications that would enable BSC to plan and coordinate material and labor needs and schedules on a "critical path" basis. Instead, LMC controlled the process and essentially spoon-fed BSC its work orders on a daily basis. . . . While Willis did consider the changes and redirections by LMC as a factor affecting BSC's efficiency, he did not identify specific instances where this factor came into play. In addition, he did not consider whether delays in delivery of owner-furnished equipment contributed to BSC's inefficiency.

The issue here is whether BSC spent too much time in constructing the Dredge. One way to make this determination would be to start by comparing BSC's actual hours against a baseline number, for example, the number of hours required to construct the Dredge under perfect conditions, that is, starting with a complete set of plans and specifications. The reasons for or causes of the variation could then be explained by comparing what should have occurred in the process under perfect conditions in terms of job sequencing and scheduling, use of labor, and ordering of materials, with what occurred during the actual construction. Another method, or possibly just a variation, which is similar to the process this Court uses for determining hours reasonably expended for attorney fee awards, would be to determine a reasonable number of hours for each separate job or task, compare it to the number of hours actually incurred for that job or task, and then determine what factors contributed to excessive hours on that particular job. Willis' approach, in contrast, starts with his conclusion that BSC was inefficient and then works backward for reasons to explain this conclusion without focusing in on the specific facts and circumstances of the case. In a case such as this, it is the particular facts rather than general conclusion that are important. [FN6]

> **FN6.** One of the inefficiency factors cited by Willis was BSC's sporadic, partial-hour, and partial-day use of employees. Willis determined

that this was a problem by examining BSC tally sheets. However, Willis' conclusion that BSC was the sole cause of this problem is based upon speculation because it is entirely possible that workers were pulled off jobs after only a few hours or minutes due to a change made by LMC. Willis did not consider whether this was a possibility, although the facts suggest that it could have been.

Second, other than citing his extensive experience in the shipbuilding industry, <u>Willis cannot explain the methodological basis for his conclusions. While Willis can cite the reasons why BSC was inefficient, he cannot explain how he arrives at the conclusion that BSC</u> was 75% responsible and LMC was 25% responsible. According to Willis, his experience is enough:

Q: My original question, sir, was precisely what you did to make that allocation. Did you do any calculation whatsoever to get to the 25 percent/75 percent allocation?

A: 25-75, yes. One-third, two-thirds. One-quarter three-quarters.

Q: Any calculations?

A: <u>I did not need to do calculations.</u>

Q: Okay.

A: <u>It was my professional judgment—and I've done it so long, I just have it in my head.</u>

(5/7/02 Hr'g Tr. at 108.) <u>In other words, "it is" because he says so.</u> However, the analytical gap here is so great that *ipse dixit* alone cannot suffice to render the opinion reliable.

Finally, because Willis cannot describe the analysis he uses to reach his conclusion, he also cannot demonstrate that whatever that analysis is, it is reliably applied to the facts. Therefore, <u>Willis' opinion will not assist the trier of fact and must be excluded as unreliable under Rule 702.</u> [Emphasis added.]

Bay Construction Co., VABCA No. 5594, et al., 02-1 BCA ¶ 31,795, 2002 WL 442118, concerned a contract for $644,375 to perform demolition and renovation at a VA medical center in San Francisco. The project was planned for 66 days but actually took 370 days to complete. No critical path schedule was required for the project. A no-cost termination was negotiated between the parties. Thereafter the contractor pursued *total time* claims for delay, based on a so-called CPM analysis, and lost efficiency, based on a so-called "measured mile" analysis.[31.2]

[31.2] The court in *Bay* also discarded the testimony of the contractor's expert as to its so-called measured mile claim. In this instance the court looked to the fact that the purported expert did not even distinguish between trades in making measured mile calculations or distinguish specific periods of change-order-impacted inefficient performance. The court stated its general findings as follows:

The case was interesting in the first instance because it expressed the court's preference for CPM proof to isolate critical path delays—even in this case, where a critical path schedule was not specified for the renovation project:

> Also, to recover under the SUSPENSION OF WORK clause, a contractor must be able to distinguish between alleged suspension and change order time, including discrete periods of delay to the critical path preceding change work, the time required to do change work, and the impact that a change may have on unchanged work. *Coates Industrial Piping, Inc.*, VABCA No. 5412, 99-2 BCA ¶ 30,479, at 7,744; *P.J. Dick Contracting, Inc.*, VABCA Nos. 3386, 3387-97, 92-1 BCA ¶ 24,599, at 122,728; *Dawson Construction Company*, VABCA Nos. 3306-3310, 93-3 BCA ¶ 26,177, at 130,314.

Further, the case is significant because a witness proffered to establish the CPM and lost-efficiency claims was judged "insufficient" because the witness's testimony was based on uncorroborated assumptions, largely conjectural testimony, and prompted testimony. In *Bay*, the expert proffered by the contractor did not actually prepare a CPM analysis, even though he claimed to have done so. For example: he did not know whether the original schedule on which he based his analysis employed "working days," "calendar days," or "performance days"; he did not actually employ logic ties to reflect the sequencing relationship between activities (e.g., precede, succeed, go on at the same time); he did not reflect early and late starts or total float calculations; he did not account for

> The Appellant wholly failed to present probative evidence of lost productivity. Again, Mr. Kim's charts and summary conclusions that Bay had lost productivity because work was in some instance done out of sequence and piecemeal in some areas fall far short of the proof we expect for such cases. His attempt at quantification, applying two methods to price Bay's alleged damages for what he said was Bay's lost productivity [,] was not compelling for many of the same reasons we articulated in our earlier discussions of his delay and suspension analysis. Bay's lack of contemporaneous project documentation of the impact of the delays and its failure to proffer credible testimony, impeached the overall reliability of its evidence. While Mr. Kim was very willing to assume Government-caused delay and interference, there was very little evidence in the record to back up his assumptions. He had even less professional experience analyzing lost productivity than he had in delay and suspension analysis.
>
> Given the size and complexity of this project, the number and nature of changes reflected in the SAs were not so momentous as to impact the project in the significant and serious ways that Appellant claims. As we recently stated in Clark Construction Group, Inc., "[t]he after-the-fact, conclusory assessments of the project managers or the opinions of its experts are not sufficient substitutes for [the contractor's] underlying obligation to contemporaneously document the severe adverse impact on labor efficiency it now claims resulted from the changes and RFIs." *Clark Construction Group, Inc.*, VABCA No. 5674, 00-1 BCA ¶ 30,870 at 152,413, citing *Fru-Con Construction Corporation v. United States*, 43 Fed. Cl. 306 (1999), aff'd 250 F.3d 762 (Fed. Cir. 2000) (Table); *Centex Bateson*, 99-1 BCA ¶ 20,153; *Triple "A" South*, 94-3 BCA ¶ 27,194. We conclude that Bay's evidence failed to provide proof of change to working conditions or loss or productivity.

time used for used submittals; he did not account for subcontractor work activities; he did not account for contractor delays (such as inadequate crew sizing); and he included days on which no contractor work was performed.

The decision stated in pertinent part:

> Mr. Kim attempted to prove Government-caused suspension by recreating the job progress using the documentary information available to him in the form of daily logs and correspondence, and inputting that information into a computer scheduling program. He based his "as-built" time analysis and testimony on uncorroborated assumptions about how the project was originally planned and performed, and at times his testimony was largely conjectural. <u>His reference to his time analysis being a "CPM analysis" is inaccurate, possibly due to his own lack of experience. His analysis is unlike any CPM analysis with which we are familiar.</u> Bay neither was required to, nor used, the critical path method [CPM] to schedule or maintain schedules for this project. Mr. Kim used a computer program to generate his chart showing supposed delays to the critical path. However, he did not generate a "CPM analysis." <u>We found his analysis to be more in the form of bar charts that we have previously held are ordinarily incapable of providing the standard of proof required to establish delays and impacts on a project.</u> *Coates Industrial Piping, Inc.*, VABCA No. 5412, 99-2 BCA ¶ 30,479 citing H.W. Detailer Co., Inc., ASBCA No. 35327, 88-2 BCA ¶ 21,612.
>
> The validity and approval of Bay's original schedule, as well as Bay's projected staffing for the project, was not satisfactorily established. Mr. Kim determined that Mr. Doerr, whom he believed had created the original schedule, had properly planned and staffed the VA project. He deduced that the schedule had been approved by the VA and was reasonable. He believed that Mr. Yu saw the project documents and prepared the undated and unsigned chart on which he based his testimony at the hearing. However, we did not find sufficient reliable factual information in the record to support his conclusions. There was neither comprehensive nor convincing evidence regarding Bay's schedule submission(s), contents or approval dates. The record did not contain updated schedules reflecting what was happening at the time the delay triggering events allegedly occurred or reflecting the schedule being modified to mitigate delays. The record deficiencies are noted regarding Bay's submittals.
>
> <u>Mr. Kim also attributed all of Bay's time loss and extended performance time to Government changes, delays and suspensions. He ignored or casually dismissed any reference to Bay's small crews and lack of progress, and did not appropriately consider any information that was unfavorable to the Appellant. That Bay was behind schedule was observed by the COTR and noted in almost every monthly progress payment report.</u> Yet, Mr. Kim downplayed these observations and concluded that his analysis showed the various Bay-caused factors raised by the Government did not in any way impact the critical path. The Appellant did not effectively address various discrepancies in the daily logs and failed to prove several of the key facts upon which it based its case. No subcontractors, who performed significant

amounts of the actual work on the job, were called to testify about Government caused delays, and there is no indication any of those subcontractors presented delay or suspension claims.

Bay also failed to establish that it exercised diligence in making its submittals, or that it could have met its planned Phase I schedule with its anticipated project staffing. The daily logs show that Bay's project crews were consistently small and that it greatly relied on subcontractors to perform much of the actual day-to-day work. The Appellant failed to convincingly address the questions raised about its inadequate staffing and failure to make progress, and how those issues related to any Government caused delays that it said occurred. Bay clearly bore some responsibility for the extended performance period, but, on the basis of the evidence before us, we were unable to determine how much of the time was due to Bay deficiencies and how much was due solely to Government delays, suspension, changes, actions or inactions. <u>Bay must account for its own delays, and its failure to acknowledge and factor them into its analysis made its analysis flawed, and its purported critical path analysis unreliable</u>. It failed to show by a preponderance of the evidence that Phase I activities were delayed and suspended solely to Government conduct, and did not meet its burden of proving that it could have and would have completed its schedule but for Government-caused delays and suspensions. *Wickham Contracting Company v. Fischer*, 12 F.3d 1574, 1581-82 (Fed. Cir. 1984); *Hensel Phelps Construction Co.*, ASBCA No. 49270, 99-2 BCA ¶ 30,531.

In all, Appellant's analysis was premised on many unconfirmed fundamental assumptions that it attempted to prove through the largely conjectural and prompted testimony of an insufficient witness. The charts Appellant generated and used at hearing, and Mr. Kim's testimony, did not convince us that Bay suffered a suspension that would be compensable under the Contract's SUSPENSION OF WORK clause. <u>Given the record before us, Mr. Kim's readiness to assume only facts favorable to Bay and his equal willingness to negate Bay's culpability for delays made his analysis neither probative nor his opinions convincing. Bay presented little credible evidence connecting suspension time sought to particular Government-caused events</u>. Bay's unsupported generalizations attributing the excessive time taken to perform the Contract work totally to Government caused delay and suspension cannot be substituted for the probative evidence necessary to sustain Appellant's burden. *Dawson*, 93-3 BCA ¶ 26,177, at 162,328 citing WRB Corporation v. United States, 183 Ct. Cl. 409,427 (1968). [Emphasis added.]

In addition, the court discarded the testimony of the government scheduling expert, because it was based on incorrect information as to actual start dates of activities. Though not significant to the ruling against the appellant, *the court thereby provided guidance on the defective nature of expert testimony, that is not supported by the record, and expressed its cynicism concerning the "inverse relation between the certainty of experts' opinion and the specificity of detail"*:

The difficulty of our task was compounded by the fact that the opposing parties presented us with two irreconcilable time analyses. We also found the Government's time analysis to be of little value. Mr. Lloyd's analysis is questionable because he appears to have used incorrect start dates based on conversations with CO Prescott. That analysis also presented an incomplete picture of what actually happened on this project. It was based on only a limited review of the Contract documents and unverified discussions with VA staff. The results of Mr. Lloyd's later analysis in which he concluded there were 78 calendar days of delay associated with change orders and 28 days of suspension time differed from an earlier version where he concluded there were 77 days of "work stoppages." On the whole, we found both Government time analyses cursory in nature, and in several instances, related testimony confusing and circuitous.

We conclude that the testimony and opinions of Messrs. Kim and Lloyd did not add much value to their respective cases. As we stated in *Dawson*: "Expert opinions offered on certain matters that clearly are not supported by the record tended to cast a shadow on the value of other opinions concerning issues where underlying factual matters were less clear."

Testimony was of particular value to the Board to the extent that the witnesses were familiar with the daily logs and other voluminous documentary evidence that constitutes the record in these appeals. For both expert and other witnesses there seemed too often to be an inverse relationship between the certainty of opinion and the specificity of detail. The more general and vague the proposition, the more certain the witnesses were.

§ 15.10   FAMILIARIZATION PHASE

Page 664, add at end of section:

See authority and discussion in new **§ 10.08** concerning negative inferences to be drawn when a claimant fails to call (or show that experts' testimony was based on) any witnesses who knew or understood what was happening on the project.

Chapter 16
CASE HISTORIES

Page 725, add new sections at end of chapter:

§ 16.08   BIG DIG

One of the recent major procurements for the Big Dig in Boston provides a number of lessons for owners as to the importance of scheduling and dispute resolution. These lessons include the necessity for:

- vigilance as to the nature and content of scheduling provisions;
- vigilance as to the maintenance of scheduling updates and their content;
- vigilance as to the content of dispute resolution provisions.

The procurement in question concerned a major cut-and-cover procurement, as well as a tunneling operation in connection with the major artery to be constructed in the area of the "South Station"—more specifically, the I-93 northbound tunnel between Congress Street and the renovation of South Station.

Certain of the contract provisions were relevant to later construction disputes. First, the specifications called for the preparation of a CPM schedule. However, the specification did not call for the activities to be resource loaded. (Remember that the only way we compute activity durations is to calculate the amount of work to be done divided by the number of resources anticipated at a given production rate.) In addition, the specification called for *monthly schedule updates.*

A later action that proved significant was the decision, during the life of the project, by the owner and the contractor to agree to a *binding disputes review board procedure, with ground rules to be set essentially by the dispute review board selected.*

The project in question experienced construction delays with the contractor behind schedule. The contractor, under an agreement with the owner, then committed to a start-over schedule with aggressive durations to recover 239 days of delay.[22]

---

[22] The 239 days were to be recovered by reducing durations for underpinning-related activities to 18 months; and by a new "block by block" approach in accomplishing utility relocation, slurry wall, deck work, and mainline excavation. This required a new traffic phasing and construction phasing plan.

After implementation of the start-over schedule, a number of problems were encountered. For example, the contractor did not produce a traffic plan to address its new means of sequencing the work under the start-over schedule, the contractor was not achieving planned durations for the cut-and-cover portion of the work (as to either fabrication or installation of the struts); and changes and changed conditions were encountered in the tunnel operation.

The facts were further complicated by the appointment of two DRBs for the project. The first DRB, which lasted through the illness of one member of the board, ruled, in response to a request by the parties, that the 10 and 10 markup covered extended duration-type costs. Approximately $100 million had been paid out in changes on the project.

A second DRB was appointed to replace the first DRB. The second DRB considered claims by the contractor for delays and extended duration expense after the commencement of the start-over schedule.

The second DRB proceeded to overturn the ruling of the first DRB relative to the 10 and 10 markup, stating that the first ruling was non-binding (the second DRB noted as an infirmity that the parties had requested the 10 and 10 ruling during the lunch period of a hearing by the parties with the first DRB).

In addition, the second DRB proceeded to hear the time and delay claims on the basis of procedures it set itself. These included such procedures as no cross-examination or questioning of witnesses; the requirement that one party not respond at hearing to the claim position put forward by the other party at hearing until rebuttal; and others.

The proof presented by the contractor at the hearing on time damages rested heavily on contemporaneous updates of the schedule, which had not been objected to by the owner (with testimony by the owner that its scheduling representative was told to essentially "cool it" and stop objecting to deficiencies after some partnering sessions). Among other problems with the contractor's contemporaneous updates was that they contained logic errors and changes and failed to correct remaining-duration estimates for excavation and strut activities to reflect what was happening in the field.[23]

The proof by the contractor at the hearings was to the effect that the critical delays to the project were located in the tunneling operation, where changes and changed conditions had been experienced.

The proof presented by the owner at the hearing was that the contractor did not follow the sequence in its recovery plan; that the contractor had failed to give the owner credit for allowing changes in traffic patterns to resequence the excavation operations; that the contractor had completely failed to achieve the aggressive durations required for the excavation operation to proceed, particularly the strut fabrication and installation; and that the updates for the project

---

[23] The default program for Primavera used on this project was to keep the original estimated duration for remaining work, regardless of whether estimates were beaten or severely exceeded, as was the case here.

were severely flawed due to logic errors, logic changes (e.g., cut logic ties), shortened durations, and the failure to meet planned durations (requiring new realistic durations for remaining work). The owner presented as-built and corrected updated schedules to establish the location of the critical path for the project in the excavation operation.

Subsequently, the board, in a decision that did not address specific questions posed by the owner, ruled for the contractor on the issue of time.

This ruling teaches us three important lessons:

First, when creating a scheduling specification, an owner should include appropriate requirements for logic and resource loading information,[24] so that the owner representatives can evaluate the substance of a schedule and object when schedules or schedule updates are unrealistic,

Second, owners should pay attention to updates as much as to original schedules. Updates with faulty information, and/or faulty logic, and/or faulty remaining durations, if are not objected to by an owner, can mean that a contractor recovers on the basis of incorrect information.

Third, remember that a binding DRB agreement is the same as a binding arbitration. Set rules that provide some modicum of due process for the parties.

§ 16.09 NOAA FACILITY

Hensel Phelps Construction Co., GSBCA Nos. 14744, 14877, 01-1 BCA ¶ 31,249 (2001), involved construction of a new National Oceanic and Atmospheric Administration (NOAA) facility in Boulder, Colorado. Hensel Phelps Construction was the general contractor on the $50 million project. Trautman & Shreve, Inc. (T&S) was the plumbing and HVAC subcontractor. The original subcontract price was $7.8 million. The facility was subdivided into four interconnected separate blocks or buildings which joined to form one large building of approximately 372,000 square feet. The buildings were separated by function. Two housed mainly offices and computer rooms. One housed laboratories. The fourth housed mechanical rooms and laboratories.

The project schedule generally called for the blocks to be constructed in sequence, beginning with D and C, and followed by B and A. T&S's plan was to assign crews for each system (HVAC piping, domestic water, natural gas, special gasses, and storm drains and sanitary waste) to blocks D and C. Upon completion, these crews would move over to blocks B and A. The crews would begin on the lowest levels and work their way to the upper levels. The plan was for T&S to have access to a level allowing completion of most piping in the ceiling space before other trades began installation. This would also permit T&S to stock a floor with all required materials at one time, so its crews would always have sufficient materials to maintain progress. Finally, under its plan, T&S would

---

[24] In this case, the contractor asserted that it did not possess a manloaded schedule.

never have members of the same crews working on different floors at the same time.

Early on in the project, major deficiencies began to surface with the plumbing and HVAC drawings. These deficiencies included conflicts in pipe sizes from drawing to drawing. T&S's project manager testified that in more than 30 years in the business, these were the most poorly coordinated drawings he had even seen. Ultimately, most of the plans required extensive revisions. Hundreds of requests for clarification were submitted to the GSA's design professionals. The GSA's responses were generally late and sometimes inadequate. To make matters worse, contrary to standard industry practice and the contractor's reading of the specifications, the GSA insisted on vibration isolation of plumbing piping throughout the project. This was not apparent from the drawings and was discovered well after construction had begun. Substantial delays and disruption resulted from retrofitting piping that already had been installed. All of these problems were exacerbated by the fact that the mechanical engineering firm that originally prepared the mechanical design had not been retained to assist the GSA's construction manager during construction.

As these problems were discovered and investigated, it became clear to the project participants that the schedule would be affected. The GSA wanted to try to keep the project on schedule. Consequently, it was agreed that T&S would add manpower to the project to overcome the impacts caused by the design problems and the changes made to the HVAC and plumbing piping. Although this agreement was not formalized in writing, the GSA's project manager acknowledged it at trial, as well as his understanding that the GSA would pay the cost of this effort. In effect, a decision was made to "accelerate" T&S's work to overcome potential impacts by adding manpower rather than waiting for a complete corrected HVAC and plumbing design. This was done to keep the project moving forward during a very tight labor market. Hensel Phelps and T&S were concerned that any work stoppage would result in the affected workers finding other jobs, because locating replacements would be difficult if not impossible. Almost five months later, the GSA contracting officer did finally issue a formal direction requiring T&S to "accelerate the schedule to mitigate the impact caused by the HVAC conflicts." *Id.* at 154,300.

Throughout the course of the project, the GSA's construction manager would not permit Hensel Phelps to reflect the schedule impact of the design changes in the monthly schedule updates until a formal contract modification was approved by the GSA. Because it usually took months or years to finalize these modifications, the updates generally did not accurately portray the current schedule's actual status.

As a result of the mechanical design deficiencies, the vibration isolation fiasco, the lack of timely and adequate design information, the multiple changes to the mechanical design, and the GSA's direction to "accelerate" by adding manpower to overcome schedule impacts, T&S could not perform in accordance with its plan. Workers from the same crews were forced to work on multiple

CASE HISTORIES § 16.09

floors at the same time. Additional supervision was required to handle the extra effort and the workers who were spread throughout the buildings. Workers had to move from location to location to address "hot spots" where other trades were also working. This "hop scotching" itself resulted in inefficiency, as well as a loss of contemplated learning curve. Constant reassignment of workers to hot spots, where they were perceived as impediments to other trades, as well as substantial retrofit and rework, also caused major worker morale problems and absenteeism.

T&S and Hensel Phelps submitted proposals to the contracting officer seeking reimbursement for the vibration isolation work and for acceleration and impact costs caused by the addition of T&S manpower, acceleration, multiple design changes and scope revisions, and the overall inadequacy of the mechanical drawings and related design information. The latter proposal covered acceleration costs and impact to base contract work. T&S, at the request of the GSA, attempted to estimate the portion of its $2.2 million proposal attributable to acceleration. In so doing, T&S advised that because the acceleration occurred while work was being impacted by various delays and disruptions, it was extremely difficult to separate acceleration costs from impact costs. T&S used the Corps of Engineers *Modification Impact Evaluation Guide* to quantify these costs.

After a series of discussions regarding the proposal and whether T&S should continue to accelerate, the GSA contracting officer denied responsibility for acceleration of T&S's work. T&S was understandably dismayed by this and responded that if the GSA refused to acknowledge acceleration, a substantial time extension would be required. Surprisingly, the GSA then unilaterally authorized a $50,000 "good faith" payment to cover the cost of the directed acceleration of the HVAC design revisions. The GSA refused to make any additional payment pending resolution of the entire proposal for acceleration and impact costs. The GSA subsequently refused any further payment, contending that even though the GSA had concluded that there had been an impact to the schedule, the contractor had failed to provide an appropriate time impact analysis for the acceleration costs. The contracting officer also noted that the GSA did not recognize the Corps' *Modification Impact Evaluation Guide*, and stated that the contractor had failed to address concerns regarding claimed impact or inefficiency costs not attributable to the GSA and projected future costs. The government also reelected to convert T&S's request to have its contract converted to a cost-reimbursement-type contract. T&S then suggested that the GSA use the inefficiency percentages contained in the Mechanical Contractors Association of America (MCAA) labor productivity bulletin to compute the value of impact and acceleration, for both changed and base contract work. The GSA responded by denying that base contract work had been impacted.

T&S and Hensel Phelps subsequently submitted claims for the cost of adding vibration isolation to plumbing piping ($583,000) and for labor productivity losses attributable to the vibration isolation change, the mechanical design deficiencies and revisions, and the acceleration directive ($2 million). The labor productivity claim sought recovery for the impacts or inefficiencies caused to base contract work. The costs were quantified using the MCAA inefficiency factor percentages. The claims were denied and litigation ensued at the GSA Board of Contract Appeals. Two attempted mediations failed to elicit any significant settlement proposals from the GSA. Throughout the claims discussions, the GSA and its counsel clung to the notion that to recover any acceleration/impact costs, T&S had to demonstrate that the work was on the project's critical path. Unfortunately for the GSA, a more realistic assessment of its exposures could have yielded a much different result.

At trial, T&S and Hensel Phelps offered testimony by an expert in labor productivity who had extensive hands-on experience in mechanical construction. The expert conducted a thorough review of the project plan, actual performance, and the project records to prepare a detailed as-built schedule and manpower curves. The expert utilized six of the MCAA inefficiency factors to evaluate productivity impacts on the plumbing and HVAC crews in each of the four buildings over the life of the project. These inefficiency factors included: Morale and Attitude, Reassignment of Manpower, Stacking of Trades, Concurrent Operations, Dilution of Supervision, and Learning Curve. For purposes of this analysis, the project was divided into three time periods. The expert performed his own analysis of the impacts on the crews in each building for each separate time period. A separate assessment was made for the impacts caused by the vibration isolation work. The expert assigned his own percentages of impact based on his experience in the industry and his understanding of the project history and conditions. These conclusions were then checked against the inefficiency percentages recommended by MCAA. In most cases the expert's percentages were conservative, falling within the range of the MCAA-recommended percentages for "minor" and "average" disruption.

The GSA's trial experts continued to maintain that the contractors' claims should be denied because the contractors had not shown that the impacted work was on the critical path. The GSA's expert witnesses suggested that the MCAA factors were out of favor and inappropriate for analysis of the contractors' claims. The GSA's construction scheduling expert suggested that a measured mile analysis was the proper approach for quantifying productivity losses on the project.

The GSBCA was impressed both with T&S's expert's credentials and with the depth of his analysis of the project. The board was quite dismissive of the government experts' presentation, lending it no credence whatsoever. The board found that a measured mile approach was not feasible under the circumstances of the case and concluded that it had little confidence in the CPM schedules on this particular project for assessing productivity losses. The GSBCA noted that Hensel Phelps's and T&S's use of the MCAA factors provided a rational basis for quantifying the claims. However, the board concluded that this pricing approach essentially altered the nature of the claim itself. Rather than viewing the claim as a classic acceleration claim, the board treated the claim as a dis-

CASE HISTORIES § 16.09

ruption claim. By casting the claim in this fashion, the contractors effectively avoided the special proof requirements ordinarily required for reimbursement of acceleration claims. It also allowed Hensel Phelps to obtain compensation for impact, not only to critical path activities but also to other activities.

> There is considerable merit in the approach ultimately hit upon by appellant for dealing with increased costs associated with the addition of manpower to the project. It circumvents the special requirements which must be met before a claimant can be reimbursed for acceleration costs—with which the Government understandably was concerned once it insisted on the claim for acceleration costs being broken out from HPCC's original impact claim. In particular it obviates the need to ensure that the additional manpower was no more than that required to overcome negative float and keep the contract on schedule. It likewise permits the claimant with the aid of its expert to assess the impact of the labor increase on base activities as opposed to critical path activities. In addition, with this approach, appellant lays aside its claim for time extensions as an alternative to acceleration. Above all, by viewing the facts related to T&S's increase in manpower as the basis for a labor productivity claim rather than an acceleration claim, the Government is thus able to honor in an acceptable fashion the commitment previously made to assist with the costs attendant to the addition of manpower to mitigate the impacts resulting from design changes and keep the project on schedule.

Id. at 154,316 (footnote omitted).

The GSBCA sustained substantially all of the contractors' claims in a decision containing more than 200 separate findings relating to labor productivity impacts on the project, the deficiencies in the mechanical drawings, and the vibration isolation changes. In one of its key holdings the board concluded:

> [W]e are most definitely convinced that GSA did in fact reach agreement with HPCC and T&S that the adverse impact of changes in the project's piping design would be mitigated by the addition of manpower to the project rather than by an extension of the contract completion date or the authorization of overtime. We likewise are convinced that, under this agreement, the Government was in some manner expected to bear the cost of these additional resources. We therefore conclude that appellant's request that it be reimbursed for the labor inefficiencies resulting from the disruption caused by the subsequent addition of manpower is entirely reasonable and should be honored by the Government in view of the agreement previously reached by the parties—provided claimant can demonstrate that the addition of manpower to the project did in fact adversely impact the unchanged work in the manner and to the degree alleged.

Id. at 154, 317.

This case illustrates the very important differences in the types of proof required for delay/acceleration claims versus disruption claims. Although CPM analysis can be extremely helpful in analyzing lost productivity or disruption claims, in certain cases it is not essential—particularly when the available schedule data is suspect through no fault of the claimant. Careful attention must be paid to the circumstances of each case. Blind reliance on CPM analysis to defend a disruption claim may well prove devastating, as this case demonstrates. Finally, this case history underscores the importance of an early and realistic evaluation of one's position. Had the government undertaken such an assessment, it might well have resolved the matter for an amount substantially less than the board's award and avoided the cost and time of a lengthy trial.

APPENDIX L
PMI'S COLLEGE OF SCHEDULING

Introducing the Project Management Institute College of Scheduling

The Project Management Institute
PMI is a non-profit professional organization dedicated to advancing the state-of-the-art in Project Management.

PMI's Objectives:
- to foster professionalism in the management of projects

- to advance the quality and range of Project Management

- to identify and promote the fundamentals of Project Management and advance the Body of Knowledge for managing projects successfully

- to provide a recognized forum for free exchange of ideas, applications, and solutions to Project Management challenges

- to stimulate the application of Project Management to the benefit of industry and the public

- to provide an interface between users and suppliers of hardware and software Project Management systems

- to collaborate with universities and other educational institutions to encourage appropriate education and career development at all levels in Project Management

- to encourage academic and industrial research in the field of Project Management

- to foster contacts internationally with other public and private organizations that relate to Project Management and cooperate in matters of common interest.

For further information about joining PMI contact the Project Management Institute at (610) 356-4600 or visit the PMI website at www.pmi.org.

COLLEGE OF SCHEDULING

CONSTRUCTION SCHEDULING

An Open Invitation from Our Chairman

If you were given the opportunity to make a positive difference in your world, wouldn't you grab it? If you were offered a way to change the future of scheduling for the better, wouldn't you jump at the challenge? Here is your chance – I hope you'll agree that you can't pass it up.

In some ways similar to the accounting crisis in the United States, there are all too many examples of unreliable reporting and a lack of intellectual rigor and discipline in the scheduling arena. Your membership in the PMI College of Scheduling is, therefore, critical to seeing that this changes. The goal of the College of Scheduling is to promote accurate, honest schedules throughout the world in order to reverse the trends mistakenly (and at times intentionally) created by years of abuse and neglect. It is the College's objective to establish:

> standards of practice in preparing, executing and maintaining network analysis systems; communication and protocol standards for scheduling software makers to ensure the integrity of such systems; and standards for validating the qualifications of "scheduling practitioners" and "scheduling experts."

It has been said that "it is . . . the responsibility of the expert to operate the familiar and that of the leader to transcend it." As an experienced leader in the industry, you share a responsibility with other leaders to enhance confidence in the integrity of schedules. By sharing project experiences, and providing education and training in scheduling and time management, you and other college members will help to establish a knowledge base on which current and future generations may draw.

As someone involved extensively in the scheduling arena since 1966, I urge you to be a part of this dynamic organization. You will have an opportunity to put your own ideas into practice and potentially change the way scheduling is perceived in every industry in the world.

We have assembled a distinguished Board of Directors to lead this effort including Gordon Davis, Tom Driscoll, Dick Faris, Pat Galloway, Jim O'Brien and Stu Ockman; and we have recently received our charter for the College from PMI. However, we need your help to achieve our mission and carry forward the challenge of professional and ethical scheduling practices. Make your vision part of scheduling reality. Join the College of Scheduling today.

Jon Wickwire

Our Vision

To be recognized as a dynamic organization of professionals dedicated to promoting the expectation and implementation of accurate, ethical schedules throughout the world.

Our Mission

To provide a forum for Professionals to promote excellence in scheduling through networking, sharing project experiences, providing and receiving training, providing support and encouragement for the ongoing development of the PMI Body of Knowledge in the areas of scheduling and time management, and supporting project managers in their PMP certification efforts.

Our Approach

Our approach is a multi-pronged process for promoting our *Vision* and achieving our *Mission*:

The individual prongs include:

- Holding an annual PMI College of Scheduling Seminar/Symposium every spring beginning in 2004.
- Working with PMI to update the Time Management section of the PMBOK and to develop a Practice Standard for Scheduling.
- Establishing a Board of Directors made up of leaders both in the field of scheduling and in service to PMI
- Working with PMI to establish standards for scheduling software to encourage development of more accurate schedules.

APPENDIX L

- Establishing a website (operational at www.pmicos.org).
- Establishing a Yahoo Group for communicating directly among members (operational at pmicos@yahoogroups.com).
- Providing education and training in scheduling and time management.
- Establishing a global presence supported by a virtual organization and E-communications to realize our mission.

Our Three-Year Plan

April 2003 – New Time Management Section of PMBOK
Fall 2003 – Call for Papers for First College of Scheduling Seminar/Symposium
September 2003 – 2nd Annual Membership Campaign
October 2003 – 2nd Annual Business Meeting at PMI Congress in Baltimore
December 2003 – Reach 1,000 Members
April 2004 – First College of Scheduling Annual Seminar/Symposium in Montreal
Spring 2004 – Draft Practice Standard for Scheduling
December 2004 – Reach 2,000 Members
Spring 2005 – Draft Practice Standard for Scheduling Software
April 2005 – 2nd Annual Seminar/Symposium
December 2005 – Reach 3,250 Members

How to Join?

Fill out the enclosed registration form and return it today. For members of PMI, the annual membership fee is $20. If you are not a member of PMI, a fee of $149 covers a one-year membership to both PMI and the College of Scheduling.

Complete the registration form and send or fax to the Project Management Institute. Or apply on line at www.pmi.org.

For further information about the College, contact Stu Ockman at (610) 566-1241 or visit our website at www.pmicos.org.

Registration Form

Project Management Institute
College of Scheduling

Name

Title

Organization

Address

City, State, ZIP

Country

Telephone (day)   (evening)

FAX   E-Mail Address

Annual membership:
   I am a PMI member ($20) ____
   non-member ($149)* ____

* Includes first year PMI membership dues

☐ Check enclosed payable to the Project Management Institute

☐ Charge my credit card   ☐ VISA ☐ MasterCard
        ☐ American Express ☐ Diners Club

Card Number _____

Expiration Date ____ Signature _____

Send payment to: Project Management Institute
Four Campus Boulevard
Newtown Square, PA 19073-3299
USA
Telephone: (610) 356-4600

or FAX: (610) 356-4647

Our Board of Directors

CHAIRMAN – JON M. WICKWIRE is a shareholder in the law firm of Wickwire Gavin, P.C., and is President of Construction Strategies, Inc., a construction-consulting firm providing Alternative Dispute Resolution and strategic planning services to the construction industry. For more than 25 years, he has been actively involved in the construction industry, analyzing and resolving performance problems, preparing major systems claims, and serving as lead counsel on large claims and litigation. He has published extensively on using critical path method techniques in contract claims and is nationally recognized as the premier legal historian in this field.

PRESIDENT – STUART OCKMAN is President of Ockman & Borden Associates, project management consultants specializing in project planning and control, claims management and claims avoidance. He has over 25 years experience in engineering and construction management utilizing computerized project management systems for scheduling, estimating, cost control and financial analysis of projects including rapid transit systems, refuse-fired steam generating plants, food processing facilities, power plants and industrial research centers.

VICE-PRESIDENT – EDUCATION & TRAINING
JAMES J. O'BRIEN, PE, PMP, is co-founder of O'Brien Kreitzberg, the nation's oldest and largest firm specializing in program and construction management. Jim has been involved with CPM scheduling since 1962. McGraw-Hill first published his book, *CPM in Construction Management*, in 1965. The 5th edition of the book (co-authored by Frederick L. Plotnick, Esq., PE) was published in 1999.

VICE-PRESIDENT – FINANCE
J. GORDON DAVIS, PhD, is Chief Executive Officer of Davis Consulting Group, a firm providing project coordination and expediting services to owners, developers, designers, and contractors. He has more than twenty-five years of project management experience designing and implementing management systems for a wide variety of projects both in North America and abroad. Gordon also has assisted several large corporations in developing improved organizational structures for more effective project management

VICE-PRESIDENT – GLOBAL SERVICES
RICHARD K. FARIS is co-founder, co-owner, and President of Primavera Systems, the nation's 25th largest PC-based software company. The company's focus is solely on project management software solutions. Dick has led new product development and technical support services at Primavera for nearly 20 years. Under his guidance, Primavera has successfully kept pace with the innovations in computer hardware and software, developing more than 60 releases of twelve distinct project management products.

VICE-PRESIDENT – PROGRAMS
PATRICIA D. GALLOWAY is Chief Executive Officer and President of The Nielsen-Wurster Group, an international management-consulting firm with offices throughout the United States, Europe and Asia-Pacific. Pat provides management consulting, risk management and dispute resolution services on projects around the world. She is a recognized leader in project controls, risk analysis, and delay and disruption. In August 2002, Ms. Galloway became the first woman selected to serve as President of the American Society of Civil Engineers.

VICE-PRESIDENT – PUBLICITY
THOMAS J. DRISCOLL is a Senior Vice President with URS Corporation. Tom has more than 25 years of experience as a planning engineer, project manager, project executive, and as President of an international project management consulting organization. He has authored numerous publications and has participated as a lecturer in more than 300 seminars on such topics as program, project, and construction management; project controls, scheduling, productivity measurement, delay analysis and claims avoidance.

APPENDIX M
UNIFIED FACILITIES GUIDE SPECIFICATIONS FOR NETWORK ANALYSIS SYSTEMS (FEB. 2003)

```
**************************************************************************
USACE / NAVFAC / AFCESA               UFGS-01321N (February 2003)
                                      ------------------------------
Preparing Activity: NAVFAC            Superseding
                                      UFGS-01321N (December 2002)

           UNIFIED FACILITIES GUIDE SPECIFICATIONS

        Revised throughout - changes not indicated by CHG tags
**************************************************************************
```

SECTION TABLE OF CONTENTS

DIVISION 01 - GENERAL REQUIREMENTS

SECTION 01321N

[DESIGN-BUILD]NETWORK ANALYSIS SCHEDULES (NAS)

02/03

PART 1   GENERAL

  1.1   DESCRIPTION
  1.2   SUBMITTALS
  1.3   SCHEDULE ACCEPTANCE
    1.3.1   Schedule Acceptance Prior to Start of Work
    1.3.2   Acceptance
  1.4   SOFTWARE
  1.5   QUALIFICATIONS
  1.6   NETWORK SYSTEM FORMAT
    1.6.1   Diagrams
    1.6.2   Schedule Activity Properties and Level of Detail
      1.6.2.1   Activity Categories
      1.6.2.2   Project Milestones
      1.6.2.3   Activity Identification (ID) and Description
      1.6.2.4   Activity Code Dictionary and Values
      1.6.2.5   Cost and Resource Loading
      1.6.2.6   Anticipated Weather Delays
      1.6.2.7   Schedule Software Settings and Restrictions
    1.6.3   Required Tabular Reports
  1.7   SUBMISSION AND ACCEPTANCE
    1.7.1   Preliminary Meeting
    1.7.2   Design Network Analysis Schedule
    1.7.3   Construction Network Analysis Schedule
    1.7.4   Review and Evaluation
    1.7.5   Baseline Network Analysis Schedule
    1.7.6   Monthly Network Analysis Updates
    1.7.7   Summary Network
    1.7.8   As-Built Schedule
  1.8   CONTRACT MODIFICATION
    1.8.1   Time Impact Analysis:

SECTION 01321N   Page 1

CONSTRUCTION SCHEDULING

```
    1.8.2   No Reservation-Of-Rights
  1.9   CHANGES TO THE NETWORK ANALYSIS SCHEDULE
  1.10  FLOAT
    1.10.1  Definitions of Float
    1.10.2  Ownership of Float
    1.10.3  Negative Float
  1.11  THREE-WEEK LOOK AHEAD SCHEDULE
  1.12  WEEKLY COORDINATION MEETING
  1.13  CORRESPONDENCE AND TEST REPORTS

PART 2   PRODUCTS


PART 3   EXECUTION


-- End of Section Table of Contents --
```

APPENDIX M

```
*************************************************************************
USACE / NAVFAC / AFCESA                 UFGS-01321N (February 2003)
                                        -------------------------------
Preparing Activity: NAVFAC              Superseding
                                        UFGS-01321N (December 2002)

                    UNIFIED FACILITIES GUIDE SPECIFICATIONS

            Revised throughout - changes not indicated by CHG tags
*************************************************************************

                                SECTION 01321N

                 [DESIGN-BUILD ]NETWORK ANALYSIS SCHEDULES (NAS)
                                    02/03
```

```
*************************************************************************
            NOTE: This guide specification covers the
            preparation and use of Design-Build Network Analysis
            Schedules and Design-Bid-Build Network Analysis
            Schedules and as such must be edited for the
            acquisition method used. As prescribed in FAR
            36.515, the Contracting Officer may insert the
            clause "Schedules for Construction Contracts" (FAR
            52.236-15) in solicitations and contracts when a
            fixed-price construction contract is contemplated,
            the contract amount is expected to exceed the
            simplified acquisition threshold, and the period of
            actual work performance exceeds 60 days. This
            clause may be inserted in such contracts when work
            performance is expected to last less than 60 days
            and an unusual situation exists that warrants
            impositions of the requirements. This clause should
            not be used in the same contract with clauses
            covering other management approaches for ensuring
            that a contractor makes adequate progress.
            Coordination is required with other Division 1
            specifications when Network Analysis Schedules is
            not specified.

            Coordinate selection of the scheduling specification
            (either 01320 or 01321) with the administrating
            ROICC Office.

            Comments and suggestion on this specification are
            welcome and should be directed to the technical
            proponent of the specification. A listing of the
            technical proponents, including their organization
            designation and telephone number, is on the Internet.

            Recommended changes to a UFGS should be submitted as
            a Criteria Change Request (CCR).
```

SECTION 01321N   Page 3

CONSTRUCTION SCHEDULING

Use of electronic communication is encouraged.

Brackets are used in the text to indicate designer choices or locations where text must be supplied by the designer.

****
****
NOTE: This guide specification requires project costs to be loaded into the schedule and assigned to activities. When using this section, delete the requirement for "Schedule of Prices" in Section 01200 "Price and Payment Procedures".
****

PART 1   GENERAL

1.1   DESCRIPTION

****
NOTE: Edit the following paragraph as applicable for Design-Build or Design-Bid-Build contracts.
****

The network analysis system shall consist of the network analysis schedule (diagram) and associated reports. The scheduling of all[design,] procurement and construction shall be the responsibility of the Contractor. [All design and construction][Construction] increments will be interrelated on a single schedule that represents the entire project duration from Contract Award to the Contract Completion Date. Schedule updates will build upon each other and will include [design and]construction increments as they are detailed, submitted and accepted. Submission of progress and revision data will be used to measure work progress, aid in the evaluation for requests for time extensions, and to provide the basis of all progress payments. The Critical Path Method (CPM) of network calculation shall be used to generate the project schedule and will utilize the Precedence Diagram Method (PDM) to satisfy both time and cost applications. All progress payment amounts will be derived from and tied to the cost-loaded schedule activities.

For consistency, when scheduling software terminology is used in this specification, the terms in Primavera's scheduling programs are used. Primavera Project Planner, P3, Primavera Project Manager, SureTrak and PrimeContract are registered trademarks or service marks of Primavera Systems, Inc. Adobe and Acrobat are registered trademarks of Adobe Systems Incorporated.

1.2   SUBMITTALS

****
NOTE: Submittals must be limited to those necessary for adequate quality control. The importance of an item in the project should be one of the primary factors in determining if a submittal for the item should be required.

SECTION 01321N   Page 4

APPENDIX M

A "G" following a submittal item indicates that the submittal requires Government approval. Some submittals are already marked with a "G". Only delete an existing "G" if the submittal item is not complex and can be reviewed through the Contractor's Quality Control system. Only add a "G" if the submittal is sufficiently important or complex in context of the project.

For submittals requiring Government approval on Army projects, a code of up to three characters within the submittal tags may be used following the "G" designation to indicate the approving authority. Recommended codes for Army projects are "RE" for Resident Engineer approval, "ED" for Engineering approval, and "AE" for Architect-Engineer approval. Codes following the "G" typically are not used for Navy projects.

Submittal items not designated with a "G" are considered as being for information only for Army projects and for Contractor Quality Control approval for Navy projects.
****

Government approval is required for submittals with a "G" designation; submittals not having a "G" designation are for information only or as otherwise designated. When used, a designation following the "G" designation identifies the office that will review the submittal for the Government. The following shall be submitted in accordance with Section 01330 SUBMITTAL PROCEDURES:

SD-01 Preconstruction Submittals

    [Qualifications; G]

    Standard Activity ID Dictionary; G

    [Design Network Analysis Schedule; G]

    Construction Network Analysis Schedule; G

    Baseline Network Analysis Schedule; G

SD-07 Certificates

    Monthly Network Analysis Updates; G

    [Summary Network; G]

SD-11 Closeout Submittals

    As-Built Schedule; G

CONSTRUCTION SCHEDULING

1.3   SCHEDULE ACCEPTANCE

Review comments made by the Government on the Contractor's schedule(s) will not relieve the Contractor from compliance with requirements of the Contract Documents. The Contractor is responsible for scheduling, sequencing, and prosecuting the Work to comply with the requirements of the Contract Documents. Government acceptance extends only to the activities of the Contractor's schedule that the Government has been assigned responsibility for and agrees it is responsible. The Government will also review for contract imposed schedule constraints and conformance, and cost loading of the CPM activities. Comments offered on other parts of the schedule, which the Contractor is assigned responsibility, are offered as a courtesy and are not conditions of Government acceptance; but are for the general conformance with established industry schedule concepts.

1.3.1   Schedule Acceptance Prior to Start of Work

[Unless stipulated otherwise as part of the Contract Award, the design work may be started prior to submittal and acceptance of the Design Network Analysis Schedule by the Government, but acceptance of the Design NAS will be a condition precedent to processing any pay requests submitted by the Contractor.]The Baseline Network Analysis Schedule described in the paragraph entitled "Baseline Network Analysis Schedule" must be submitted and accepted by the Government before the Contractor will be allowed to start work on the construction stage(s) of the contract. Examples of construction stages are, but not limited to; demolition, site work, temporary work for construction, etc.

1.3.2   Acceptance

    a.   [When the Design Network Analysis Schedule is submitted and accepted by the Contracting Officer it will be considered the "Baseline Network Analysis Schedule for Design". The Design Network Analysis Schedule shall be updated at least monthly or submitted as part of the design submittals, whichever occurs first.]When the Construction Network Analysis Schedule is submitted and accepted by the Contracting Officer, it will then be considered the "Baseline Network Analysis Schedule". The Baseline Network Analysis Schedule will then be used by the Contractor for planning, organizing, and directing the work; reporting progress; and requesting payment for work accomplished. The schedule will be updated monthly by the Contractor and submitted monthly with the progress pay request to reflect the current status of the work. Submittal and acceptance of the [Baseline Network Analysis Schedule for Design and]Baseline Network Analysis Schedule and accurate updated schedules accompanying the pay requests are both conditions precedent to processing pay requests. Only bonds will be paid prior to acceptance of the Baseline Schedule(s).

    b.   Submittal of the Network, and subsequent schedule updates, will be understood to be the Contractor's representation that the submitted schedule meets all of the requirements of the Contract Documents, accurately reflects the work accomplished, and that

APPENDIX M

Work will be executed in the sequence indicated on the submitted schedule.

1.4   SOFTWARE

****
          NOTE: Contact the Administering ROICC Office to
          determine which software will be used on the
          project.
****

The scheduling software that will be utilized by the Government on this project is [SureTrak by Primavera Systems, Inc.][Primavera Project Planner (P3) by Primavera Systems, Inc.]. Notwithstanding any other provision in the contract, schedules submitted for this project must be prepared using either Primavera P3 or Primavera SureTrak (files saved in Concentric P3 format). The Contractor shall provide electronic files saved in a format that is compatible with the Contracting Officer's current software version. Submission of data from another software system where data conversion techniques or software is used to import into Primavera's scheduling software is not acceptable and will be cause for rejection of the submitted schedule.

[1.5   QUALIFICATIONS

****
          NOTE: The requirement for a full time scheduler
          will be used very infrequently and only on projects
          that are large and complex enough to warrant the
          additional expense. A part time scheduler can be
          specified (and part time defined) when complexity
          and size does not warrant a full time scheduler and
          the ROICC does not want emphasis of the duty left to
          the discretion of the Contractor. Lastly, the
          office may choose to not designate full or part time
          and leave the emphasis of the duty to the
          Contractor. Before editing the following paragraph,
          coordinate with the ROICC Office.
****

The Contractor shall designate a [full time][part time] Scheduler that will be responsible for the development, preparation, and maintenance of an accurate, computerized Network Analysis Schedule. [Full time is defined as the scheduler being on-site during normal work hours to perform on-site coordination, attending project meetings, and updates. The Scheduler shall have no other duties than scheduling for this contract.] [Part time is defined as the Scheduler performing [on-site] coordination, attending project meetings, and updates for [_____] hours per work week.]The Scheduler shall have previously developed, created and maintained at least [2][_____] previous computerized schedules of similar size and complexity of this contract. A resume outlining the qualifications of the Scheduler shall be submitted for acceptance to the Contracting Officer. If at a later date, the Contracting Officer considers the Contractor's Scheduler to be incompetent or objectionable, the Contractor will propose a new

CONSTRUCTION SCHEDULING

Scheduler, meeting the qualification requirements. Payments will not be processed until an acceptable Scheduler is provided.

]1.6   NETWORK SYSTEM FORMAT

The system shall consist of time scaled logic diagrams and specified reports.

1.6.1   Diagrams

Show the order and interdependence of activities and the sequence in which the work is to be accomplished as planned. The basic concept of a network analysis diagram will be followed to show how the start of a given activity is dependent on the completion of preceding activities and how its completion restricts or restrains the start of following activities. Diagrams shall be [organized by [Work Phase][Area Code] and] sorted by Early Start Date and will show a continuous flow from left to right with no logic (relationship lines) from right to left. With the exception of the Contract Award, Project Start and Project Completion milestone activities, no activities will be open-ended; each activity will have predecessor and successor ties. The diagram shall clearly show the activities of the critical path. Once an activity exists on the schedule it may not be deleted and must remain in the logic. No more than [20][____] percent of the activities may be critical or near critical. Critical will be defined as having zero days of Total Float. "Near critical" will be defined as having Total Float in the range of [1 to 14][[____] to [____]] days. Show the following information on the diagrams for each activity:

   a.   Activity ID

   b.   Activity Description

   c.   Original Duration in Work Days

   d.   Remaining duration

   e.   Actual Duration in Work Days

   f.   Early Start Date

   g.   Early Finish Date

   h.   Total Float

Provide network diagrams on ANSI E sheets. Updated diagrams shall show the date of the latest revision.

1.6.2   Schedule Activity Properties and Level of Detail

****
               NOTE: A good knowledge of construction and
               scheduling are required when determining the number
               of activities for a network analysis schedule.
               Factors such as the nature of the work, geographical

APPENDIX M

>   location, completion time, complexity (the
>   complexity of a project is related to the number of
>   specification sections, the number of buildings,
>   special phasing requirements and special quality
>   control requirements), cost of maintaining each
>   activity throughout the life of the contract and
>   level of use by field management personnel must be
>   considered. Contact the administrating ROICC Office
>   when determining the number of construction
>   activities.
>
>   *Important-When selecting the number of activities,
>   please keep in mind the cost added to the contract.
>   A schedule needs to be maintained throughout the
>   life of the contract and the use of too many
>   activities will unnecessarily increase the total
>   contract cost.
>
>   Use your best judgment for selecting number of
>   activities. (Ex: A contract to stripe a 500-mile
>   stretch of highway may have a project cost of
> $6,000,000 but it should not require between 1000 to
>   2000 activities).
> **

Numbering shall be assigned so that, in general, predecessor activity numbers are smaller numerically than the successor activity numbers. Skip numbering shall be used on the network to allow insertion of additional activities for contract modifications and logic changes. The minimum number of construction activities in the final network diagram shall be [_____]. Activity categories included in the schedule are specified below.

1.6.2.1   Activity Categories

> **
>   NOTE: Include the following paragraph in Design
>   Build projects. Remove the first bracketed phrase
>   if Fast-Tracking will not be used on this project.
> **

>   [a. Design Activities: Requirements for the activities related to
>   design shall be included as separate activities in the project
>   schedule. Design activities shall include, but are not limited
>   to; the Design Notice to Proceed, Contractor's various stages of
>   design, application for and receipt of permits required,
>   Contractor's constructibility reviews, submittal of design
>   packages to Government, Government's design review periods,
>   specified design meetings, transition periods prior to
>   Construction Notice to Proceed, [(including Notices to Proceed for
>   each Fast-Track Phase as indicated in other sections of this
>   specification and as directed by the Contracting Officer)]etc.
>   The Government review period shall be from the time the design is
>   received by the Government to the time it is sent back to the
>   Contractor; mail time will not be included in the Government

SECTION 01321N   Page 9

CONSTRUCTION SCHEDULING

review period. Design activities will be linked to their associated Procurement and/or Construction Activities.

If the Government's action on any submittal is "Disapproved" or "Revise and Resubmit", a new series of Design Activities will be inserted into the schedule. Predecessor for the new design preparation activity will be the original approval activity and the successor of the new approval activity will be the next design step (in-progress or final) activity.]

b. Procurement Activities: Tasks related to the procurement of material or equipment shall be included as separate activities in the project schedule. Examples of procurement activities include, but are not limited to; Material/equipment submittal preparation, submittal and approval of material/equipment; delivery of O&M manuals; material/equipment fabrication and delivery, delivery of extra parts, extra stock, special tools, notification of Government Furnished Material/Equipment delivery requirement, etc. As a minimum, separate procurement activities will be provided for every specification section. If the Contractor intends on using Just-In-Time (JIT) delivery methods, the schedule will show each JIT delivery with relationship tie to the Construction Activity specifically for the JIT delivery. Material and equipment for which payment will be requested in advance of installation shall be cost-loaded with the procurement costs. All activities within a procurement process/cycle will have a unique identifier in the activity code to show their relationships and will extend to the related construction activities (i.e., CSI Code).

If the Government's action on any submittal is "Disapproved" or "Revise and Resubmit", a new series of Procurement Activities will be inserted into the schedule. Predecessor for the new submittal preparation activity will be the original approval activity and the successor of the new approval activity will be the fabrication/deliver activity for the equipment or material.

****
NOTE: Remove the bracketed phrase if Fast-Tracking will not be used in the project.
****

c. Government Activities: Government and other agency activities that could impact progress shall be clearly identified. Government activities include, but are not limited to; Government approved submittal reviews, Government conducted inspections/tests, environmental permit approvals by State regulators, utility outages, Notice(s) to Proceed [(including Notices to Proceed for each Fast-Track Phase as indicated in other sections of this specification and as directed by the Contracting Officer)]and delivery of Government Furnished Material/Equipment. Show activities indicating Government furnished materials and equipment utilizing delivery dates indicated in "FAR 52.245-2, Government Property (Fixed-Price Contracts)." Government

APPENDIX M

   activities will be driven by calendars that reflect Saturdays, Sundays and all Federal Holidays as non-work days.

   d. Construction Quality Management (CQM) Activities: CQM Activities will identify the Preparatory Phase and Initial Phase for each Definable Feature of Work identified in the Contractor's Quality Control Plan. These activities will be added to each 3-Week Look Ahead Schedule referenced in the paragraph entitled "THREE-WEEK LOOK AHEAD SCHEDULE" and will also be included in each monthly update referenced in the paragraph entitled "Monthly Network Analysis Updates". The Follow-up Phase will be represented by the Construction Activities in the Baseline Schedule and in the schedule updates.

   e. Construction Activities: Construction activities shall include, but are not limited to: Tasks related to mobilization or demobilization; the installation of temporary or permanent work by tradesman; testing and inspections of installed work by technicians, inspectors or engineers; start-up and testing of equipment; commissioning of building and related systems; scheduling of specified manufacture's representatives; Punch Out Inspection; Pre-Final Inspection, Final Acceptance Inspection; final clean-up; training to be provided; and administrative tasks necessary to start, proceed with, accomplish or finalize the contract. No onsite construction activity shall have a duration in excess of 20 working days. Contractor activities will be driven by calendars that reflect Saturdays, Sundays and all Federal Holidays as non-work days.

****
      NOTE: Include Hammock Activities if Summary
      Networks will be requested or if repetitive groups
      of activities will be used in a project (e.g.
      similar housing units being built several times
      over). Also include if Summaries will assist in
      keeping Customer or Management appraised of progress.
****

   [f. Hammock (Summary) Activities: The Contractor shall include special activities that are a summary of a chain of activities. The start of the activity will be the start date of the first activity in the chain and the finish date will be the finish date of the last activity in the chain. Generalized work sequences, Area Codes and Phase Codes will be summarized.]

1.6.2.2   Project Milestones

Dates shall be shown on the diagram for the start of the project, any contract required interim start and completion dates, contract completion date and other significant milestones.

   a. Project Start Date Milestones: The schedule shall start no earlier than the Contract Award Date and the project duration (Day 1) will start on the Notice-to-Proceed (NTP) date. The Contractor

CONSTRUCTION SCHEDULING

shall include as the first milestone in the schedule, an activity named "Contract Award". Another milestone shall be included that will be named "Start Project".[Additional milestones shall be included for Design NTP for each design increment and Construction NTP for each construction increment.] The Contract Award and Project Start milestones shall have mandatory start constraint dates equal to the Contract Award and NTP dates, respectively.

b. Constraint of Last Activity Milestone: The Contractor shall include as the last activity in the project schedule, an activity named "End Project". The "End Project" activity shall have a mandatory finish constraint equal to the contract completion date for the project. Calculation of project updates shall be such that if the finish of the last activity falls after the contract completion date, then the float calculation shall reflect negative float on the critical path.

c. Early Project Completion: In the event the Contractor's project schedule shows completion of the project prior to the contract completion date, the Contractor shall include an activity named "Contractor Early Completion". The activity shall be a milestone with an unconstrained date representing the Contractor's Early Completion date.

d. Substantial Completion: If the Contractor elects to include an activity for Substantial Completion, then it is agreed that Substantial Completion will be the point in time that the Government considers the project is complete and ready for its intended use. The activity will be named "Substantial Completion". The activity shall be a milestone with an unconstrained date representing the Contractor's Substantial Completion date.

****
NOTE: Include the following three paragraphs when the project includes the requirement for Phased Construction.
****

[e. Phase Start Milestone: The Contractor shall include as the first activity for a project phase, an activity named "Start Phase X", where "X" identifies the phase of work. The "Start Phase X" activity shall have an unconstrained start date equal to the date of the Phase NTP. This unconstrained start date is not a release from contractually required start dates, but is left unconstrained to allow the schedule logic to calculate without hindrance.

f. End Phase Milestone: The Contractor shall include as the last activity in a project phase, an activity named "End Phase X" where "X" identifies the phase of work. The "End Phase X" activity shall have an unconstrained late finish date equal to the contract phase completion date. This unconstrained completion date is not a release from contractually required finish dates, but is left unconstrained to allow the schedule logic to calculate without

APPENDIX M

hindrance.

g. Early Phase Completion: If the Contractor expects to finish prior to the contract phase completion date, the milestone will show an early finish date equal to the Contractor's early finish date. The name of the activity will be "Early Phase Completion" and will have an unconstrained date representing the Contractor's early phase completion date.]

1.6.2.3 Activity Identification (ID) and Description

a. Standard Activity ID Dictionary: The Contractor shall submit the coding scheme for Schedule Activity Numbers that shall be used throughout the project. The coding scheme submitted shall list the values for each activity code category and translate those values into project specific designations. Code length shall not exceed [10][_____] characters. Once accepted, the coding scheme will be used for the duration of the project.

b. Activity Description: Each activity shall have a narrative description consisting of a Verb or work function (e.g.; form, pour, excavate), an Object (e.g.; slab, footing, under floor plumbing), and Area (e.g.; 3rd floor, northeast quadrant, basement).

1.6.2.4 Activity Code Dictionary and Values

The Contractor shall establish the activity codes identified in this specification. The codes will have values assigned that will allow the scheduling program to sort, select, group and organize the activities in the schedule. Activity codes include, but are not limited to, the following codes:

****
NOTE: Include the following paragraph when the project includes the requirement for Phased Construction.
****

[a. Phase Code: If phasing is specified in the contract, all activities shall be identified in the project schedule by the Phase Code in which the activity occurs. Activities shall not be contained in more than one Phase.]

****
NOTE: Use the following paragraph only when Fast-Tracking is required or is an option.
****

[b. Fast-Track Code: All Activities shall be identified in the project schedule according to the design phase and its corresponding construction increment. An example of activities that would have a common Fast-Track Code is the foundation design activities and the corresponding foundation construction

CONSTRUCTION SCHEDULING

activities. Individual activities shall not be contained in more than one fast-track code.]

c. Area Code: All activities shall be identified in the project schedule by the Area Code in which the activity occurs. Activities shall not be contained in more than one Area Code. Area is defined as distinct separations in construction, such as a story of construction, separate structure, usage or function difference, utility distribution systems, etc.

d. Responsibility Code: All activities in the project schedule shall be identified with the party responsible to perform the task. Responsibility includes, but is not limited to; the Prime Contractor, subcontracting firm, or Government agency performing a given task. Activities shall not belong to more than one responsible party. The responsible party for each activity shall be identified by a responsibility code. For example, a responsibility code value, "ELEC", may be identified as "Electrical Subcontractor".

e. CSI Code: All activities in the project schedule shall be identified with its respective 5-digit Specification Section number. Activities shall not belong to more than one Section number. If an activity does not have an applicable CSI Code, (such as "Mobilize"), the code will be "00000".

f. Drawing Code: All activities in the project schedule shall be identified with its respective project Drawing Code. The Drawing Code is the Sheet Number on the primary project drawing, which indicates the work to be performed. Activities shall not belong to more than one Drawing Code. Examples of Drawing Codes are "C-10", "C.10" or "C10". The code system will allow organizing all activities by Drawing Code in alpha and numeric order. If an activity does not have an applicable Drawing Code, (such as "Mobilize"), the code will be "00000".

g. Modification Code: The Modification Code shall identify activities that are modified or added by contract modification. Activities shall not belong to more than one Modification Code. The Government will assign the modification number, which will be shown on the SF 30. Use a shortened version of the modification number for the code (e.g.; A00010 = 010).

h. Request for Equitable Adjustment (REA) or Claim Code: Activities that are modified or added, as a result of a Contractor's REA or Claim shall be identified by a code generated by the Contractor. Activities shall not belong to more than one REA or Claim Code.

1.6.2.5 Cost and Resource Loading

a. Cost Loading Activities:[Costs for incremental design preparation will be assigned to the respective design phase submittal milestone(s).] Equipment costs will be assigned to their respective Procurement Activities (i.e., the delivery

APPENDIX M

milestone activity). Costs for installation of the material/equipment (labor, construction equipment, and temporary materials) will be assigned to their respective Construction Activities. The value of inspection/testing activities will not be less than [10][_____] percent of the total costs for Procurement and Construction Activities. Evenly disperse overhead and profit to each activity over the duration of the project. The total of all cost loaded activities; including costs for material and equipment delivered for installation on the project, and labor and construction equipment loaded construction activities, shall total to 100 percent of the value of the contract.

b. Quantities and Units of Measure: Each cost loaded activity will have a detailed breakdown of the contract price, giving quantities for each of the various kinds of work, unit prices, etc.

****
NOTE: The information required by the following paragraphs is optional. Tracking of actual resources is typically not needed for routine work. Labor and equipment loaded schedules are of primary importance to the Contractor in deciding the most efficient use of personnel resources and optimizing equipment usage and is the basis of activity duration estimates. Since these decisions are the responsibility of the Contractor's management process, the information value to the Contracting Officer is in assuring that the planned labor and equipment are being supplied throughout the course of the project.
****

[c. Labor Resource Loading: As part of the Baseline Schedule development each construction activity shall have an estimate of the number of workers per day by trade, hours per day by trade and total expected hours used by trade during the execution of the activity. If no workers are required for an activity, then the activity shall be identified as using zero workers per day. [Actual labor resource expended on an activity will be recorded in the monthly updated schedules and will coincide with entries made in the Daily Reports.]

d. Equipment Resource loading: As part of the Baseline Schedule development each construction activity shall have an estimate of the equipment used per day, number of units per day and total expected hours for each piece of equipment used during the duration of the activity. Include a description of the major items of construction equipment planned for each construction activity on the project. The description shall include the year, make, model, and capacity. If no equipment is required for an activity, then the activity shall be identified as using zero equipment per day.[Actual equipment resource expended on an activity will be recorded in the monthly updated schedules and will coincide with entries made in the Daily Reports.]]

CONSTRUCTION SCHEDULING

1.6.2.6   Anticipated Weather Delays

Schedule activity duration(s) shall be formulated with allowance for normal adverse weather conditions. Any activity duration, which could be impacted by normally anticipated adverse weather (precipitation, high or low temperature, wind, etc.), due to the time period that the Contractor has scheduled the work, shall include an adjustment to include the anticipated weather delay. The Contractor shall anticipate delay by comparing the contractually imposed environmental restrictions in the Contract Documents to the National Oceanic and Atmospheric Association's (NOAA) historical monthly averages for the NOAA location [at (Enter NOAA Station here)][closest to the project site]. The number of anticipated adverse weather delays allocated to an activity will be reflected in the activity's calendar. A lost workday, due to weather conditions, is defined as a day in which the Contractor's workforce cannot work 50 percent or more of the day. The Contractor shall immediately notify the Contracting Officer when a lost day has occurred due to weather and will record on the Daily Reports, the occurrence of adverse weather and resultant impact to the normally scheduled work. If the number of actual adverse weather delay days exceeds the number of days anticipated, the Contracting Officer will convert any qualifying delays to calendar days, giving full consideration for equivalent fair weather work days and issue a modification in accordance with the contract clauses.

1.6.2.7   Schedule Software Settings and Restrictions

   a.   Activity Constraints: Date/time constraint(s), other than those required by the contract, will not be allowed unless accepted by the Contracting Officer. Contractor will identify any constraints proposed and provide an explanation for the purpose of the constraint in the Narrative Report.

   b.   Lags: Lags will not be used when the creation of an activity will perform the same function (e.g., concrete cure time). Lag durations contained in the project schedule shall not have a negative value. Contractor will identify any lag proposed and provide an explanation for the purpose of the lag in the Narrative Report.

   c.   Default Progress Data Disallowed: Actual Start and Finish dates shall not be automatically updated by default mechanisms that may be included in the CPM scheduling software system. Actual Start and Actual Finish dates on the CPM schedule shall match the dates provided from Contractor Quality Control and Production Reports. These reports will be the sole basis for updating the schedule. Work activities will be updated by actual work progression rather than being cash flow driven. Actual labor and equipment hours used on activities will be derived from the Daily Reports.

   d.   Software Settings: The updating of percent of payment and actual to date of any activity shall be independent functions; program features that calculate one of these parameters from the other shall be disabled. Schedule calculations and Out-of-Sequence

APPENDIX M

progress (if applicable) shall be handled through Retained Logic, not Progress Override. All activity durations and float values will be shown in days, time will not be shown in the duration display. Date format will be DDMMMYY (i.e., 11DEC02). Default activity type will be set to "Task".

1.6.3   Required Tabular Reports

****
              NOTE: Consult with the ROICC Office to identify
              which of the following reports will be needed.
              Always include Earned Value Report and Log Report.
****

The following reports will be based on the information in the paragraph entitled "Diagrams" and included with the schedule submittals and in each updated schedule submission provided on disk by the Contractor:

   a. Earned Value Report: Listing all activities having a budget amount and cost. A compilation of total earnings on the project from the notice to proceed to the most recent monthly progress payment request and the difference between the previous request amount and the current payment request amount. Sort report first by resource and then by activity.

   b. Log Report: With each updated schedule submission, provide a computer generated Log Report using a recognized schedule comparison software listing all changes made between the previous schedule and current updated schedule. Identify the name of the previous schedule and name of the current schedule being compared. This report will as a minimum show changes for: Added & Deleted Activities, Original Durations, Remaining Durations, Activity Percent Complete, Total Float, Free Float, Calendars, Descriptions, Constraints (added, deleted or changed), Actual Starts/Finishes, Added/Deleted Resources, Resource Quantities, Costs, Resource Percents, Added/Deleted Relations, Changed Relation Lags, Changed Driving Relations, and Changed Critical Status.

   [c. Activity ID Report: By activity number in ascending order showing the current status of all activities.]

   [d. Total Float Report: List of all activities by total float in ascending order and then in order of [activity number][early start date].]

   [e. Early Start Report: By earliest allowable start dates and then in order of activity number.]

   [f. 30-Day Look Ahead: Activities in progress or scheduled to start or finish within the next 30 calendar days of the project Data Date or is continuing through the 30 day period.]

   [g. Predecessor/Successor Report: By activity number from lowest to

SECTION 01321N   Page 17

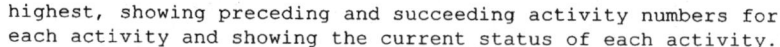

highest, showing preceding and succeeding activity numbers for each activity and showing the current status of each activity.]

****
NOTE: Include the following two paragraphs if
resource loading is specified in the paragraph
entitled "Cost and Resource Loading". If resource
loading is required, determine if only the Baseline
Network Analysis Schedule will be loaded or if
actual resource allocation is tracked in each
update. Tracking actual resources will increase the
cost of project scheduling and the information
should be available from the Daily Reports.
****

[h. Labor Staffing Report and Histogram: With each Baseline Network Analysis Schedule submittal[and each updated schedule], a planned early and planned late[versus actual] labor resource report and histogram will be provided.[The report and histogram shall be based upon and shall be in agreement with, the number of shifts and crew sizes by craft, in the Baseline Network Analysis Schedule (planned) and the Monthly Network Update (actual). Included in the report will be a tabular listing of each trade that worked on the activities during the construction period.]

i. Equipment Usage Report and Histogram: With each Baseline Network Analysis Schedule submittal[and each updated schedule], a planned early and planned late[versus actual] equipment resource report and histogram will be provided.[The report and histogram shall be based upon and shall be in agreement with the equipment allocation in the Baseline Network Analysis Schedule (planned) and the Monthly Network Update (actual). Included in the report will be a tabular listing of equipment (by year, make and model) that worked on the activities during the construction period.]]

1.7   SUBMISSION AND ACCEPTANCE

1.7.1   Preliminary Meeting

Prior to the preparation of the Construction Network Analysis Schedule for acceptance; the Contracting Officer, Contractor and the scheduler shall participate in a preliminary meeting to discuss the proposed schedule and requirements of this section prior to submission of the network.

[1.7.2   Design Network Analysis Schedule

****
NOTE: When Design-Build is being used in a project,
use this paragraph. When the Fast-Tracking is
required or an option for the project, include the
first bracketed sentence of this paragraph.
****

****

APPENDIX M

```
            NOTE: When WebCM is a requirement on this project,
            use the second set of bracketed sentences and delete
            the third bracketed sentence of this paragraph.
**************************************************************************
```

Submit the Design Network Analysis Schedule defining the planned operations during the design phase(s) of the contract. The general (summarized) approach for the construction phase(s) of the project shall also be indicated. Cost of activities expected to be completed or partially completed before submission of the Baseline Network Analysis Schedule shall be included.[When the project is being Fast-Tracked, the Design Network Analysis Schedule shall include all fast-tracked design phases, including the required or proposed design submittals within each phase that will occur during the duration of the project.] Submit three copies of both the design network diagrams and reports listed in paragraph entitled "Required Tabular Reports." In accordance with paragraph entitled "Monthly Network Analysis Updates" the design network may be used for requesting progress payments for a period not to exceed the design phase(s) of the contract. Submittal and acceptance of the Design Network Analysis Schedule is condition precedent to the processing of the Contractor's pay requests on this schedule. The activities and relationships of the design schedule shall coincide and mesh with the activities of the Baseline Network Analysis Schedule. As part of this submittal, provide the Project Name format (and Project Group Name if used) that will be used by the Contractor to identify initial schedule submittals, updates, fragnets, changes, etc. [Backed-up native files (.prx or .stx) for the schedule submittal will be posted to the NAVFAC WebCM internet site, as directed by the Contracting Officer. The project schedule will also be posted in the format specified as an Adobe PDF file with no relationship lines displayed in the graphic.][Include [1 copy][____ copies] of the Design Network Analysis Schedule on electronic media that is acceptable to the Contracting Officer.]]

1.7.3   Construction Network Analysis Schedule

```
**************************************************************************
            NOTE:  Include the first set of brackets if the
            project is Design Build, the second set of brackets
            will be used for Design-Bid-Build. When
            Fast-Tracking is required or an option for the
            project, include the third set of brackets.
**************************************************************************
```

```
**************************************************************************
            NOTE: When WebCM is a requirement on this project,
            use the fourth set of bracketed sentences and delete
            the fifth bracketed sentence of this paragraph.
**************************************************************************
```

[If design must be completed and accepted prior to construction, submit][Submit] the complete network analysis schedule and obtain acceptance prior to starting construction work.[If the project will be Fast-Tracked, each construction stage will be built upon the previous Fast-Tracked Baseline Schedule (including any interim updates thereto) and accepted prior to starting that stage of the construction work.] Submit

CONSTRUCTION SCHEDULING

[three][____] copies of the diagrams described in the paragraph entitled "Diagrams" and the reports listed in the paragraph entitled "Required Tabular Reports". As part of this submittal, provide the Project Name format (and Project Group Name if used) that will be used by the Contractor to identify initial schedule submittals, updates, fragnets, changes, etc. [Backed-up native files (.prx or .stx) for the schedule submittal will be posted to the NAVFAC WebCM internet site, as directed by the Contracting Officer. The project schedule will also be posted in the format specified as an Adobe PDF file with no relationship lines displayed in the graphic.][Include [1 copy][_____ copies] of the Construction Network Analysis Schedule on electronic media that is acceptable to the Contracting Officer.]

1.7.4   Review and Evaluation

After the Government's review(s) of the [Design Network Analysis Schedule and]Construction Network Analysis Schedule, the Contractor shall meet with the Contracting Officer to discuss the review and evaluation of the NAS submittal. Revisions necessary as a result of this review shall be resubmitted for acceptance within 10 calendar days after the meeting.

1.7.5   Baseline Network Analysis Schedule

Once review comments are resolved and the Contracting Officer has accepted the [Design Network Analysis Schedule and]Construction Network Analysis Schedule, the Contractor shall within 5 calendar days furnish:

    a. [Two][_____] copies of the network diagrams.

    b. [Two][_____] copies of the reports listed in paragraph entitled "Required Tabular Reports".

    [c. [Two][_____] copies of the Cash Flow S-Curve indicating the cash flow based upon both the projected early and late finish dates.]

```
**************************************************************************
                NOTE: When WebCM is a requirement on this project,
                use the third set of bracketed sentences and delete
                the fourth bracketed sentence of this paragraph.
**************************************************************************
```

    d. [Two][_____] sets of data disks containing the project schedule shall be provided for the initial submission and every periodic project update. [Backed-up native files (.prx or .stx) for the schedule submittal will be posted to the NAVFAC WebCM internet site, as directed by the Contracting Officer. The project schedule will also be posted in the format specified as an Adobe PDF file with no relationship lines displayed in the graphic.]Data shall be submitted on electronic media that is acceptable to the Contracting Officer. A permanent exterior label shall be affixed to each disk submitted. The label shall indicate the type of schedule ([Design NAS,]Construction NAS, Baseline, Update, Recovery, Change, etc.), full contract number, Project Name used to identify project in scheduling software, contract name & location, data status date, diskette number with total number of

APPENDIX M

diskettes in set, software name and version used to run the
schedule, and the name and telephone number of person responsible
for the schedule.

For major revisions, updates or changes to the network diagrams, once
accepted by the Contracting Officer, the Contractor shall submit these same
diagrams and reports.

1.7.6   Monthly Network Analysis Updates

At monthly intervals the Contractor and Government representatives will
meet to jointly update the project schedule and agree on percentage of
payment for each activity progressed during the update period. The purpose
of the meeting is to determine progress payment amounts for each activity,
allow all parties to evaluate project status at the data date, provide a
complete and accurate update of [design,]procurement and construction
progress, create an historical record of the project and establish
prediction of completion date(s) based upon current status. The Contractor
is responsible to gather all supporting documentation, present the update
data for the schedule and record the meeting minutes. All progress payment
amounts will be derived from and tied to the cost-loaded schedule
activities. Submit at monthly intervals a report of the actual [design and
]construction progress by updating the required reports and the time scaled
logic diagram. Meeting to update the schedule and the submission of an
error free, acceptable updated schedule to the Government is a condition
precedent to the processing of the Contractor's pay request. As a minimum,
the following actions will be accomplished during the meeting:

   a. Identify activities started and completed during the previous
       period and enter the Actual Start and Actual Finish dates. It
       will be understood that Actual Start is defined as the date that
       work begins on an activity with the intent to pursue the work
       represented by the activity to substantial completion, and Actual
       Finish is defined as the date that the activity's work is
       substantially complete to the point that its successor activity(s)
       may begin.

   b. Show estimated duration (in workdays) to complete each activity
       started but not completed (remaining duration).

   c. Indicate percentage of cost payable and percent of work complete
       as separate and independent entries for each activity. The
       assignment of an Actual Finish date to an activity does not imply
       that the activity's percent of payment will be statused to 100%.

   d. Reflect changes in the network diagram. All changes (i.e.,
       remaining duration changes, logic changes, new logic, conformed
       change orders, new activities, changes due to Conformed
       Modifications, changes in work sequence, entry of as-built
       relationship logic, etc.) shall be recorded and a note added to
       the activity log field. The log shall include as a minimum, the
       date and reason for the change, and description of the change.

   e. Submit [two][____] copies of a Narrative Report describing: 1)

SECTION 01321N   Page 21

CONSTRUCTION SCHEDULING

Progress made in each area of the project; 2) Changes in the following; activities, original durations, logic interdependencies, milestones, planned sequence of operations, critical path, and resource and loading; 3) Pending items and status thereof, including permits, change orders, and time extensions; 4) Status of Contract Completion Date and interim milestones; 5) Current and anticipated delays (describe cause of the delay and corrective action(s)); and 6) Description of current and future schedule problem areas. Each entry in the narrative report will cite the respective Activity ID and Activity Description.

    f. Submit [two][_____] copies of the reports listed in paragraph entitled "Required Tabular Reports".

    g. [Two][_____] hard copies of the network diagrams and [two][_____] sets of data disks.

    h. Submit [two][_____] copies of the Update Meeting minutes.

[1.7.7   Summary Network

****
NOTE: Before specifying Summary Networks, verify with the ROICC Office that the Summary will be useful on the project being designed. Choose type of summary to be provided. Area Code will be the typical sequence to choose unless the project is Phased, at which time either (but not both) may be chosen.
****

A summary network shall have the same network format as the Baseline Network Analysis Schedule. The summary network will contain a minimal number of activities that represent the general approach of work sequence. The Summary will be a time-scaled logical sequence of [Phase Code][Area Code]. The Contractor shall submit a summary network diagram along with the Baseline Network Analysis Schedule. A summary network update shall be submitted every [6][_____] months during the contract duration and immediately following acceptance of each major schedule change. Submit the following:

    a. [Two][_____] copies of the summary network diagram.

    b. [Two][_____] copies of the Activity ID Report.

    c. [Two][_____] copies of the Total Float Report.

    d. [Two][_____] copies of the Earned Value Report indicating the actual cash flow for the current updated (not summary) network based upon both the early and late start schedules.

]1.7.8   As-Built Schedule

APPENDIX M

```
*************************************************************************
            NOTE:  Before specifying As-Built Schedules, verify
            with the ROICC Office that the schedule will be
            required.
*************************************************************************
```

As a condition precedent to the release of retention and making final payment, the Contractor shall submit an "As-Built Schedule", which is the last schedule update. The As-Built Schedule shall reflect the exact manner in which the project was actually constructed (including actual start and finish dates, activities, sequences, and logic) and shall be certified by the Contractor's Project Manager and Construction Scheduler as being a true reflection of the way the project was actually constructed. If more than one person filled the position(s) during the course of the project, each person will provide certification for the period of time they were responsible.

1.8   CONTRACT MODIFICATION

When a contract modification to the work is required, submit proposed revisions to the network with a fragnet and a cost proposal for each proposed change. All modifications shall be incorporated into the network analysis system as separately identifiable activities broken down and inserted appropriately on the first update following issuance of a directive to proceed with the change. Submit [two][_____] copies of the Total Float Report, Log Report and a copy of the proposed Time Impact Analysis on disk, with the cost proposal. Unless the Contracting Officer requests otherwise, only conformed contract modification fragnets will be added into the subsequent monthly updates. All revisions to the current baseline schedule activities that are necessary to further refine the schedule so that the changed work activities can be logically tied to the schedule shall be made. Financial data shall not be incorporated into the schedule until the Contracting Officer signs the contract modification.

1.8.1   Time Impact Analysis:

The Time Impact Analysis method shall be used by the Contracting Officer and Contractor in determining if a time extension or reduction to the contract milestone date(s) is justified. The Contractor shall provide a Time Impact Analysis to the Contracting Officer for any proposed contract change or as support for a Value Engineering Proposal, Variance Request, Claim or Request for Equitable Adjustment by the Contractor. Submit the Time Impact Analysis schedule, reports, etc. on disk and as a printed/plotted hardcopy.

   a. The Contractor shall submit a Time Impact Analysis (TIA) illustrating the influence of each change or delay on the Contract Completion Date or milestones. Unless the Contracting Officer requests an interim update to the schedule, the current monthly updated schedule accepted by the Government shall be used to display the impacts of the change. Unless requested by the Contracting Officer, no other non-conformed changes will be incorporated into the schedule being used to justify the change impact.

CONSTRUCTION SCHEDULING

   b. Each TIA shall include a Fragmentary Network (fragnet) demonstrating how the Contractor proposes to incorporate the impact into the project schedule. A fragnet is defined as the sequence of new activities and/or activity revisions, logic relationships and resource changes that are proposed to be added to the existing schedule to demonstrate the influence of impacts to the schedule. The fragnet shall identify the predecessors to the new activities and demonstrate the impacts to successor activities. The Contractor shall provide a hardcopy printout of the fragnet activities and relationships being added and also insert the fragnet into the most current, accepted Monthly Network Analysis Update, run the schedule calculations and submit the impacted schedule with the proposal, claim, etc. Include a narrative report describing the effects of new activities and relationships to interim and contract completion dates, with each TIA. Submit time extension requests with a Time Impact Analysis and three hardcopies of the fragnet, impacted schedule (with fragnet loaded), Total Float Report, Narrative Report and Log Report.

   c. Following the Contractor's receipt of a contract modification on a Standard Form 30 signed by the Government; all changes in the fragnet used to determine impacts, shall be incorporated into the schedule. Changes will occur during the next monthly schedule update meeting.

1.8.2   No Reservation-Of-Rights

All direct costs, indirect costs, and time extensions will be negotiated and made full, equitable and final at the time of modification issuance.

1.9   CHANGES TO THE NETWORK ANALYSIS SCHEDULE

If changes in the method of operating and scheduling are desired, the Contracting Officer shall be notified in writing stating the reasons for the change. If the Contracting Officer considers these changes to be of a major nature, the Contractor may be required to revise and submit for acceptance, without additional cost to the Government, the network diagrams and required reports. A change may be considered of a major nature if the estimated time required or actually used for an activity or the network logic has varied from the original plan to a degree that there is a reasonable doubt as to the effect on the contract completion date(s)[or phase completion dates]. Changes that affect activities with adequate float time shall be considered a major change when their cumulative effect could extend the contract completion date.

1.10   FLOAT

Use of float suppression techniques, such as; preferential sequencing (arranging critical path through activities more susceptible to Government caused delay), lag logic restraints, zero total or free float constraints, extended activity times, or imposing constraint dates other than as required by the contract, shall be cause for rejection of the project

APPENDIX M

schedule or its updates. The use of Resource Leveling (or similar software features) used for the purpose of artificially adjusting activity durations to consume float and influence the critical path is expressly prohibited.

1.10.1   Definitions of Float

Free Float is the length of time the start of an activity can be delayed without delaying the start of a successor activity. Total Float is the length of time along a given network path that the actual start and finish of activity(s) can be delayed without delaying the project completion date. Project Float is the length of time between the Contractor's Early Completion (or Substantial Completion or similar activity) and the Contract Completion Date.

1.10.2   Ownership of Float

Float available in the schedule, at any time shall not be considered for the exclusive use of either the Government or the Contractor. During the course of contract execution, any float generated due to the efficiencies of either party is not for the sole use of the party generating the float; rather it is a shared commodity to be reasonably used by either party. Efficiencies gained as a result of favorable weather within a calendar month, where the number of days of normally anticipated weather is less than expected, will also contribute to the reserve of float. A schedule showing work completing in less time than the Contract time, and accepted by the Government, will be considered to have Project Float. Project Float will be a resource available to both the Government and the Contractor. No time extensions will be granted nor delay damages paid unless a delay occurs which impacts the Project's critical path, consumes all available float or contingency time, and extends the work beyond the Contract Completion Date.

1.10.3   Negative Float

Negative float will not be a basis for requesting time extensions. Any extension of time will be addressed in accordance with the paragraphs entitled "CONTRACT MODIFICATION". Scheduled completion date(s) that extend beyond the contract[or phase] completion date(s) (evidenced by negative float) may be used in computations for assessment of payment withholdings. The use of this computation is not to be construed as a means of acceleration.

1.11   THREE-WEEK LOOK AHEAD SCHEDULE

****
            NOTE: Consult with the local ROICC Office if the
            bracketed phrase will be used.
****

To provide a more detailed day-to-day planning of upcoming construction work, the Contractor shall prepare and issue detailed work plans that coordinate with and supplement the above defined network analysis. The work plans shall be keyed to the CPM activity numbers and shall be submitted each week and shall show the project activities that will occur

CONSTRUCTION SCHEDULING

during the current and following two-week interval. Additionally, the critical path activities are to be identified on the 3-Week Look Ahead Schedule. The schedule will be a bar chart type schedule prepared by the Contractor in sufficient detail to define the work to be accomplished, the crews, construction tools and equipment to be used during the current and next two-week interval. The bar charts shall be formatted to allow reproduction on 8 1/2 by 11 sheets. Three copies of the bar chart schedules shall be delivered to the Contracting Officer[not less than 3 work hours prior to the start of the weekly coordination meeting].

[1.12   WEEKLY COORDINATION MEETING

****
        NOTE: Consult with the local ROICC Office on
        whether to use this paragraph.
****

In conjunction with the receipt of the 3-Week Look Ahead Schedule, a coordination meeting will be held each week [on-site][in the Contracting Officer's conference room] to discuss the work schedule. The Contractor shall make a presentation of the previously submitted and current 3-Week Look Ahead Schedule to the Contracting Officer so as to provide an overview of the project's schedule and provide an opportunity to discuss items of coordination. Consideration of materials, crews, and equipment shall be addressed to ascertain their respective availability. The meeting shall identify actions necessary to provide adherence to the 3-Week Look Ahead Schedule and the overall network for the project defined above. The Contractor will take meeting minutes. All meeting minute entries will be keyed to the schedule activity number(s) being addressed. Within one day of the meeting, the Contractor will provide a draft copy of the meeting minutes to the Contracting Officer for review and comment. Final copies of the minutes containing the comments provided by the Contracting Officer will be issued within 3 days of the meeting.

]1.13   CORRESPONDENCE AND TEST REPORTS

All correspondence (e.g., letters, Requests for Information (RFIs), e-mails, meeting minute items, Production and QC Daily Reports, material delivery tickets, photographs, etc.) shall reference the Schedule Activity Number(s) that are being addressed. All test reports (e.g., concrete, soil compaction, weld, pressure, etc.) shall reference the Schedule Activity Number(s) that are being addressed.

PART 2   PRODUCTS

Not used.

PART 3   EXECUTION

Not used.
         -- End of Section --

APPENDIX N

UNIFIED FACILITIES GUIDE SPECIFICATIONS FOR NETWORK ANALYSIS SYSTEMS (APR. 2002)

```
*************************************************************
USACE / NAVFAC / AFCESA            UFGS-01321N (April 2002)
                                   -------------------------
Preparing Activity: NAVFAC         Superseding
                                   UFGS-01321N (February 2002)

             UNIFIED FACILITIES GUIDE SPECIFICATIONS

         Revised throughout - changes not indicated by CHG tags
*************************************************************

                        SECTION TABLE OF CONTENTS

                      DIVISION 01 - GENERAL REQUIREMENTS

                              SECTION 01321N

                       NETWORK ANALYSIS SCHEDULES (NAS)

                                   04/02


PART 1   GENERAL

    1.1    DESCRIPTION
    1.2    SUBMITTALS
    1.3    SCHEDULE ACCEPTANCE
       1.3.1    Schedule Acceptance Prior to Start of Work
       1.3.2    Acceptance
    1.4    SOFTWARE
       1.4.1    Computer Hardware
       1.4.2    Software Training
    1.5    QUALIFICATIONS
    1.6    NETWORK SYSTEM FORMAT
       1.6.1    Diagrams
       1.6.2    Quantity and Numbering of Activities
          1.6.2.1    HVAC TAB Activities
          1.6.2.2    Procurement Activities
          1.6.2.3    Government Activities
          1.6.2.4    Construction Activities
          1.6.2.5    Anticipated Weather Delays
          1.6.2.6    Activity Properties
       1.6.3    Mathematical Analysis
       1.6.4    Additional Requirements
       1.6.5    Required Reports
    1.7    SUBMISSION AND ACCEPTANCE
       1.7.1    Preliminary Meeting
       1.7.2    Schedule Development Session:
       1.7.3    Preliminary Network Analysis Schedule
       1.7.4    Network Analysis Schedule
       1.7.5    Review and Evaluation
       1.7.6    Accepted Network Analysis Schedule
       1.7.7    Monthly Network Analysis Updates


                     SECTION 01321N    Page 1
```

CONSTRUCTION SCHEDULING

```
      1.7.8    Summary Network
      1.7.9    As-Built Schedule
   1.8    CONTRACT MODIFICATION
      1.8.1    Time Impact Analysis:
      1.8.2    No Reservation-Of-Rights
   1.9    CHANGES TO THE NETWORK ANALYSIS SCHEDULE
   1.10   FLOAT
      1.10.1   Definitions of Float or Slack
      1.10.2   Ownership of Float
      1.10.3   Negative Float
   1.11   TIME EXTENSIONS
   1.12   MONTHLY COORDINATION MEETING
   1.13   BIWEEKLY WORK SCHEDULE
   1.14   WEEKLY COORDINATION MEETING
   1.15   CORRESPONDENCE AND TEST REPORTS

PART 2   PRODUCTS


PART 3   EXECUTION


-- End of Section Table of Contents --
```

APPENDIX N

```
***************************************************************
USACE / NAVFAC / AFCESA              UFGS-01321N (April 2002)
                                     -------------------------------
Preparing Activity: NAVFAC           Superseding
                                     UFGS-01321N (February 2002)

              UNIFIED FACILITIES GUIDE SPECIFICATIONS

          Revised throughout - changes not indicated by CHG tags
***************************************************************

                         SECTION 01321N

                  NETWORK ANALYSIS SCHEDULES (NAS)
                              04/02

***************************************************************
```

> NOTE: This guide specification covers the preparation and use of a contractor prepared Network Analysis Schedules. This section will be used on most projects in lieu of Section 01320, "Construction Progress Documentation." Section 01320 shall be used only when a hand-drawn bar chart is required for management and oversight of a project. As prescribed in FAR 36.515, the Contracting Officer may insert the clause "Schedules for Construction Contracts" (FAR 52.236-15) in solicitations and contracts when a fixed-price construction contract is contemplated, the contract amount is expected to exceed the simplified acquisition threshold, and the period of actual work performance exceeds 60 days. This clause may be inserted in such contracts when work performance is expected to last less than 60 days and an unusual situation exists that warrants impositions of the requirements. This clause should not be used in the same contract with clauses covering other management approaches for ensuring that a contractor makes adequate progress. Coordination is required with other Division 1 specifications when Network Analysis Schedules is not specified.
>
> Comments and suggestion on this specification are welcome and should be directed to the technical proponent of the specification. A listing of the technical proponents, including their organization designation and telephone number, is on the Internet.
>
> Recommended changes to a UFGS should be submitted as a Criteria Change Request (CCR).
>
> Use of electronic communication is encouraged.

SECTION 01321N   Page 3

CONSTRUCTION SCHEDULING

>   Brackets are used in the text to indicate designer
>   choices or locations where text must be supplied by
>   the designer.
> **
> **
>   NOTE: This guide specification requires project
>   costs to be loaded into the schedule and assigned to
>   activities. When using this section, delete the
>   requirement for "Schedule of Prices" in Section
>   01200 "Price and Payment Procedures".
> **

PART 1   GENERAL

1.1   DESCRIPTION

Prepare a progress chart pursuant to the clause entitled "FAR 52.236-15, Schedules for Construction Contracts" of the Contract Clauses that shall consist of a network analysis system. The network analysis system shall consist of the network analysis schedule (diagram), mathematical analysis, and associated reports. The scheduling of construction shall be the responsibility of the Contractor. Submission of progress and revision data will be used to measure work progress, aid to evaluate time extensions, and provide basis of all progress payments. The Critical Path Method (CPM) of network calculation shall be used to generate the project schedule and will utilize the Precedence Diagram technique to satisfy both time and cost applications. All progress payment amounts will be derived from and tied to the cost-loaded schedule activities.

1.2   SUBMITTALS

> **
>   NOTE: The "G" in submittal tags following each
>   submittal item indicates Government acceptance and
>   should be retained. Add "G" in submittal tags
>   following any added submittals that are determined
>   to require Government acceptance. Submittal items
>   not designated with a "G" will be approved by the QC
>   organization.
> **

Submit the following in accordance with Section 01330, "Submittal Procedures."

   SD-01 Preconstruction Submittals

      [Qualifications; G]

      Standard Activity Coding Dictionary

      [Schedule Development Session scheduler/planner; G]

      [Preliminary Network Analysis Schedule; G]

SECTION 01321N   Page 4

APPENDIX N

        Network Analysis Schedule; G

        Accepted Network Analysis Schedule; G

        Summary Network

        As-Built Schedule

    SD-07 Certificates

        Monthly Network Analysis Updates; G

    SD-11 Closeout Submittals

1.3   SCHEDULE ACCEPTANCE

Review comments made by the Government on the Contractor's construction schedule will not relieve the Contractor from compliance with requirements of the Contract Documents. The Contractor is responsible for scheduling, sequencing, and prosecuting the Work to comply with the requirements of the Contract Documents. Government acceptance extends only to the activities of the contractor's schedule that the Government has been assigned responsibility for and agrees it is responsible. The Government will also review for contract imposed schedule constraints and conformance, and cost loading of the CPM activities. Comments offered on other parts of the schedule which the Contractor is assigned responsibility are offered as a courtesy and are not conditions of government acceptance; but are for the general conformance with established industry schedule concepts.

[1.3.1   Schedule Acceptance Prior to Start of Work

****
        **NOTE: Prior to including or editing this paragraph,
        contact the ROICC Field Office to determine if the
        contractor will be allowed to start work prior to
        acceptance of the project schedule.**
****

The Accepted Network described in the paragraph entitled "Accepted Network Analysis Schedule" must be submitted and accepted by the government before the contractor will be allowed to start work.

]1.3.2   Acceptance

      a.   When the Accepted Network Analysis Schedule is submitted and accepted by the Contracting Officer, it will be considered the "Baseline CPM Schedule". The Baseline CPM Schedule will then be used by the Contractor for planning, organizing, and directing the work; reporting progress; and requesting payment for work accomplished. The schedule will be updated monthly by the Contractor and submitted monthly with the progress pay request to reflect the current status of the work. [For payment requests made after the period covered by the Preliminary Schedule,] The

CONSTRUCTION SCHEDULING

submittal and acceptance of the Accepted Network Analysis Schedule and accurate updated schedules accompanying the pay requests are both conditions precedent to processing pay requests. Only bonds will be paid prior to acceptance of the Accepted Network Analysis Schedule.

b. Submittal of the Network, and subsequent schedule updates, will be understood to be the Contractor's representation that the submitted schedule meets all of the requirements of the Contract Documents, accurately reflects the work accomplished, and that Work will be executed in the sequence indicated on the submitted schedule.

1.4   SOFTWARE

****
NOTE: Check with the ROICC Field Office for local personal computer (PC) equipment capacity and edit as appropriate. The Contractor's software may require more computer capacity than the ROICC Field Office has available, in which case, subject to the written approval of the Contracting Officer, the contract may include the requirement for the contractor to provide hardware and software necessary to allow the government to monitor work progress and process payments. At the end of the contract term, this equipment software may be specified to remain the property of the contractor or become government property as determined to be most cost effective by the Contracting Officer. Should this equipment be specified to become government property, all property control regulations must be followed.
****

****
NOTE: Include the bracketed sentences requiring Primavera software for LANTDIV, PACDIV and SOUTHDIV projects. Consult with the EFD/EFA 05 and/or Field Office to determine which software will be used. As a general guide; for projects less than $5 Mil use SureTrak and for projects $5 Mil and greater use P3.
****

[The scheduling software that will be utilized by the government on this project is [SureTrak by Primavera Systems, Inc.] [Primavera Project Planner (P3) by Primavera Systems, Inc. If the contractor chooses to use an equally capable program, the contractor shall convert all data into Primavera Machine Readable Format (Lotus, D-Base, Excel, etc.) prior to submission of all schedule inputs, included but not limited to the initial schedule, monthly updates, and changes to the schedule. It is the responsibility of the Contractor to ensure all data elements and logic required by this specification are kept intact during the conversion to Primavera. If scheduling software other than Primavera is being used,

APPENDIX N

provide]] [Provide] a licensed copy of the Contractor's scheduling software and data. The software will be the most current version available and will be compatible with all MS-Windows operating systems (e.g., Win NT, Win 95, etc.). The scheduling software package shall contain all user manuals normally provided by the software distributor. If the Contractor upgrades their software during the course of the contract, the upgrade shall also be provided to the Contracting Officer. The software will remain the property of the government.

[1.4.1   Computer Hardware

[The network analysis software shall be capable of running on a [Government owned] [Contractor provided] personal computer.] [Provide and maintain a [_____] personal computer (PC) capable of running the network analysis software specified herein.] All necessary software and hardware will be provided to make the system a complete and useable package.] [Provide a [_____] [printer] [plotter] with necessary cables. The contractor PC will remain the property of the [Contractor] [Government].

][1.4.2   Software Training

****
           NOTE: Select and edit this paragraph when training
           is needed. Coordinate with the ROICC Field Office.
****

[If software other than Primavera is used by the Contractor, provide][Provide] schedule software training for [two] [_____] Government personnel. A firm accredited by the scheduling software manufacturer, as their authorized trainer shall conduct the training. The training shall last a minimum of 24 hours per individual. Provide course material the training firm normally distributes at their software classes. Provide all necessary materials and equipment to conduct the training. The Contractor shall provide training within 10 working days after notification to the Contractor, by the Contracting Officer. Unless agreed to by the Contracting Officer, the training site shall be at the Contracting Office.

][1.5   QUALIFICATIONS

****
           NOTE: Before editing the following paragraph,
           coordinate with the ROICC Field Office.
****

The Contractor shall designate a [full time] [part time] Scheduler that will be responsible for the development, preparation, and maintenance of an accurate, computerized Network Analysis Schedule. [Part time is defined as the scheduler performing on-site coordination, attending project meetings, and updates for [_____] hours per work week.] The Scheduler shall have previously developed, created and maintained at least [2] [_____] previous computerized schedules of similar size and complexity of this contract. A resume outlining the qualifications of the scheduler shall be submitted for acceptance to the Contracting Officer. If at a later date, the Contracting Officer considers the Contractor's Scheduler to be incompetent or

CONSTRUCTION SCHEDULING

objectionable, the Contractor will propose a new Scheduler, meeting the qualification requirements. Payments will not be processed until an acceptable Scheduler is provided.

]1.6   NETWORK SYSTEM FORMAT

The system shall consist of time scaled logic diagrams accompanying mathematical analyses and specified reports.

1.6.1   Diagrams

Show the order and interdependence of activities and the sequence in which the work is to be accomplished as planned. The basic concept of a network analysis diagram will be followed to show how the start of a given activity is dependent on the completion of preceding activities and how its completion restricts or restrains the start of following activities. Diagrams shall be [organized by [Work Phase][Area Code] and] sortedby Early Start Date and will show a continuous flow from left to right with no logic (relationship lines) from right to left. With the exception of the Project Start and Project Completion milestone activities, no activities will be open-ended; each activity will have predecessor and successor ties. The diagram shall clearly show the activities of the critical path. No onsite construction activity shall have duration in excess of 20 working days. Once an activity exists on the schedule it may not be deleted and must remain in the logic. No more than [20] [____] percent of the activities may be critical or near critical. Critical will be defined as having zero days of Total Float. "Near critical" will be defined as having Total Float in the range of [1 to 14] [[____] to [____]] days. Show the following information on the diagrams for each activity:

   a.   Activity/Event Number

   b.   Activity Description

   c.   Original Duration in work days

   d.   Actual Duration in Work Days

   e.   Early Start Date

   f.   Early Finish Date

   g.   Total Float (or Slack)

   h.   Responsibility Code

Provide network diagrams on ANSI E sheets. Updated diagrams shall show the date of the latest revision.

1.6.2   Quantity and Numbering of Activities

****
          **NOTE: A good knowledge of construction is required
          when determining the numbers of activities for a**

APPENDIX N

network analysis. Factors such as the nature of the work, geographical location, completion time, complexity ("the complexity of a project is related to the number of specification sections, the number of buildings, special phasing requirements and special quality control requirements"), cost of maintaining each activity throughout the life of the contract and level of use by field management personnel must be considered. As a general rule, use the following guidance:

PROJECT CONSTRUCTION COST	NUMBER OF CONSTRUCTION ACTIVITIES RECOMMENDED
Up to $1,000,000	150 $\pm$ activities
$1,000,000 to $2,000,000	150 to 200 activities
$2,000,000 to $5,000,000	200 to 1000 activities
$5,000,000 to $10,000,000	1000 to 2000 activities
Over $10,000,000	2500 $\pm$ activities

*Important

-When selecting the number of activities, please keep in mind the cost added to the contract. An activity needs to be maintained throughout the life of the contract and the use of too many activities will unnecessarily increase the total contract cost.

-The guidance provided above is meant as GUIDANCE. Use your best judgement for selecting number of activities. Some contracts may require less number of activities than recommended amounts. (Ex: A contract to stripe a 500-mile stretch of highway may have a project cost of $6,000,000 but it should not require between 1000 to 2000 activities).

****

Numbering shall be assigned so that, in general, predecessor activity numbers are smaller numerically than the successor activity numbers. Skip numbering shall be used on the network to allow insertion of additional activities for contract modifications and logic changes. The minimum number of construction activities in the final network diagram shall be [_____]. Types of activities included in the schedule are specified below.

[1.6.2.1   HVAC TAB Activities

****
NOTE: This paragraph will be used only when HVAC Testing, Adjusting and Balancing work is specified in the contract specifications.
****

Requirements for the activities related to HVAC TAB work, Section entitled,

"HVAC Testing/Adjusting/Balancing," are specified in Section entitled, "Price and Payment Procedures."

1.6.2.2   Procurement Activities

Tasks related to the procurement of material or equipment shall be included as separate activities in the project schedule. Examples of procurement activities include, but are not limited to: Material/equipment submittal preparation, submittal and approval of material/equipment; delivery of O&M manuals; material/equipment fabrication and delivery, delivery of extra parts, extra stock, special tools, notification of Government Furnished Material/Equipment delivery requirement, etc. As a minimum, separate procurement activities will be provided for every specification section. If the Contractor intends on using Just-In-Time (JIT) delivery methods, the schedule will show each JIT delivery with relationship tie to the Construction Activity specifically for the JIT delivery. Material and equipment for which payment will be requested in advance of installation shall be cost-loaded with the procurement costs. All activities within a procurement process/cycle will have a unique identifier in the activity code to show their relationships and will extend to the related construction activities (i.e., Work Category).

If the Government's action on any submittal is "Disapproved" or "Revise and Resubmit", a new series of Procurement Activities will be inserted into the schedule. Predecessor for the new submittal preparation activity will be the original approval activity and the successor of the new approval activity will be the fabrication/deliver activity for the equipment or material.

1.6.2.3   Government Activities

Government and other agency activities that could impact progress shall be clearly identified. Government activities include, but are not limited to; Government approved submittal reviews, Government conducted inspections/tests, utility outages, Notice(s) to Proceed and delivery of Government Furnished Material/Equipment. Show activities indicating Government furnished materials and equipment utilizing delivery dates indicated in "FAR 52.245-2, Government Property (Fixed-Price Contracts)." Government activities will be driven by calendars that reflect Saturdays, Sundays and all Federal Holidays as non-work days.

1.6.2.4   Construction Activities

Construction activities shall include, but are not limited to: Tasks related to mobilization/demobilization; the installation of temporary or permanent work by tradesman; testing and inspections of installed work by technicians, inspectors or engineers; start-up and testing of equipment; commissioning of building and related systems; scheduling of specified manufacture's representatives; final clean-up; training to be provided; and administrative tasks necessary to start, proceed with, accomplish or finalize the contract. Contractor activities will be driven by calendars that reflect Saturdays, Sundays and all Federal Holidays as non-work days.

1.6.2.5   Anticipated Weather Delays

APPENDIX N

Schedule activity duration(s) shall be formulated with allowance for normal adverse weather conditions. Any activity duration which could be impacted by normally anticipated adverse weather (precipitation, high or low temperature, wind, etc.), due to the time period which the Contractor has scheduled the work, shall include an adjustment to include the anticipated weather delay. The Contractor shall anticipate delay by comparing the contractually imposed environmental restrictions in the Contract Documents to the National Oceanic and Atmospheric Association's (NOAA) historical monthly averages for the NOAA location [at (<u>Enter NOAA Station here</u>)] [closest to the project site]. The number of anticipated adverse weather delays allocated to an activity will be reflected in the activity's calendar. A lost workday, due to weather conditions, is defined as a day in which the contractor's workforce cannot work 50 percent or more of the day. The Contractor shall immediately notify the Contracting Officer when a lost day has occurred due to weather and will record on the Daily Reports, the occurrence of adverse weather and resultant impact to the normally scheduled work. If the number of actual adverse weather delay days exceeds the number of days anticipated, the Contracting Officer will convert any qualifying delays to calendar days, giving full consideration for equivalent fair weather work days and issue a modification in accordance with the contract clauses.

1.6.2.6 Activity Properties

Schedule activities will have the following properties:

a. Standard Activity Coding Dictionary: The Contractor shall submit a coding scheme for Schedule Activity Numbers that shall be used throughout the project. The coding scheme submitted shall list the values for each activity code category and translate those values into project specific designations. Code length shall not exceed [10] [____] characters. Once accepted, the coding scheme will be used for the duration of the project.

b. Activity Description: Each activity shall have a narrative description consisting of a Verb or work function (e.g.; form, pour, excavate), an Object (e.g.; slab, footing, underfloor plumbing), and Area (e.g.; 3rd floor, northeast quadrant, basement).

****
NOTE: Include the following paragraph when the project includes the requirement for Phased Construction.
****

[c. Work Phase: If phasing is specified in the contract, all activities shall be identified in the project schedule by the phase of work in which the activity occurs. Activities shall not be contained in more than one Work Phase.]

d. Work Category: All Activities shall be identified in the project schedule according to the work category which best describes the

CONSTRUCTION SCHEDULING

activity. Examples of work categories are procurement, government, and construction activities that are all related to a single Definable Feature of Work. Activities shall not be contained in more than one Work Category.

e. Area Code: All activities shall be identified in the project schedule by the Area Code in which the activity occurs. Activities shall not be contained in more than one Area Code. Area is defined as a distinct separation in construction, such as a story of construction, separate structure, usage or function difference, utility distribution systems, etc.

f. Responsibility Code: All activities in the project schedule shall be identified with the party responsible to perform the task. Responsibility includes, but is not limited to; the prime contractor, subcontracting firm, or Government agency performing a given task. Activities shall not belong to more than one responsible party. The responsible party for each activity shall be identified by a responsibility code. For example, a responsibility code value, "ELEC", may be identified as "Electrical Subcontractor."

g. CSI Code: All activities in the project schedule shall be identified with its respective 5-digit Specification Section number. Activities shall not belong to more than one Section number. If an activity does not have an applicable CSI Code, (such as "Mobilize"), the code will be "00000".

h. Drawing Code: All activities in the project schedule shall be identified with its respective project drawing code. The drawing code is the Sheet Number on the primary project drawing which indicates the work to be performed. Activities shall not belong to more than one Drawing Code. Examples of Drawing Codes are "C-10", "C.10" or "C10". The code system will allow organizing all activities by drawing code in alpha and numeric order. If an activity does not have an applicable Drawing Code, (such as "Mobilize"), the code will be "00000".

i. Modification Code: The Modification Code shall identify activities that are modified or added by contract modification. Activities shall not belong to more than one Modification Code. The Government will assign the modification number, which will be shown on the SF 30. Use a shortened version of the modification number for the code (e.g.; A00010 = 010).

j. Request for Equitable Adjustment (REA) or Claim Code: Activities that are modified or added, as a result of a Contractor's REA or Claim shall be identified by a code generated by the Contractor. Activities shall not belong to more than one REA or Claim Code.

k. The Three Phases of Control (Preparatory, Initial, and Follow-up): For each Definable Feature of Work identified in the Contractor's Quality Control Plan, include an activity for the Preparatory Phase. The Initial Phase and Follow-up Phase will be represented

APPENDIX N

by the Construction Activities in the schedule.

l. Project Milestone Dates: Dates shall be shown on the diagram for the start of the project, any contract required interim start and completion dates, contract completion date and other significant milestones.

m. Scheduled Project Duration: The schedule duration shall extend from notice-to-proceed to the contract completion date.

n. Project Start Date Milestones: The schedule shall start no earlier than the contract award date and the project duration (Day 1) will start on the Notice-to-Proceed (NTP) date. The Contractor shall include as the first activity in the schedule, an activity named "Contract Award" and another activity on the NTP date named "Start Project". Both activities will be zero duration, with constrained start dates equal to the contract award and NTP dates.

o. Constraint of Last Activity Milestone: The Contractor shall include as the last activity in the project schedule, an activity named "End Project". The "End Project" activity shall be zero duration with a mandatory finish constraint equal to the contract completion date for the project. Calculation of project updates shall be such that if the finish of the last activity falls after the contract completion date, then the float calculation shall reflect negative float on the critical path.

p. Early Project Completion: In the event the Contractor's project schedule shows completion of the project prior to the contract completion date, the Contractor shall include an activity named "Contractor Early Completion". The activity shall be a zero duration milestone with an unconstrained date representing the Contractor's Early Completion date.

q. Substantial Completion: If the contractor elects to include an activity for Substantial Completion, then it is agreed that Substantial Completion will be the point in time that the Government considers the project is complete and ready for its intended use. The activity will be named "Substantial Completion". The activity shall be a zero duration milestone with an unconstrained date representing the Contractor's Substantial Completion date.

****
NOTE: Include the following three paragraphs when the project includes the requirement for Phased Construction.
****

[r. Phase Start Milestone: The Contractor shall include as the first activity for a project phase, an activity named "Start Phase X", where "X" identifies the phase of work. The "Start Phase X" activity shall be zero duration with an unconstrained start date equal to the date of the Phase NTP. This unconstrained start date

SECTION 01321N   Page 13

CONSTRUCTION SCHEDULING

is not a release from contractually required start dates, but is left unconstrained to allow the schedule logic to calculate without hindrance.

s. End Phase Milestone: The Contractor shall include as the last activity in a project phase, an activity named "End Phase X" where "X" identifies the phase of work. The "End Phase X" activity shall be zero duration with an unconstrained late finish date equal to the contract phase completion date. This unconstrained completion date is not a release from contractually required finish dates, but is left unconstrained to allow the schedule logic to calculate without hindrance.

t. Early Phase Completion: If the contractor expects to finish prior to the contract phase completion date, the milestone will show an early finish date equal to the Contractor's early finish date. The name of the activity will be "Early Phase Completion" and will be zero duration with an unconstrained date representing the contractor's early phase completion date.]

****
NOTE: Include Summary Activities if Summary Networks will be requested or if repetitive groups of activities will be used in a project (e.g. similar housing units being built several times over). Also include if Summaries will assist in keeping Customer or Higher Management appraised of progress.
****

[u. Summary (a.k.a., Banding or Hammock) Activities: The Contractor shall include special activities that are a summary of a chain of activities. The start of the activity will be the start date of the first activity in the chain and the finish date will be the finish date of the last activity in the chain. Generalized work sequences, Categories of Work and all Phase of Work activity chains will be summarized.]

v. Activity/Event Constraints: Date/time constraint(s), other than those required by the contract, will not be allowed unless accepted by the Contracting Officer.

w. Leads and Lags: Leads or lags will not be used when the creation of an activity will perform the same function (e.g., concrete cure time). Lag durations contained in the project schedule shall not have a negative value. The use of any lead or lag will be explained in the Narrative Report.

x. Default Progress Data Disallowed: Actual Start and Finish dates shall not be automatically updated by default mechanisms that may be included in the CPM scheduling software system. Actual Start and Actual Finish dates on the CPM schedule shall match the dates provided from Contractor Quality Control and Production Reports. These reports will be the sole basis for updating the schedule.

APPENDIX N

Work activities will be updated by actual work progression rather than being cash flow driven. The updating of the percent complete and the remaining duration of any activity shall be independent functions; program features that calculate one of these parameters from the other shall be disabled. Out-of-Sequence progress (if applicable) shall be handled through Retained Logic, not the Default Option of Progress Override. Actual labor and equipment hours used on activities will be derived from the daily reports.

1.6.3   Mathematical Analysis

The network diagram mathematical analysis shall include a tabulation of each activity shown on the detailed network diagrams. Provide the following information as a minimum for each activity:

a. Activity/Event number

b. Activity/Event description

c. Estimated duration of activities (by work days)

d. Earliest start date (by calendar date)

e. Earliest finish date (by calendar date)

f. Actual start date (by calendar date)

g. Actual finish date (by calendar date)

h. Latest start date (by calendar date)

i. Latest finish date (by calendar date)

j. Total float or slack

k. Material/Equipment costs will be assigned to their respective Procurement Activities (i.e., the delivery activity). Costs for installation of the material/equipment (labor, construction equipment, and temporary materials) will be assigned to their respective Construction Activities. The value of inspection/testing activities will not be less than [10] [_____] percent of the total costs for Procurement and Construction Activities. Evenly disperse overhead and profit to each activity over the duration of the project.

l. Responsibility code (including prime contractor, subcontractors, suppliers, Government, or other party responsible for accomplishment of an activity.)

m. Area Code

n. Manpower required (crew size)

o. Percentage of activity duration completed

SECTION 01321N   Page 15

CONSTRUCTION SCHEDULING

    p.   Contractor's earnings based on accepted work-in-place.

The program or means used in making the mathematical computation shall be capable of compiling the total value of completed and partially completed activities. The program shall also be capable of accepting revised completion dates as modified by approved time extensions and recompilation of tabulation dates/costs and float accordingly. The total of all cost loaded activities; including costs for material and equipment delivered for installation on the project, and manpower and construction equipment loaded construction activities, shall total to 100 percent of the value of the contract.

[1.6.4   Additional Requirements

****

NOTE: The information required by the following paragraphs are optional and typically not needed for routine work. Include on projects with critical completion dates. Manpower and equipment loading schedules are of primary importance to the Contractor in deciding the most efficient use of personnel resources and optimizing equipment usage and is the basis of activity duration estimates. Since these decisions are the responsibility of the Contractor's management process, the information value to the Contracting Officer is in assuring that the planned manpower and equipment are being supplied throughout the course of the project.

****

In addition to the tabulation of activities, in the Paragraph entitled "Mathematical Analysis", include the following data:

    a.   On-site manpower loading schedule: Each construction activity shall have an estimate of the number of workers per day by trade, man-hours per day by trade and total expected hours used by trade during the execution of the activity. If no workers are required for an activity, then the activity shall be identified as using zero workers per day.

    b.   Equipment loading schedule: Each construction activity shall have an estimate of the equipment used per day, number of units per day and total expected hours for each piece of equipment used during the duration of the activity. Include a description of the major items of construction equipment planned for each construction activity on the project. The description shall include the year, make, model, and capacity. If no equipment is required for an activity, then the activity shall be identified as using zero equipment per day.

]1.6.5   Required Reports

****

SECTION 01321N   Page 16

APPENDIX N

> NOTE: Consult with the ROICC Field Office to identify which of the following reports are preferred. Always include Earned Value Report and Log Report.

****

The following reports will be made available in the schedule submittals and in each updated schedule submission provided on disk by the Contractor:

a. By the preceding event number from lowest to highest and then in the order of the following activity number (Activity Identification Report) showing the current status of all activities.

b. By the amount of total float, from lowest to highest and then in order of [activity number] [early start date] (Total Float or Slack Report) showing all incomplete activities.

c. By latest allowable start dates and then in order of activity numbers (Late Start Report).

d. Earned Value Report listing all activities having a budget amount and cost. A compilation of total earnings on the project from the notice to proceed to the most recent monthly progress payment request and the difference between the previous request amount and the current payment request amount. Sort report first by resource and then by activity.

e. By earliest allowable start dates and then in order of activity number (Early Start Report).

f. By tasks scheduled to start and finish by the end of the next pay period (30-Day Look Ahead).

g. With each updated schedule submission, provide a computer generated Log Report using a recognized schedule comparision software listing all changes made between the previous schedule and current updated schedule. Identify the name of the previous schedule and name of the current schedule being compared. This report will as a minimum show changes for: Added & Deleted Activities, Original Durations, Remaining Durations, Activity Percent Complete, Total Float (or Slack), Free Float, Calendars, Descriptions, Constraints (added, deleted or changed), Actual Starts/Finishes, Added/Deleted Resources, Resource Quantities, Costs, Resource Percents, Added/Deleted Relations, Changed Relation Lags, Changed Driving Relations, and Changed Critical Status.

h. By the activity number from lowest to highest, showing preceding and succeeding activity numbers for each activity (Predecessor/Successor Report), and showing the current status of each activity.

****

SECTION 01321N   Page 17

CONSTRUCTION SCHEDULING

****
NOTE: Include the following two paragraphs if the requirements of the paragraph entitled "Additional Requirements" are specified.
****

[i. Manpower staffing report and histogram: With each update schedule, a planned early and planned late versus actual labor resource histogram will be provided. This histogram shall be based upon and shall be in agreement with, the number of shifts and crew sizes by craft, in the Accepted Network Analysis Schedule (planned) and the Monthly Network Update (actual). Included in the report will be a tabular report that will list each trade to the activities that were worked on during the construction period.

j. Equipment usage report and histogram: With each update schedule, a planned early and planned late versus actual equipment resource histogram will be provided. This histogram shall be based upon and shall be in agreement with the equipment allocation accepted on the Accepted Network Analysis Schedule (planned) and the Monthly Network Update (actual). Included in the report will be a tabular report that will list equipment (by make and model) to the activities that were worked on during the construction period.]

1.7 SUBMISSION AND ACCEPTANCE

1.7.1 Preliminary Meeting

At the Pre-Construction Conference, the Contracting Officer, Contractor and major subcontractors shall participate in a preliminary meeting to discuss the proposed schedule and requirements of this section prior to submission of the network. The definition of a "major subcontractor" is one that exceeds [5] [_____] percent of the contract value.

[1.7.2 Schedule Development Session:

****
NOTE: Contact the ROICC Field Office before including this paragraph in the specifications. If included, editing of the paragraph will be coordinated with the Representative. This paragraph will typically be used only on large, complex or schedule sensitive projects.
****

[Upon completion of the 90 day (Preliminary) Network Analysis Schedule, and] Prior to the submission of the Network Analysis Schedule, the Contractor shall conduct a Schedule Development Session. The Schedule Development Session shall include procurement of on site services of an expert scheduler/planner for not less than a [5] [_____] day period. The Contractor's choice of Schedule Development Session scheduler/planner is subject to the acceptance of the Contracting Officer. The scheduler/planner shall facilitate the session on site [and shall be fluent in the English language]. The scheduler/planner shall have at least [10] [_____] years experience developing construction project schedules with

APPENDIX N

scheduling software programs that the contractor intends to use. Unless agreed to by the Contracting Officer, the session shall be conducted at the Office of the Contracting Officer. The Contractor is responsible for providing the necessary equipment for the session which, as a minimum, includes a personal computer (PC), a computer display projector to facilitate group viewing, and a printing device. During the session the facilitator [shall provide all necessary training to participants and] shall lead the development of the project's schedule. As a minimum, the scheduler/planner shall facilitate development of activity coding and work breakdown structures; establishment of procurement, government, and construction activities; activity relationship; resourcing; budgeted costs; and reports to be used during the project. Members of the Contracting Officer's staff will attend the session as well as [members of the designer of record,] [customer who will occupy the facility,] [major subcontractors (those which exceed [5] [_____] percent of the contract value), and] the Contractor's home and field project management staff. [Past experience has revealed that these services do not exist in [Indicate project location] which has resulted in the Contractor forming agreements with Scheduling Firms [in the United States] to meet the terms of the specification requirement.] All costs associated with the Schedule Development Session are to be borne by the Construction Contractor.]

[1.7.3   Preliminary Network Analysis Schedule

****
            **NOTE: This paragraph should only be used on complex
            contracts. Do not use this paragraph on contracts
            that require an Accepted Network Analysis Schedule
            to be submitted and accepted by the Government prior
            to beginning work.**
****

Submit a preliminary network defining the planned operations during the first [90] [_____] calendar days after contract award within [20] [_____] days after contract award. The general approach for the balance of the project shall be indicated. Cost of activities expected to be completed or partially completed before submission and acceptance of the Accepted Network Analysis Schedule should be included. Submit three copies of both the preliminary network diagrams and required reports listed in paragraph entitled "Required Reports." In accordance with paragraph entitled "Monthly Reports," the preliminary network may be used for requesting progress payments for a period not to exceed 90 calendar days after receipt of "Contract Award." Submittal and acceptance of the Preliminary Network is condition precedent to the processing of the Contractor's pay requests on this schedule. Payment requests after the first [90] [_____] calendar day period shall be based upon the Accepted Network Analysis Schedule. The activities and relationships of the preliminary schedule shall coincide and mesh with the activities of the Network Analysis Schedule. As part of this submittal, provide the Project Name format (and Project Group Name if used) that will be used by the Contractor to identify initial schedule submittals, updates, fragnets, changes, etc. Include [1] [_____] copy of the Preliminary Network Analysis Schedule on 3.5" disk(s).

]1.7.4   Network Analysis Schedule

CONSTRUCTION SCHEDULING

```
*************************************************************
          NOTE: In the first sentence, remove the language in
          the brackets if the schedule is to be submitted
          prior to allowing the contractor to commence work.
          If a Preliminary Schedule is required remove the
          language for Project Name format.
*************************************************************
```

Submit the complete network system, consisting of the network mathematical analysis and network diagrams[, within 40 [_____] calendar days after contract award]. Submit [three] [_____] copies of the diagrams described in the paragraph entitled "Diagrams", the required reports listed in the paragraph entitled "Required Reports ", [and] the analysis described in the paragraph entitled "Mathematical Analysis" [and information required by the paragraph entitled "Additional Requirements"]. [As part of this submittal, provide the Project Name format (and Project Group Name if used) that will be used by the Contractor to identify initial schedule submittals, updates, fragnets, changes, etc.] Include [1 copy] [_____ copies] of the Network Analysis Schedule on 3.5" disk(s) formatted to hold 1.44 MB of data.

1.7.5   Review and Evaluation

After the Government's review, the Contractor shall meet with the Contracting Officer to discuss the review and evaluation of the NAS submittal. Revisions necessary as a result of this review shall be resubmitted for acceptance within 10 calendar days after the meeting.

1.7.6   Accepted Network Analysis Schedule

Once review comments are resolved and the network has been accepted by the Contracting Officer, the Contractor shall within 5 calendar days furnish:

    a.   [Two] [_____] copies of the network diagrams

    b.   [Two] [_____] copies of the required reports listed in paragraph entitled "Required Reports"

    c.   [Two] [_____] copies of the "Mathematical Analysis".

    d.   [Two] [_____] copies of the Cash Flow Report indicating the cash flow based upon both the early and late start schedules.

    e.   [Two] [_____] copies of each major subcontractor's statement certifying their concurrence with the Contractor's Accepted Network Analysis Schedule. Each certifying statement will be made on the subcontractor's letterhead.

    f.   [Two] [_____] sets of data disks containing the project schedule shall be provided for the initial submission and every periodic project update. Data shall be submitted on 3.5: disk(s), formatted to hold 1.44 MB of data. A permanent exterior label shall be affixed to each disk submitted. The label shall indicate the type of schedule (Preliminary, NAS Submittal, Accepted,

APPENDIX N

Update, Recovery, or Change), full contract number, Project Name used to identify project in scheduling software, contract name & location, data status date, diskette number with total number of diskettes in set, software name and version used to run the schedule, and the name and telephone number of person responsible for the schedule.

For major revisions, updates or changes to the network diagrams, once accepted by the Contracting Officer, the Contractor shall submit these same diagrams and reports.

1.7.7   Monthly Network Analysis Updates

At monthly intervals the Contractor, Government representatives and major subcontractors will meet to jointly update the project schedule and agree on percentage of payment for each activity progressed during the update period. The purpose of the meeting is to determine progress payment amounts for each activity, allow all parties to evaluate project status at the data date, provide a complete and accurate update of procurement and construction progress, create an historical record of the project and establish prediction of completion date(s) based upon current status. The Contractor is responsible to gather all supporting documentation propose the update data for the schedule and record the meeting minutes. All progress payment amounts will be derived from and tied to the cost-loaded schedule activities. Submit at monthly intervals a report of the actual construction progress by updating the required reports, the time scaled logic diagram, and mathematical analysis. Meeting to update the schedule and the submission of an error free, acceptable updated schedule to the Government is a condition precedent to the processing of the Contractor's pay request. As a minimum, the following actions will be accomplished during the meeting:

   a. Identify activities started and completed during the previous period and enter the Actual Start and Actual Finish dates.

   b. Show estimated duration (in workdays) to complete each activity started but not completed (remaining duration).

   c. Indicate percentage of cost payable for each activity.

   d. Reflect changes in the network diagram. All changes (i.e., duration changes, logic changes, new logic, conformed change orders, new activities, changes due to Conformed Modifications, changes in work sequence, etc.) shall be recorded and a note added to the activity log field. The log shall include as a minimum, the date and reason for the change, and description of the change.

   e. Submit [two] [____] copies of a Narrative Report describing: 1) Progress made in each area of the project; 2) Changes in the following; activities, original durations, logic interdependencies, milestones, planned sequence of operations, critical path, and resource and loading; 3) Pending items and status thereof, including permits, change orders, and time extensions; 4) Status of Contract Completion Date and interim milestones; 5) Current and anticipated delays (describe cause of the delay and corrective action(s)); and 6) Description of current and future schedule problem areas. Each entry in the narrative report will cite the respective Activity ID and Activity Description.

    f. Submit [two] [_____] copies of the required reports listed in paragraph entitled "Required Reports".

    g. Submit [two] [_____] copies of the Update Meeting minutes.

[1.7.8   Summary Network

****
NOTE: Before specifying Summary Networks, verify with the ROICC Field Office that the Summary will be useful on the project being designed. Choose type of summary to be provided.
****

A summary network shall have the same network form as the Accepted Network Analysis Schedule. The summary network will contain a minimal number of activities that represent the general approach of work sequence. The Summary will be a time-scaled logical sequence of [Work Phases] [Work Category] [Area Code]. The Contractor shall submit a summary network diagram immediately after acceptance of the Accepted Network Analysis Schedule. A summary network update shall be submitted every [6] [_____] months during the contract duration and immediately following acceptance of each major schedule change. Submit the following:

    a. [Two] [_____] copies of the summary network diagram.

    b. [Two] [_____] copies of the Activity Identification Report.

    c. [Two] [_____] copies of the Total Float (or Slack) Report.

    d. [Two] [_____] copies of the Earned Value Report indicating the actual cash flow for the current updated (not summary) network based upon both the early and late start schedules.

][1.7.9   As-Built Schedule

****
NOTE: Before specifying As-Built Schedules, verify with the ROICC Field Office that the schedule will be required.
****

As a condition precedent to the release of retention, the last update of the schedule submitted shall be identified by the Contractor as the "As-Built Schedule". The As Built shall reflect the exact manner in which the project was actually constructed (including actual start and finish dates, activities, sequences, and logic) and shall be certified by the Contractor's Project Manager and Construction Scheduler as being a true

APPENDIX N

reflection of the way the project was actually constructed. If more than one person filled the position(s) during the course of the project, each person will provide certification for the period of time they were responsible.

11.8 CONTRACT MODIFICATION

When a contract modification to the work is required, submit proposed revisions to the network with a fragnet and a cost proposal for each proposed change. All modifications shall be incorporated into the network analysis system as separately identifiable activities broken down and inserted appropriately on the first update following issuance of a directive to proceed with the change. Submit [one copy] [_____ copies] of the Total Float Report, Log Report and a copy of the proposed Time Impact Analysis on disk, with the cost proposal. Unless the Contracting Officer requests otherwise, only conformed contract modification fragnets will be added into the subsequent monthly updates. All revisions to the current baseline schedule activities that are necessary to further refine the schedule so that the changed work activities can be logically tied to the schedule shall be made. Financial data shall not be incorporated into the schedule until the contract modification is signed by the Contracting Officer.

1.8.1 Time Impact Analysis:

Time Impact Analysis shall be used by the Contracting Officer in determining if a time extension or reduction to the contract milestone date(s) is justified. The Contractor shall provide a Time Impact Analysis to the Contracting Officer for any proposed contract change or as support for a Value Engineering Proposal, Claim or Request for Equitable Adjustment by the Contractor.

    a. The Contractor shall submit a Time Impact Analysis (TIA) illustrating the influence of each change or delay on the Contract Completion Date or milestones. Unless the Contracting Officer requests an interim update to the schedule, the current monthly updated schedule accepted by the government shall be used to display the impacts of the change. Unless requested by the Contracting Officer, no other non-conformed changes will be incorporated into the schedule being used to justify the change impact.

    b. Each TIA shall include a Fragmentary Network (fragnet) demonstrating how the Contractor proposes to incorporate the impact into the Project Schedule. A fragnet is defined as the sequence of new activities and/or activity revisions, logic relationships and resource changes that are proposed to be added to the existing schedule to demonstrate the influence of impacts to the schedule. The fragnet shall identify the predecessors to the new activities and demonstrate the impacts to successor activities. Include a narrative report describing the effects of new activities and relationships to interim and contract completion dates, with each TIA.

CONSTRUCTION SCHEDULING

c. Following the Contractor's receipt of a contract modification on a Standard Form 30 signed by the Government; all changes in the fragnet used to determine impacts, shall be incorporated into the schedule. Changes will occur during the next monthly schedule update meeting.

1.8.2   No Reservation-Of-Rights

All direct costs, indirect costs, and time extensions will be negotiated and made full, equitable and final at the time of modification issuance.

1.9   CHANGES TO THE NETWORK ANALYSIS SCHEDULE

If changes in the method of operating and scheduling are desired, the Contracting Officer shall be notified in writing stating the reasons for the change. If the Contracting Officer considers these changes to be of a major nature, the Contractor may be required to revise and submit for acceptance, without additional cost to the Government, the network diagrams and required sorts. A change may be considered of a major nature if the estimated time required or actually used for an activity or the network logic is varied from the original plan to a degree that there is a reasonable doubt as to the effect on the contract completion date(s) [or phase completion dates]. Changes that affect activities with adequate float time shall be considered a major change when their cumulative effect could extend the contract completion date.

1.10   FLOAT

Use of float suppression techniques, such as; preferential sequencing (arranging critical path through activities more susceptible to government caused delay), special lead/lag logic restraints, zero total or free float constraints, extended activity times, or imposing constraint dates other than as required by the contract, shall be cause for rejection of the project schedule or its updates. The use of Resource Leveling (or similar software features) used for the purpose of artificially adjusting activity durations to consume float and influence the critical path is expressly prohibited.

1.10.1   Definitions of Float or Slack

Free Float is the length of time the start of an activity can be delayed without delaying the start of a successor activity. Total Float is the length of time along a given network path that the actual start and finish of activity(s) can be delayed without delaying the project completion date. Project Float is the length of time between the Contractor's Early Completion (or Substantial Completion) and the Contract Completion Date.

1.10.2   Ownership of Float

Float available in the schedule, at any time shall not be considered for the exclusive use of either the Government or the Contractor. During the course of contract execution, any float generated due to the efficiencies of either party is not for the sole use of the party generating the float; rather it is a shared commodity to be reasonably used by either party.

APPENDIX N

Efficiencies gained as a result of favorable weather within a calendar month, where the number of days of normally anticipated weather is less than expected, will also contribute to the reserve of float. A schedule showing work completing in less time than the Contract time, and accepted by the Government, will be considered to have Project Float. Project Float will be a resource available to both the Government and the Contractor. No time extensions will be granted nor delay damages paid unless a delay occurs which impacts the Project's critical path, consumes all available float or contingency time, and extends the work beyond the Contract Completion Date.

1.10.3   Negative Float

Negative float will not be a basis for requesting time extensions. Any extension of time will be addressed in accordance with the Paragraph "Time Extensions". Scheduled completion date(s) that extend beyond the contract [or phase] completion date(s) (evidenced by negative float) may be used in computations for assessment of payment withholdings. The use of this computation is not to be construed as a means of acceleration.

1.11   TIME EXTENSIONS

Extension of time for performance required under the clauses entitled "Changes," "Differing Site Conditions," "Default (Fixed-Price Construction)" or "Suspension of Work" will be granted only to the extent that equitable time adjustments for the activity or activities affected exceed the total float or slack along the network paths involved at the time Notice to Proceed was issued for the change. The Contractor acknowledges and agrees that delays in activities which, according to the network analysis schedule, does not in fact actually affect any milestone completion dates or the contract completion date shown on the CPM network at the time of delay, will not be a basis for a contract extension. Submit time extension requests with a Time Impact Analysis and three copies of the Total Float (or Slack) Report, Narrative Report and Log Report.

[1.12   MONTHLY COORDINATION MEETING

****
           NOTE: Consult with the local ROICC Field Office on
           whether to use this paragraph. Include this
           paragraph for larger or more complex projects.
****

In conjunction with receipt of the Monthly Network Update submission, a coordination meeting will be held each month [on site] [in the Contracting Officer's conference room] to discuss the report. The Contractor shall make a presentation of the previously submitted and current Monthly Network Update to the Contracting Officer so as to provide an overview of the project's schedule and provide an opportunity to discuss items of coordination.

]1.13   BIWEEKLY WORK SCHEDULE

****

CONSTRUCTION SCHEDULING

> **NOTE:** Consult with the local ROICC Field Office on whether to use this paragraph. Include this paragraph for larger or more complex projects.

To provide a more detailed day-to-day planning of upcoming work, the Contractor shall prepare and issue detailed work plans that coordinate with and supplement the above defined network analysis. The work plans shall be keyed to the CPM activity numbers and shall be submitted each week and shall show the projects activities that will occur during the following two-week interval. Additionally, the critical path activities are to be identified on the Biweekly Work Plan. The detail work plans are to be bar chart type schedules prepared by the Contractor in sufficient detail to define the work to be accomplished, the crews, construction tools and equipment to be used during the current and next two-week interval. The bar charts shall be formatted to allow reproduction on 8 1/2 by 11 sheets. Three copies of the bar chart schedules shall be delivered to the Contracting Officer not less than 3 work hours prior to the start of the weekly coordination meeting.

[1.14   WEEKLY COORDINATION MEETING

> **NOTE:** Consult with the local ROICC Field Office on whether to use this paragraph. Include this paragraph for larger or more complex projects.

In conjunction with the receipt of the Bi-Weekly Work Schedule, a coordination meeting will be held each week [on site] [in the Contracting Officer's conference room] to discuss the work schedule. The Contractor shall make a presentation of the previously submitted and current Bi-Weekly Work Schedule to the Contracting Officer so as to provide an overview of the project's schedule and provide an opportunity to discuss items of coordination. Consideration of materials, crews, and equipment shall be addressed to ascertain their respective availability. The meeting shall identify actions necessary to provide adherence to the Bi-Weekly Work Schedule and the overall network for the project defined above. The Contractor will take meeting minutes. All meeting minute entries will be keyed to the schedule activity number(s) being addressed. Within one day of the meeting, the Contractor will provide a draft copy of the meeting minutes to the Contracting Officer for review and comment. Final copies of the minutes containing the comments provided by the Contracting Officer, will be issued within 3 days of the meeting.

]1.15   CORRESPONDENCE AND TEST REPORTS

All correspondence (e.g., letters, Requests for Information (RFIs), e-mails, meeting minutes, Production and QC Daily Reports, material delivery tickets, photographs, etc.) shall reference the Schedule Activity Number(s) that are being addressed. All test reports (e.g., concrete, soil compaction, weld, pressure, etc.) shall reference the Schedule Activity Number(s) that are being addressed.

TABLE OF CASES

References are to sections.

A

Alcan Elec. & Eng'g Co., Inc. v. Samaritan Hosp., 9.08[G][2]

B

Bay Constr. Co., 8.11, 10.08, 12.14, 15.02

C

Cable & Computer Tech., Inc., 9.08[M], 12.14

Charles G. Williams Constr., Inc. v. White, 12.14

F

Fire Sec. Sys., Inc., 8.11, 9.08[G][2], 9.08[G][3]

Fraya, 9.11

G

Gladwynne Constr. Co. v. Mayor & City Council of Baltimore, 9.08[G][2], 12.14

J

Jimenez, Inc., 9.06[E], 9.06[F], 9.08[D]

L

Lake Mich. Contractors, Inc. v. Manitowoc Co., Inc., 15.02

Lummus Global Amazonas, S.A. v. Aguaytia Energy del Peru, 13.03[A]

M

Manuel Bros., Inc. v. United States, 9.08[G][2]

N

Nicon, Inc. v. United States, 12.14

P

PCL Constr. Servs., P. Inc. v. United States, 9.08[G][2]

P.J. Dick Inc. v. Secretary of Veterans Affairs, 9.06[E], 9.06[F], 9.08[D], 9.08[E], 9.08[M], 12.14

R

RPR & Assocs., Inc. v. University of North Carolina-Chapel Hill, 9.08[A], 9.08[G][2],

R.W. Granger & Sons, Inc. v. City Sch. Dist. of Albany, 5.04[C], 9.08[A], 9.11

S

Sauer v. Danzig, 9.08[G][2]

Slidell, Inc. v. Millennium Inorganic Chems., Inc., 9.08[A]

Stone & Webster, 9.11, 11.03

Sherman R. Smoot Corp., 15.02

INDEX

References are to sections, chapters (Ch.), and appendices (App.).

B

Breach of contract
    network analysis schedule, failure to provide, 9.11

C

Case studies
    Big Dig, 16.08
    College of Scheduling brochure, App. L

P

Plans and specifications
    Unified Facilities Guide Specifications (Apr. 2002), 4.14, App. N
    Unified Facilities Guide Specifications (Feb. 2003), 4.14, App. M

T

Time delay claims
    failure to call witness with actual knowledge, 10.08